For the Duration *plus* Six Months

Major Silveo G. Colletti, USAF, Retired

The opinions expressed in this manuscript are solely the opinions of the author and do not represent the opinions or thoughts of the publisher. The author has represented and warranted full ownership and/or legal right to publish all the materials in this book.

For the Duration Plus Six Months
All Rights Reserved.
Copyright © 2016 Major Silveo G.Colletti, USAF Retired
v1.0

Cover Image © 2016 Suzette Colletti. All rights reserved - used with permission.

This book may not be reproduced, transmitted, or stored in whole or in part by any means, including graphic, electronic, or mechanical without the express written consent of the publisher except in the case of brief quotations embodied in critical articles and reviews.

Outskirts Press, Inc.
http://www.outskirtspress.com

ISBN: 978-1-4787-2580-0

Outskirts Press and the "OP" logo are trademarks belonging to Outskirts Press, Inc.

PRINTED IN THE UNITED STATES OF AMERICA

Table of Contents

Chapter 1............Welcome to the Army

Chapter 2............Langley Field, Hampton, Virginia

Chapter 3............Walter Reed Hospital, Army Medical Center, Washington DC

Chapter 4............Back to Langley Field

Chapter 5............Nashville, Tennessee. Welcome to the Air Corps

Chapter 6............Preflight Training, Maxwell Army Air Base, Montgomery, Alabama

Chapter 7............Primary Flight Training, Carlstrom Field, Arcadia, Florida

Chapter 8............Basic Flight Training, Bainbridge, Georgia

Chapter 9............Twin Engine Advanced Pilot Training, Moody Field, Valdosta, Georgia

Chapter 10...........Aerial Gunnery School, Tyndall Field, Panama City, Florida

Chapter 11...........Bombardier School, Victorville Army Air Base, Victorville, California

Chapter 12...........Cross-Country to New Jersey and Back

Chapter 13...........B24 Training, March Field, Riverside, California

Chapter 14...........Island Hopping and Jungle Survival Training

Chapter 15...........408th Squadron, Owi Island, Dutch East Indies

Chapter 16...........Anguar, Palau Island Group

Chapter 17...........Welcome to Samar, the Kitchen is Open

Chapter 18...........Clark Field, Luzon, Philippine Islands

Chapter 19...........Okinawa, Japan

Chapter 20...........Georgia, Florida, and a Mop of Red Hair

Chapter 21...........Home and Everything After

Chapter 22...........Final Thoughts

Chapter 23...........Today

Chapter 24...........Duty Tours, Bases, Military Addresses and Biography

Preface

What I had not realized (and was totally unprepared for) was the great emotional impact I would experience when I began to write about the four years I served during WWII. What quickly became apparent was the fact that to write it was to relive it. One recalled moment would bring to mind forgotten detail, which in turn, would rekindle another memory. Events that had been blurred by the passing of time slowly came into sharp focus and I found myself in a *time warp*. Once again, it was October 20, 1941, the day I was drafted -- the day when it all began.

There is little doubt that the years I spent in the Army and Air Corps during WWII were a very significant part of my life. There were days and nights when it was, among other things, lonely, tiring uncomfortable, confusing, difficult, miserable, tormenting, boring and dangerous. Yet, it cannot be denied that very often we were able to see the humorous side of things and laugh despite the hardships (mud, poor food, disease,) tense situations or ridiculous moments (the day the wind blew the roof off the latrine) that we had experienced. Perhaps it was the sense of camaraderie we shared, which made it easier to keep our heads on straight, but whatever it was, a good laugh at the right time worked wonders. Fortunately, there always seemed to be someone, somewhere who had the ability to come up with the right comment at the right moment.

I was very fortunate to have survived the war unscathed with the realization that the time spent in uniform had proved to be a most valuable learning experience. Without question, I was a better man because of it. More than ever, I was able to appreciate many of the things in our daily existence which we all take for granted, such as privacy and the freedom to make our own decisions. I came away with a clearer perspective and deeper understanding of how to make the distinction between the important and trivial things in our daily existence. That ability made it easy to put the emphasis where it belonged, on (among other things) character, relationships, family and most of all, love shared with the right person. In that respect I have been truly blessed because the Gods were smiling down on me the day I met, and later married, the girl who has been my wife, mother of our five children, companion and everything else for the past sixty-eight years. Every time I look in a mirror I find myself saying to the reflected image, "you lucky dog, you've got it all," and no one knows it better than I!

1

WELCOME TO THE ARMY

I am quite certain that most everyone in the city of Linden, New Jersey, saw nothing unusual about the morning of October 20, 1941. It was a typical fall day, but not for the group of men who had received notices to report to the local library at ten in the morning. This surely was not a typical day for them because their draft number, 158, had come up and they would soon be inducted into the Army to serve for a period of one year.

A few words of greeting were spoken to the assembled group by a member of the draft board, who wished us well and instructed us to answer to roll call. At its conclusion, we were told to stand, raise our right hand and recite the pledge of allegiance to the United States of America. He then congratulated us, for we were officially on the government payroll. Pay: Twenty-one dollars a *month*. We who had been drafted were now in the Army of the United States. Some men in the group had volunteered before being drafted, and when sworn in, became members of the United States Army. There was a difference. We were draftees, they were Regular Army. We soon learned that the Regular Army men were paid first on payday.

I can still hear the laughter and snide remarks when I had previously told my friends of my imminent change of status: "Look who is going to be a soldier, Ha! Ha! I'll sleep soundly because you will be on duty to watch over the country. Have they made you a General yet? No? How come? Cheer up, it's only for one year and the sooner you go in the sooner you will be out."

After swearing in, we were told to line up to begin the march from the library to Wood Avenue and then an additional half a mile to the railroad station. A small band had been assembled and the new recruits and band marched down the main street of town. Why we were given a rousing sendoff was something I never quite understood since our only accomplishment, unfortunately, was to be one of the first to be drafted while we were not at war. Friends and family met us at the train station and after kissing everyone goodbye for the third time, we boarded the train to Fort Dix, New Jersey.

There was another *Welcome to the Army* speech upon our arrival at Fort Dix followed by a march to our designated camp area. After roll call, we received tent assignments, information regarding the location of the mess hall, latrines, etc., and what was on tomorrow's schedule. Questions were asked and answered and then it was time for lunch (mess).

The arrival at Fort Dix had been very confusing. Where do I go? What am I supposed to do? Do I salute, ignore officers or just pretend that I don't see them? Since we were not in uniform, we carried on as civilians. In the afternoon, I located my assigned tent and met the three total strangers who would be my tent mates. Moving in was simple, having no personal possessions except toilet articles and the clothes I was wearing. Without doubt, this had been the strangest day of my life. Lying on my cot that first evening, my thoughts turned to what the next twelve months might bring and wondering how difficult it would be to adjust to my new status: Private Silveo Gaetano Colletti, 32185829, Army of the United States.

The Greatest Guy in the World was Aboard that Draft Train

FAMOUS WAR-TIME PICTURE

The above picture, widely circulated by the press, depicts "Linden," a loyal canine looking wistfully after his adopted soldier master who had just left on a troop train after a furlough at the home of Mr. Charles Buchar, 322 West Linden Avenue, "Linden's" owner. After that day canine instinct impelled "Linden" to give a farewell visit and longing look to all men in khaki who left from Linden, N. J.

"Welcome Home To Our Veterans"[1] parade handout, April 6, 1946.

This radical change in the lives of the young men of America came about on September 16, 1940 when President Franklin Roosevelt signed into law the Selective Service Training and Service Act and thereby established the first *peacetime* military draft in the history of the United States. I registered for the draft on October 16, 1940 and by law, was required to carry my registration certificate at all times. In July of 1941, I was ordered to take a physical exam at the Armory in Elizabeth, and await further instructions. The memory of that physical is still fresh in my mind despite the fact that it happened seventy-five years ago.

It began with the filling out of forms, which asked for information about childhood diseases, history of broken bones, etc. Upon completion, we were told to disrobe, except for our shorts, and report to the first room, which might have been where blood was drawn. It might be appropriate to mention at this time, that we were living in a rather conservative world in the early forties. People were not prudes, but we certainly spoke, dressed and behaved much differently than is the case today. A good example of this was what was being worn when swimming. Men still had to wear a top to their bathing suit, and the women, in their one-piece suits, were more covered than exposed.

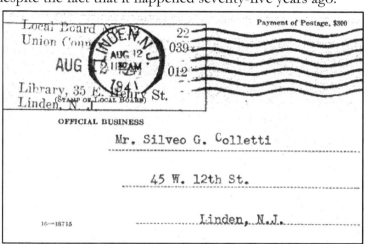

The physical had been set up as a sort of assembly line with men walking through the halls, from room to room, where the examining doctor would check eyes, heart, etc. in keeping with his specialty. What little remained of our sense of modesty, however, came to an end when we were told to remove our shorts for the next exam which would be a check for hernia. The doctor was seated in a chair, squarely before me, and it was done by pressing up in

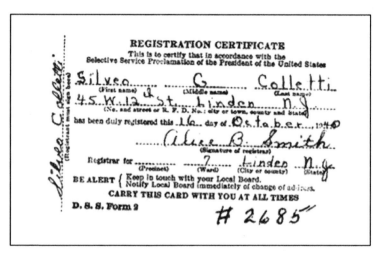

the crotch area with an extended finger. I was told to cough while he pressed, and to turn my head to one side. (The coughing makes it easier for him to make his diagnosis.) Unfortunately, many of the men forgot to turn their heads and coughed into the doctor's face. The expression of disgust on the doctor's face said it all. (This incident in our physical exam took on a life of its own. I guarantee that you can bring a smile to the face of any ex-serviceman if you were to simply ask him to cough. He would know immediately where you were coming from for we all had had this experience somewhere in our military career!) Of course, the genital area came in for its share of attention; and upon completion, was followed by a rectal exam. I am quite sure that most of us were in agreement regarding our feelings upon completion of the physical: Areas that once had been private were now in the public domain.

The interval between the physical and the notification of my draft status would prove to be a time when my imagination ran the gamut from being classified 4F, physically unfit, or 1A, fit and ready for active duty. There were other classifications, for example, which would exempt a man because he had an essential defense job. It was not unusual to see men dancing with glee after being rejected because of a bad heart, flat feet, poor eyesight or some ailment which would make then unfit for active duty. I could not begin to understand how anyone could be *happy* to learn that they had a major physical ailment, regardless of the fact that it disqualified them. The year of service would soon be over, but the bad heart or bad vision would be there for life. I could only speculate about the draft board's decision while I waited to receive my classification notice. It was a disruptive time, for there was no motivation to do anything worthwhile, as I wondered about my uncertain future.

* * * * *

It was August 8, 1938 when I began to work with Dad in New York City, he being the sole proprietor of a small jewelry shop, commuting by train from Linden via the *Pennsylvania Railroad*. There were days when the daily ride and the jostling and pushing crowds could be tiring and aggravating, but I did like the jewelry business. Whenever possible, I took advantage of spare moments to tinker with old watch movements that were out of order and were in need of repair. Of course, the fact that I didn't have a clue as to what I was doing just made it more fun.

There was a letter in the mailbox when I returned home from work one evening. It was postmarked August 12, 1941 and it conveyed the news that I had been classified 1A and should remain alert for further notices. At last, the uncertainty was over since I knew that the next notice would be the one that would call me to active duty. Shortly thereafter, I was instructed to report for induction into the Army on October 20, 1941. I had two weeks in August, the month of September and twenty days in October to do all the things I enjoyed doing, and I made the most of it. Much to my surprise, I was given a going away party at the home of Frank Krysiak, the superintendent of recreation for the city of Linden. All my good friends of the Linden Model Aircraft Club were present, and I received typical gifts of stationery, toilet articles, etc. It was fun, but obviously, it did have a downside knowing that I would soon be saying goodbye.

More than once during my last few weeks at home, I thought about the family I would soon be leaving and which I certainly would miss.

Chapter 1

About the Agency

News & Public Affairs

Publications

History Records

What Happens in a Draft

Fast Facts

SELECTIVE SERVICE LOTTERY

If and when the Congress and the President reinstate a military draft, the Selective Service System would conduct a National Draft Lottery to determine the order in which young men would be drafted.

The lottery would establish the priority of call based on the birth dates of registrants. The first men drafted would be those turning age 20 during the calendar year of the lottery. For example, if a draft were held in 1998, those men born in 1978 would be considered first. If a young man turns 21 in the year of the draft, he would be in the second priority, in turning 22 he would be in the third priority, and so forth until the year in which he turns 26 at which time he is over the age of liability. Younger men would not be called in that year until men in the 20-25 age group are called.

Because of the enormous impact of this lottery, it would be conducted publicly, with full coverage by the media. Accredited observers from public interest groups will have full access to observe the proceedings.

To make the lottery as fair as possible, the National Institute of Standards and Technology (NIST) developed a unique random calendar and number selection program for Selective Service. Using this random selection method for birthdays, each day of the year is selected by computer in a random manner, and that date is placed in a capsule. The capsules are then loaded in a large drum on a random basis. By the same method, numbers from 1 to 365 (366 for men born in a leap year) are also selected in a random fashion, placed in capsules, and the capsules are placed into a second drum. The process, repeated a second time, results in two sets of drums. Official observers certify that the capsule-filling and drum-loading were conducted according to established procedures. This certification is secured to each drum; they are sealed and placed in secure storage. Should a lottery be conducted, one of the first actions would be an inspection of these stored drums and the selection of a set to be used in the lottery.

Here is how the lottery would work: One capsule is drawn from the drum containing birth dates January 1 through December 31. One capsule is then drawn from the drum containing the sequence numbers from 1 through 365 (366 if the draft will call men born during a leap year) and the date and number are paired to establish the sequence number for each birth date. This is done in full view of all observers, officials, and the media.

For example, if the date of August 4 is drawn first from the "date" drum, and the sequence number of 32 is drawn from the "number's" drum at the same time, then those men turning 20 on August 4 would be ordered for induction processing only after men whose birthdays drew sequence numbers 1 through 31. The drawings continue until all 365 (or 366) birthdays of the year are paired with a sequence number.

After the lottery is completed and results certified, the sequence of call is transmitted to the Selective Service System's Data Management Center. Almost immediately the first induction notices are prepared and sent via mailgram to men whose birth dates drew the lowest lottery numbers.

This system, based on random selection of birth dates, with the order of priority for reporting assigned in a scientifically random manner, is a fair and equitable method of calling men to serve.

Pop, James Salvatore Colletti, was born in Palermo, Sicily on May 24, 1883, the son of a merchant sea captain. Mom, nee, Rosalia Gullo, came from the little town of Bivona which was not very far from Palermo. Her birth date was February 12, 1883, the daughter of an olive oil merchant. I do not have exact dates, but I believe that they both arrived in the United States shortly after the turn of the century. Mom was part of the great wave of people that came through Ellis Island, but what was unusual about Pop, however, was that he came to the United States as a stowaway. He served a hitch in the United States Navy (information is scant, but it was before they were married) aboard the USS *Brooklyn*, and his commanding officer was Admiral Sigsbee. There was a framed picture of his ship in their home and I still remember some of the stories he told about his days in uniform. Their first child, Domenick was born on February 5, 1908 and the family grew with the addition of Salvatore, October 14, 1910, Joseph, May 18, 1913, Angelina, December 1, 1915, and me, Silveo, September 13, 1919, at 411 2nd Avenue, New York City. We moved to Linden, New Jersey in 1925.

We were a typical Italian family, close and emotional. The display of affection was commonplace, hugging or kissing when greeting family or relatives and never resorting to an impersonal handshake. Mom and Pop were never reluctant to embrace in the presence of their children when he left for work in the morning and returned at night, and we grew up thinking that every family behaved that way. Little did we know. English and Italian were spoken at home, but we encouraged them to speak English and with our help, they also learned how to read newspapers printed in English. The amusing aspect of their marriage, however, was how completely different they were, but there was no doubt that they loved each other dearly.

Mom was *Queen Victoria;* prim, proper and intolerant of bad behavior. She was about five feet two, a hundred and fifteen pounds and it was not unusual to see her wearing silk stockings and high heels while doing housework. She went to church regularly and so did Pop -- so to speak. Someone said that he was seen in church once, but his church attendance consisted of driving her there and picking her up when Mass was over. He was the typical *good old boy* who loved to play poker (never lost), enjoyed having a few drinks and always felt that there was sufficient time for a few more hands and one last glass of beer. He loved opera and had a fairly good singing voice, but trying to hit the high note in "Sorrento" was always his downfall. He had a short fuse, was difficult to work with, but we all knew that his outbursts could be easily dismissed as puffery. It was a happy environment, especially during the holidays, when people grouped around the piano and sang while Domenick played.

I was thirteen years old when Franklin Roosevelt was elected president. I remember the speech in which he told the American people "the only thing we had to fear was fear itself," for the country was locked in a depression with many people out of work and barely surviving. In an effort to help, soup kitchens (which were small trucks with a tank full of soup on board) would be sent through the city. They would come down the street very slowly, and those who were in need and who could swallow their pride, would bring a pot or bucket out to the truck and have it filled. It wasn't much, but for some it might have been the best meal of the day. Money was scarce and what little there was had to be used wisely and not spent frivolously. Entertainment? When we could scrape enough money together we went to the movies, but for the most part the streets and open fields were where we spent our spare time. During the summer, it was softball and pitching horseshoes. In the fall, those of us who were *loaded* would buy a pair of Union Hardware roller skates which sold for about a dollar and a half. The Linden Recreation Commission would rope off a city street (selecting one which was smoothly paved) and we would join the crowd and skate until our legs ached. The open field at the end of the street was our playground, and we usually played football until it became too dark to see. When the weather turned cold, ice skating became the sport of the day at the various lakes or ponds, and after skating, we would get together at someone's house for hot cocoa. No one had any money to speak of so we took advantage of what was free and made the most of it. Looking back, I realized that the youths of my era differed from the kids of today. The kids of my youth were participants; whereas the kids of today are inclined to be spectators, watching a game on TV or in person at the stadium. This was not an option for us so we played the game instead of watching it. Without a doubt, I have always felt that *we* were the more fortunate ones. Go to summer camp? That was for the well to do kids, whose parents could afford it, so my summers were always spent at home. I had never spent a night *sleeping over* at a friend's house, for that was not in my lifestyle.

In 1938, five members of the Linden Model Aircraft Club went to Washington DC to participate in the formation of a group which would be known as the Academy of Model Aeronautics. We spent the night there and returned the next day. The only reason I mention it is because it was the first and only time I had ever spent a night away from home. To sum up, here was a less than well-traveled individual who now found himself in a unique situation. I truly wondered how well I could adjust.

Silveo, Cranford, NJ 1940

First model airplane contest sponsored by City of Linden Recreation Commission. July 1935, Athletic Field.
This is where I met Carl "Zom" Frank (3rd from left.)

It was cold the next morning when we were awakened at reveille, and we shivered as we marched to the mess hall, still dressed in our inadequate civilian clothes. Another first time experience was my introduction to the so-called *mess kit*, which was made of aluminum and opened up to form two separate pans. An aluminum cup and eating utensils were also included. We joined the others in line (cafeteria-style) where food was plopped into the open pan, and we then looked for an open table. After eating, we washed our mess kits in the three clean garbage cans that were filled with steaming water. I stuck my mess kit into the first one which contained soap and then into the second and third which were rinses. Because of the steam, I could not judge the water level in the last rinse and plunged my hand into the hot water. It hurt, but I shrugged it off and hoped that it would not be too bad.

At our next assembly, we were given two identification tags which had our name, address, next of kin, blood type, religion and Army Serial Number (which would be referred to as ASN in the future) stamped into the metal. There was a hole at the end of the tag through which we threaded a string, tied a knot and then added the other one about an inch or so above the first. Being separated, they did not jingle as we moved about. We wore them around our neck with explicit instructions *never* to take them off regardless of what we were doing. Of course, no one called them identification tags -- the common name was *dog tags*. It wasn't till months later that I learned why two tags were issued. If killed, one remained with the body and the other one would be used for record keeping purposes. Another use would be to identify a gravesite.

The clothing issue followed, and it too was a new experience. We were given a form which listed the various items of clothing we would be issued, and in the appropriate space, entered the sizes we wore. Next, we received two large bags, the so-called A and B barracks bags, told to strip naked, put our civilian clothes in one bag and then follow directions. The first stop was for underwear; long underwear. I received three pair, was told to try one on, and if it fit, leave it on and put the other two in the barracks bag and proceed to the next counter. There, another item of clothing was issued, and we proceeded from counter to counter until the issue was completed. We emerged from the building wearing a complete uniform down to winter overcoat, hat and gloves and scratching every part of our bodies. The itching was caused by the long underwear and the dozens of tags that were attached to every item of clothing. The supply sergeant came to our rescue and advised us to team up with someone and let him remove the tags from your clothes while you did the same for him. It was a slow process since many tags were hidden and not found until later. Just about the time you thought you had removed them all, you became aware that there was irritation in an unmentionable place. It was at that moment that we began to laugh, as we looked at each other standing there, completely dressed from head to toe, in our new uniforms. Now we were soldiers! As for the long underwear, I wore the tormenting thing for two more days until I could tolerate it no more. I dug into my barracks bag, pulled out my shorts and put them on, being completely convinced that I would rather be cold than uncomfortable.

Although this happened in 1941, I can easily recall the thoughts that were going through my head at the end of the day. To be uprooted from the lifestyle I knew and to make the transformation from civilian to soldier would require mental and physical adjustments. The more I thought, the more I realized that it would help to have some kind of *philosophy of life* to make it easier to cope with events and situations that I never before had to face. After some thought, what came to mind was an old adage which I am sure we have all heard: "Everything happens for the best." A good argument could probably be made that it was too simplistic and unsupportable, that too often the setbacks we suffered proved that everything did not happen for the best. This might be true, but when I look back and re-examine the facts that led me to make certain decisions, it did seem that everything did happen for the best. It was important, however, to look at the total picture and not one isolated incident. It was at that moment that I knew I had taken the first most important step toward putting my mind at ease. Serving one year in the Army would not be a problem. Whatever will be, will be. *Everything happens for the best.*

Putting the uniform on for the first time made little difference in the mentality of the new draftees since we were still thinking as civilians. That would begin to change, however, when we were shipped out of Fort Dix on the third day for our new station, Camp Lee, Petersburg, Virginia. It was located about thirty-five miles south of Richmond, Virginia, was very rich in Civil War history, but was a town that had little appeal for those who were free to leave the post.

Camp Lee was a basic training base where civilians were hopefully turned into soldiers. I was assigned to the medical department, a decision made by higher ups and in which I had no voice. (It might have just as easily been the infantry or field artillery or any other branch, if that was where men were needed.) We were to be trained as medical personnel with various skills, but that would come later. For now, the day was spent learning how to fall in, salute, march, do close order drill and all the other routines that were so typical of

Camp Lee, Petersburg, Virginia

army life. I was in the 4th platoon, composed of forty men and who were then divided into four squads of ten, with the tallest men in the front and the shortest to the rear. (This made it easier to blindly follow the man at the head of the platoon, which was good because we didn't have a clue as to where we were going or what we were supposed to be doing.) The platoon sergeant was William T. Boyce and he was assisted by corporals Myslinsky, Perry and Skaggs. Boyce was strict but fair. He would turn red with rage when we goofed up, but I liked him and we all got along quite well. Myslinsky, Perry and Skaggs were also easy to get along with so the military atmosphere was a pleasant one. I was now in a standard army barracks, having a lower and upper floor, with twenty men on each floor. My bed was the fourth one on the left on the upper floor. As you entered from the side door, a stairway led upstairs and a turn to the right and down led to the latrine and what we called the *standard quartermaster six-seater*. This was a long, rectangular box with appropriate holes cut into it. I, for one, felt no need to have company when heeding the call of nature and the lack of privacy was a radical departure from civilian life. A row of sinks lined the back wall, and a mirror was mounted over each sink. Showers were off to one side and once again, one did not lack for company when it was time to bathe. All in all, it was like living stark naked in a fish bowl.

Obviously, adjusting to this aspect of army life would take time. The interior of the barracks was bare wood (yellow pine) and the splintered, unpainted floor would snag the mop when we performed the daily house cleaning rituals. There were daily inspections, but the Saturday morning inspection was the most important one. Buckets and mops were always in short supply, which made it necessary to cooperate in order to allow every one the opportunity to get the job done. I distinctly recall the rumor that we were going to have a *GI Party* our first Friday evening at Camp Lee. Little did we, the greenhorns, realize that a GI party was not fun time, but rather an evening spent dusting, mopping, cleaning and arranging personal effects in preparation for the Saturday morning inspection.

Poor inspections, we soon learned, led to KP duty. Within three days, we knew that it was going to be a long year, longer than the Selective Service Board told us we had to serve. (By way of clarification: The abbreviation "GI" stands for *Government Issue*. How it became mutated into *GI Joe* or *GI Party* has always been a mystery to me, since we were not *issued*.)

The barracks fronted onto a very large area where we would assemble for all our formations, parades and drill. There was no grass, just loose sand such as you would find at the seashore. It got into everything and it was almost impossible to play baseball or football because it was difficult to run or pivot.

It didn't take long to discover what army life was all about. I was assigned to KP a few days later, and the day started about four in the morning. As luck would have it, the next day was Saturday and that meant a major inspection of the kitchen. The cook was nuts. He had us disconnect the stoves and scrub down the wall behind them. We scrubbed the ceilings, walls and floors and in between did other tasks such as washing all the large vats and cookware that was used in preparing food. The detail lasted twenty-four hours. I had been in the Army just three days, but that was long enough to convince me to seek a commission, if ever given the opportunity, since commissioned officers were above KP.

My first bout with KP brought to mind a very popular song, written by Johnny Mercer, which cleverly captured and described the life of the *new soldier*, "GI Jive."[2]

Chapter 1

"GI Jive"
This is the G. I. Jive
Man alive
It starts with the bugler blowin' reveille
over your bed when you arrive
Jack, that's the G. I. Jive
Roodley-toot
Jump in your suit
Make a salute
Boot!!
After you wash and dress
More or less
You go get your breakfast in a beautiful little
cafe they call "The Mess"
Jack, when you convalesce
Outta your seat
Into the street
Make with the feet
Reet!!
If you're a P-V-T, your duty
Is to salute to L-I-E-U-T
But if you brush the L-I-E-U-T
The M-P makes you K-P on the Q-T
This is the G. I. Jive
Man alive
They give you a private tank that features a little
device called "fluid drive"
Jack, after you revive
Chuck all your junk
Back in the trunk
Fall on your bunk
Clunk!!
This is the G. I. Jive
Man alive
They give you a private tank that features a little
device called "fluid drive"
Jack, if you still survive
Chuck all your junk
Back in the trunk
Fall on your bunk
Clunk!!
Soon you're countin' jeeps
But before you count to five
Seems you're right back diggin' that G. I. Jive

October 1941

11

Slowly we learned about attention, how to salute, fall in, fall out, normal interval, short interval, about face, column left, column right, to the rear march, flanking movements, halt and probably others that I have forgotten. Some of us caught on quickly, but a few just never got the hang of it. I remember one poor soul called Domenic who was very bad. The whole platoon was to march in a competition and our sergeant put him on sick call so that he would not be in ranks, knowing that he was certain to louse it up. There was guard duty to *pull*. We didn't have rifles so the guards walked their posts with broomsticks. What little equipment we did have was left over from WWI. We were issued gas masks of that vintage which had to be carried every time we fell out for training. It didn't take us long to realize that they were useless. We removed the masks from their pouch, left them in the barracks and filled the pouch with candy snacks, bananas or whatever we had that was usually sent to us from home. Obviously, we were learning the ropes!

It was getting cold and we had to pull fireman duty. This involved keeping watch on the soft-coal furnaces of four barracks and shoveling coal when needed to keep the fires burning. This, of course, was an all night duty.

If there were no duty assignments, we would go to the PX where the jukebox was playing continuously. One could almost say that we went to war listening to "Chattanooga Choo Choo" and "In the Mood" by the Glenn Miller Orchestra. The biggest activity of the evenings, however, was letter writing.

Without question, the receipt of mail was the greatest morale booster. Mail call was the highlight of the day and answering letters was what we did religiously. We were a bunch of draftees, not military men, and we were here because the government decided that this was where we had to be. Mail was our lifeline and the Army was well aware of it.

Fortunately, there was always someone in the group who could be counted on to keep everybody laughing, either by deed or by intent. The entire barracks had a great time with an incident that involved letter writing. First, it is necessary to explain that one of the most popular songs of the day was titled "Jim"[3] by Jimmy Dorsey's Orchestra, and sung by Helen O'Connell. Part of the lyric was, "Jim doesn't ever bring me pretty flowers, Jim doesn't try to soothe my lonely hours, don't know why I'm so crazy for Jim."[3] Across the aisle from me, Sammy C. was busy writing a letter. What was unusual was that he recited out loud that which he was writing. Some of it was quite nasty—so much so that someone asked,

"Sammy who in hell are you writing that nasty stuff to?"

Sammy answered, "My girlfriend."

We all asked "Why?"

He replied, "Well you see, Christmas is coming and I don't want to spend the money for a Christmas present. I want to get her angry with me, until after Christmas, and then I'll write something nice to her and patch it all up."

The laughter was spontaneous and the die was cast. From that moment on, Sammy C. ceased to exist. From that moment on he was, "Call me Jim." -- "Call me Jim, do you want to go to the PX? -- Call me Jim, do you want to go to the movies?" and so it went day in and day out.

"Jim"

Jim doesn't ever bring me pretty flowers, Jim never tries to cheer my lonely hours
Don't know why I'm so crazy for Jim.
Jim never tells me I'm his heart's desire, I never seem to set his love afire,
Gone are the years I've wasted on him.
Sometimes when I get feeling low, I say let's call it quits
Then I hang on and let him go, breaking my heart in bits.
Someday I know that Jim will up and leave me,
But even if he does you can believe me, I'll go on carrying the torch for Jim.

* * * * *

Basic training was where we learned how to be a soldier and additionally, how to perform those tasks that would be our responsibility as members of the medical department. Our classroom was the outdoors, usually the area between two barracks. We were issued a folding chair and the call to class was a whistle blast followed by the order, "Fall out with chairs." The instructor was usually a commissioned officer and the subject might be, "How to Dig a Slit Trench Latrine," or "How to Purify Water to Make It Safe to Drink" or whatever the Army thought we needed to know once we got into the field. Of course, there was always someone in the group who managed to find a way to add humor to the subject matter. The humor was very well received and made it easier to overcome the boredom that would come with the details of how to dig a latrine trench. Who cared? Another day might bring instruction in how to bandage various wounds, and of course, first aid. Actually, it was information that anyone might find useful whether in uniform or civilian life. There would be a few hours of classes and then more marching and drilling. There was always an inspection and the ritual of shining shoes and making up drum-tight beds never ceased.

The men in the infantry had to carry a rifle, but we in the medical department had our own specialty: a litter. We were divided into groups of four and each group was assigned a litter. One of the four was designated litter bearer, and it was his responsibility to carry it when the blast of the whistle was followed by the order, "Fall out with litters." Wouldn't you know that it was usually the smallest of the four men who had to carry the litter up and down the stairs?

One of the best laughs of the day occurred the day we were going to learn how to retrieve wounded people from the battlefield. We marched into the pine forests onto the *battlefield* which was a hilly, forested area. Scattered through the area were the *wounded*, lying on the ground, very comfortable in the warm sun, waiting to be placed on the litter to be carried to the hospital area. Each *casualty* had been identified with a particular type wound, and it was our job to make certain we didn't add to his *injuries* as we picked him up and placed him on the litter. Our wounded soldier turned out to be Norman Spector, he being over six feet tall and weighing more than two hundred pounds. We were on the slope of a hill and Spector made certain that he didn't make it any easier for us to get him on the litter. This was finally accomplished, but that was just the beginning of our troubles. Because of the slope of the hill, one litter bearer had to raise his end up high while the other bearer had to double up, keeping his hands close to the ground. The wounded man must always be kept level, or so we were told, and we tried to do our best. Well, as it turned out we almost *killed* Norman because we slipped while going downhill and dumped him on the ground!

Norman Spector was from Rutherford, New Jersey, and was a dentist in civilian life, but he was not exempt from basic training. The day our training was completed he was commissioned a first lieutenant and we pinned his bars on his shoulders. One minute he was a twenty-one dollar a month private and then, a moment later, became an officer. It was a pleasure to salute him.

4th Platoon, Camp Lee, Petersburg, Virginia. Friday, November 28, 1941. Norm Spector (with pipe) sitting on ground in front.

We were into November now and gradually settling into the daily routine. The nearest city was Petersburg, which was historically rich, but provided little insofar as entertainment was concerned. The PX and the theater were the most we could look forward to while on the base. Richmond was only about thirty-five miles away, and we were permitted to leave the post if we had no duty assignments such as guard duty or KP. Buses were provided for the trip there and back and it was usually our destination. Saturday morning always began with an inspection and a parade on the drill field. After that, we were free to leave the post for the weekend, returning early Sunday evening. In Richmond, the local armory had hundreds of cots spread across the floor and that was where I would spend the night. The town was peaceful and pretty and one of the friendliest places a serviceman would ever find. It was not unusual for one of the citizens to invite a soldier, who was a perfect stranger and whom he might have seen on the street, to come to his home for dinner.

One of my fondest memories of Richmond was the dances held on Saturday night at the Mosque Ballroom. It was very large with round, marble columns every twenty feet or so spread over the entire dance floor. On this particular evening, the band played a conga, and it didn't take but half a minute to have a few hundred people doing the *one, two, three, KICK* which is the conga beat. The leader started to weave snake-like, from one column to the next, and with that number of people in the line, neither the beginning nor the end of the line could be seen. As is typical of the conga, it kept going and going until people began to drop out due to sheer fatigue. The band could be heard but could not be seen, being hidden from view by the dancers. It was probably one of the most fun filled evenings of my short Army career. Leaving the ballroom, at the end of the dance, I could not help but sing the Cuban conga:

"I Came, I Saw, I Conga'd"[4]
I came, I saw, I conga'd, I came, I saw, I conga'd
It's plain to see you conquered me.
Each time I shake a shoulder, I get a little bolder,
A dance like this deserves a kiss.
One two three kick! One two three kick!

I went to bed that night doing the conga in my dreams.

Colletti, far right in front.

With the coming of November, our thoughts turned to Thanksgiving. Since our induction, none of us had gotten leave and the anticipation of going home *in uniform* was building up. At one of our outdoor meetings, our commanding officer informed us that half of the platoon could go home for Thanksgiving and half for Christmas. We would draw lots and were permitted to exchange with someone if we had drawn the wrong holiday. I chose Christmas. Needless to say, the days seemed to drag until Thanksgiving finally arrived. All went well. Those who chose Thanksgiving, received their three-day passes, went home and returned. Soon it would be our turn.

I had gone to Richmond, on this particular Saturday in December, and spent the night in the local armory. In the early afternoon, I returned to Camp Lee and after mess, wrote a few letters and went to bed at lights out. At two o'clock in the morning, the lights were turned on, followed by a loud, ear piercing, startling whistle blast and the shouted command to "Turn in your gas masks on the double!" In a panic, most of us tried to remember where we had put them. Fortunately, we managed to comply with the order while asking,

"What's going on?"

"The Japanese have bombed Pearl Harbor" was the reply.

"Where is Pearl Harbor? What is Pearl Harbor?"

"It is a major Navy and Army Air Corps base in the Hawaiian Islands," was the answer. Apparently, the Government was alarmed of the possibility of a surprise gas attack to the west coast of the United States. Obsolete or not, they were gathering all the masks they could locate, including ours. We had a few more hours of sleep before reveille, but I'm sure most of us were just lying there, wide-awake, wondering what it all meant.

The following morning, December 8, 1941, the entire complement of 22,000 men assembled in the very large parade ground that had a public address system. President Franklin Roosevelt spoke and made his famous "Day of Infamy" speech in which he said that a state of war now existed between Japan and the United States. After the speech, we returned to our barracks and were told by our commanding officer that all leaves had been cancelled for we were now at war. In addition, our initial obligation to serve for one year had now been changed to "*for the duration plus six months.*" It was also emphasized that we *serve at the convenience of the government and the President, since he is the Commander in Chief.* Almost as one, a chorus of voices boomed out,

"How about our Christmas leave?" We argued that the other half of the platoon had gone home for Thanksgiving, that it wasn't fair, how can you do this?

The reply was, "Bring me your T.S. Card and I'll punch it."

That comment was followed by the question, "What's a T.S. Card?" The answer was somewhat less than profound when they explained that it meant *tough shit*. We realized that fair or not, there was nothing we could do about it.

The frivolous, lighthearted attitude that had prevailed quickly gave way to a much more serious contemplation of what the future held in store. That night at chow, the commanding officer informed us of the alert plan that had been developed. We were to keep out packs rolled and ready in the event of a perceived emergency. At a given signal, the lights would be extinguished, we were to grab our equipment and exit the barracks as quickly as possible and march to a previously selected wooded area about a mile from camp, where we would take cover.

The declaration of war resulted in a change in our schedule. What was supposed to have been a twelve-week training period would be shortened and we would soon be shipped out to another base.

Speculation and confusion was the order of the day. No one knew anything and you had your pick of which rumor to believe.

The next few days were filled with thoughts of where we would be sent. Naturally, we all hoped that it would be somewhere close enough to home; close enough to make it possible to use a three-day pass. A few days later, we had our answer. We were told that we were going to an airbase, Langley Field, Hampton, Virginia. We would be the medical detachment team attached to the airbase. It was farther from home, but I was very happy to learn of our destination.

Best Platoon Award December 21, 1941

I had always been interested in aviation; an interest that could be traced back to Lindbergh's flight in 1927, when I was eight years old. His flight was sensational, and I'm sure that it captivated the minds of just about all the kids of my age. Reports of new speed, altitude and distance records were reported with great regularity in the newspapers; and those of us who were fascinated with flying were dubbed *air-minded*, a term that everyone has forgotten. Without looking up we could identify the plane going overhead just by the sound of its engines -- then we certainly had to look up to verify our conclusion. Building and flying model airplanes became very popular with contests being held throughout the country. Every month, we would impatiently wait for the latest issue of "Model Airplane News" to become available. I still possess copies of the magazine back to December 1932 in which my picture appears. Without doubt, going to an airbase was great news for me.

2

LANGLEY FIELD, HAMPTON, VIRGINIA

On December 18, 1941, I boarded a GI truck and departed Camp Lee for Hampton, Virginia. The most vivid memory I have of that trip was that I was numb with cold, sitting in the last seat next to the tailgate. The wind was whipping in and of course, there was no heat in the back of the truck.

My first glimpse of Langley Field was a most welcome sight after the sand of Camp Lee. The roads were paved with concrete, there was grass, brick homes and permanent buildings. We knew that it was an old established base, but we weren't prepared for what we saw. The truck convoy crossed a guarded bridge to enter the base and the road became its main thoroughfare. We proceeded about a quarter of a mile, made a right turn and then a quick left. There on the right was this very large brick building, the station hospital. The trucks pulled over to the curb and we were told to fall in on the hospital lawn. The usual roster call followed, we answered to our name, and were given barracks assignments. My group had to march back about four blocks to the main thoroughfare to T95 which was a long, low, one story building with an entrance in the middle of the building, facing the street. It was about a hundred feet long and obviously not a barracks. Upon entering, what we saw was a large room, about forty feet wide. The place was a complete mess. The floor was littered with items of equipment, canteens, clothing, shoes, writing material, mess kits, etc. Obviously, the previous occupants had to leave so quickly that they did not have enough time to pack when they shipped out December 8th, the day after the bombing of Pearl Harbor. (A few years later I learned that the unit that had pulled out in such a frantic hurry would be the very unit I would become part of; the 22nd Bomb Group.)

Cots covered the entire floor, and it was apparent that cleaning up the mess was the fist order of business. There was a large counter at one end of the room, across its width, and it had the typical layout of a quick food and beverage dispensing facility. It was obvious that the building was designed for recreational use and not as living quarters. Soon we discovered that our so-called barracks had but one toilet, one sink and no showers for about thirty-five men. To bathe we had to walk back about three blocks to barracks T66, behind the hospital, carrying needed items such as soap, towels, combs, etc. and time our bathing until the regular occupants had finished. Since it was winter, going out into the cold after showering was a rather chilling experience.

The next order of business called for a trip back to the quartermaster in the hospital area, to draw bedding equipment and a footlocker. Upon returning to my new found paradise I selected a cot, put my foot locker at the end of it, put an identification tag on the end of the cot and made up the bed. That completed the moving in process.

Day number two started with a few orientation speeches and was followed by duty assignments. I was assigned to the G.U. isolation ward which was a long, low, temporary building separated from the hospital by a wide driveway.

Chapter 2

Langley Field, January 1942

Station Hospital Langley Field January 1942

The ward consisted of three locked cells, where so-called *mental cases* were confined, an office for the nurse and one for the medical officer in charge. Closets lined the hallway leading to the ward which had beds on each side of a center aisle. My first reaction to my assignment was "Oh no!", but I soon learned that this was much better than working in the main hospital where the medical and surgical wards were located. There, the patients were in need of nursing assistance and the orderlies were referred to as *bedpan commandos*. The patients in the isolation ward, however, were known as *walking wounded* since their confinement was for things such as measles, flu, V.D. or some other ailment which did not confine them to bed. There were five orderlies assigned to the ward and every sixth night one of us remained on emergency duty through the night. This was not a bad deal because we could read, write letters or just indulge in the most popular pastime of all: killing cockroaches. While reading, it was not unusual to see a few of them start crawling across the desk and this called for an immediate use of the nearby fly swatter. We kept score of our *kills* and turned it into a game to see who could rack up the highest score.

Overall, being in the medical department was a good duty assignment. We were not a spit and polish outfit. There were people on emergency duty through the night which made it impossible to conduct daytime inspections. Of course, it was necessary to maintain army standards, but it was much more relaxed. The officers in command were professional people; doctors, dentists and nurses who did not have a militaristic point of view and who had been called up because their skills were needed. The nurses were second lieutenants, easy going and no one pulled rank unless the situation demanded it. I was in the Army, but after a few weeks, it was almost like getting up in the morning to go to work. In particular, I liked Nurse Betty Seabrooke from Erie, Pennsylvania, Carol Behyl from Wisconsin, and Wilma Stout, home state unknown. In early 1942, they were shipped out to the European Theater of Operations. I corresponded with Betty Seabrooke for a while, but then we lost track of each other.

I have always felt that the nurses never received the recognition due them. Overseas, they were exposed to the same dangers, diseases, hardships and horrible living conditions that the men faced, but seldom were given the vote of thanks to which they were entitled. They did a great job.

Writing letters was the primary connection to people back home, but the written word was no substitute for hearing a familiar voice. We bridged that gap by making long distance phone calls from the public phone located in the hospital stairwell. The best time to call was Sunday night after mess when there were fewer calls being placed. We would hurry to the booth, hoping that the line was not too long. In those days, calls were placed with the operator, and we would hang up and wait for the operator to ring back when the connection was made. We knew that it could be hours before our call was completed, so writing material and books were very much in evidence while we waited. Finally, the phone would ring and the operator would ask for the person who had called a particular number. It was important to have a good supply of coins on hand to pay for the call, and it was a very slow process. Out of consideration for the others waiting, we tried to keep our calls as short as possible. For the most part, there was very little of importance being said, but just hearing the voices of family members made it worthwhile.

The Service Club, which was just a few blocks from the hospital, was the scene of the weekly Friday night dance. There was a live GI band and they were very good. They played the same arrangements of the hit songs that the famous bands played, and we did enjoy listening to the music. Girls from neighboring towns such as Hopewell and Colonial Heights were brought in by bus, but the only problem was that the men outnumbered the girls about five or six to one. You would ask a girl for the next dance and all was fine when the music started, but shortly thereafter a whistle was blown and a new partner would cut in.

With the first dance step, the first words spoken would usually be the question, "What's your name and where are you from?" I would guess that it was not unusual for a girl to have four or five different partners for each selection played. The girls were not permitted to save a dance for anyone and, from their point of view, I would assume that they had a better time just meeting a lot of different men. What was unfortunate was that you could not stay with a partner that you had found more compatible than the others. Dance styles clashed and the girl who could waltz well might not be so good at doing the Lindy. Still, it was fun.

Without doubt, the highlight of one of the dances occurred when we pulled off a very funny stunt. I do not know who concocted the brilliant idea, but it worked beautifully. With the help and contribution of clothing from the nurses, good friend Private George Palmer was dressed in women's clothing and brought to the dance. There was a large, rotating mirrored ball on the ceiling of the dance hall and we waited until the lights were lowered and spotlights were aimed on the ball to dance *her* onto the floor. George was about five feet, eight inches tall, very nice features, a good actor and a good dancer who easily followed the lead of male partners. Of course, the first question asked upon dancing was, "What's you name and where are you from?"

"I'm from Colonial Heights and my name is Snooky LaPalma" was the answer in a girlish voice. Then the whistle would blow, a new partner would cut in and the charade would be repeated. When the lights came on, Snooky and I were ushered up to the stage and we sang, "Rose-O-Day." Only then did the men see that Snooky was wearing GI shoes!

Privates George "Snooky La Palma" Palmer & Silveo Colletti
Service Club, Langley Field, April 13, 1942

Chapter 2

We had some good news with the coming of the new year, 1942. Working hours now were from 7:30 AM to 3:30 PM and one night until 7:30 PM. Saturday and Sundays were just working days, but keeping busy made time pass more quickly. I no longer did guard duty, KP, fireman or barracks orderly duty as long as I held this job. That was a great improvement!

Another *big event* in the life of Private Colletti was the increase of pay to thirty dollars a month, at the end of January, since I had now been in uniform three months.

On February 7, 1942 I wrote the following in a letter to my friend, Carl Frank:

"Last night (Friday) I was the emergency man when a call came in regarding a mid-air collision of two P40 planes. One pilot had bailed out, but the other couldn't be found. The one who had bailed out showed up twenty-five minutes later and he was quite a mess. He had a bad scalp cut and his clothing and helmet was soaked in blood. He still had the rip cord in his hand although he had lost consciousness. A search party went out to look for the other P40 and while they were out another call came in about a Navy plane that had cracked up. A lieutenant, three other men and I went out to look for the Navy plane. It had crashed about thirty-six miles away going toward Richmond. We sloshed around in the mud (it was raining hard) and we located the wreck of a Brewster Buffalo. The plane was a mess, but the pilot escaped with just a broken arm. Later on, the pilot in the other P40 was found dead. All in all, three Navy and two Army planes cracked up last night. It was quite an experience and it is difficult to put it into words. When I returned to Langley, I had to sleep in a tent where I could be reached quickly in the event of another emergency. As you might have guessed, the tent leaked like hell and I got wet while sleeping. Ah, Army life! I'm writing this while on emergency in the hospital. This has been a very busy weekend and I sure wish I could get a breathing spell. I'm in charge of the Isolation Ward and it is a cinch as long as there is nothing wrong. In the event of a fire or air raid alert, however, I'd be busier than I have ever been in my life."

Here is a good example of how the Army works at times. In mid February, I was appointed as acting corporal but had not, as yet, been promoted to private first class. My new status put me in charge of twenty-one men. I fall them out and in at reveille and take the roll call and report to the sergeant. When inspections are held, it is my job to check on the others and direct them to fix anything which I think would not pass inspection. Keeping them quiet after lights out and getting them up on time in the morning was also my responsibility. What makes it difficult is that they are all my friends and therefore might resent the fact that I can tell them what to do. My orders were to report anyone who didn't comply with the sergeant. Fortunately, that was never necessary.

We managed to keep the jukeboxes busy playing some of the hits of the day such as "Deep in the Heart of Texas" and "Humpty Dumpty Heart" which were very popular.

As for recreation, most of us felt fortunate to be stationed at Langley Field and we quickly took advantage of the bowling alleys, PX and theater. I soon learned to disengage myself from friends who wanted to have "just one more beer and then we'll go," if I wanted to get a good seat at the movies. I fell into that trap twice and found myself sitting in the first row, so close that it became an ordeal to watch. From then on, I became a *loner* if there was a movie I wanted to see.

My *domain*, the isolation ward, was very close to the seawall on the eastern side of the base. Canoes were housed there and available for our use. When duty free, we would check one out and invite the nurses to go along as our guests. The weather was sunny and warm and for a little while, the routine of army life was forgotten. One sport which I had sorely missed was softball. It was impossible to play in the sand at Camp Lee, but here at Langley, athletic equipment and playing fields were available, and we quickly assembled a number of softball teams and began regular, scheduled play. For me, it was more than just a game. It was a connecting link to the days of civilian life I had left behind.

Hampton was the nearest town to Langley Field and transportation was no problem. Anyone in uniform walking along the road toward town could easily hitch a ride. Because of gasoline rationing, the speed limit was set to thirty-five in order to conserve fuel, and at that slower speed, drivers would be more likely to stop and offer someone a ride. The USO Club in town held a dance on Saturday night which was less crowded than the Service Club dances on the base. Occasionally, it was possible to keep a good partner for a complete dance before someone would cut in. In addition, there were facilities for writing letters and a private room with a phonograph and a nice selection of 78-rpm records.

"Tangerine"[5]
Tangerine, she is all they claim, with her eyes of night and lips as bright as flame.
Tangerine, when she dances by, senoritas stare and caballeros sigh.
And I've seen toasts to Tangerine, raised in every bar across the Argentine,
Yes, she has them all on the run, but her heart belongs to just one,
Her heart belongs to Tangerine.

Those were the words to the song which I kept singing, over and over, as I returned to the base one evening, hoping not to forget the melody or the lyric. I found it in the stack of records at the USO Club, and it was there that I heard it for the first time. It was done by the Jimmy Dorsey Orchestra, and sung by Bob Eberle and Helen O'Connell. I had brought my ten-string, tiple ukulele with me when I was drafted, and I couldn't wait to return to the barracks to work out the chord changes. Without fail, my mind reverts to that evening in 1942 every time I play that tune almost seventy-four years later.

Another big hit of that era was a song that was being sung by everyone, everywhere:

"Blues in the Night"[6]
My mama done tol' me, when I was in knee-pants
My mama done tol' me, "Son, a woman'll sweet talk
And give ya the big eye, but when the sweet talkin's done
A woman's a two-face, a worrisome thing who'll leave ya to sing the blues in the night"

Everybody knew the first few lines, but very few ever learned the entire, lengthy lyric.

* * * * *

The long wait finally came to an end when I received a five-day furlough and departed for home on the 20th of February, 1942. This would be my first time home since my induction and it was exciting just to anticipate walking through the front door in uniform.

The trip home entailed going to Old Point Comfort where rail service was available. In order not to waste precious time, I took the train that departed at midnight for the trip north, meandering through Virginia, Delaware and finally New Jersey. It made so many stops that I named it the *Milk Train* because to me it seemed to be delivering milk to every little town along the way. During the war years, civilian transportation was shunted aside and military movements had priority, which I suppose made sense. For five days, I tried to cram all the fun I could into every waking hour, seeing old friends, eating good food, being with the family, sleeping in my own bed in my own room and driving a car again. I never realized how much I would miss driving. We accept it so automatically, but when you're away and don't have a car at your disposal, all you have left is the memory. Sleep was secondary and grudgingly accepted when it no longer could be denied, but much too soon it was over and it was time to leave.

The trip back to Langley was pleasant. It took nine and a half hours and the ferry ride from Old Point Comfort was enjoyable because it wasn't cold and I could stand on the deck and watch the shore pass by. It was 7:00 PM when I signed in and the mere thought of arising at 5:15 AM was brutal. *Furlough hangover* lasted about four days during which time things got done a little slower than normal.

Early in April, the big social event of the year took place over a period of three days. Quoting from the letter to Carl Frank of April 11, 1942:

"For the past three nights I have been to the Service Club. The dance floor has been roped off for dancing and around the perimeter of the floor little concession stands have been erected. It is just like a carnival complete with popcorn and throwing balls at dolls. Busloads of girls have been brought in from the nearby towns to be our dance partners and the cost was ten cents per dance. Just to make it complete, Gene Raymond, the movie star, attended. He is a 1st Lt. in the Air Corps and is stationed here at Langley and his quarters are adjacent to my barracks. He's the same as he appears on the screen, handsome and quite friendly. He presented a pen and pencil set to a lucky ticket holder and a semi professional troupe of chorus girls put on a floor show doing, among other things, the Can Can. Last night Jimmy Stewart the screen star came down to say hello to his buddy Raymond, and then Mrs. Franklin Roosevelt put in an appearance on the base."

During those Langley Field days in April of 1942, we kept the jukeboxes going full blast playing our favorite songs: "Tangerine", "Dear Mom", "Shrine of Saint Cecilia", "This Is No Laughing Matter", "I Don't Want To Walk Without You" and "Zoot Suit."

In early May, without any fanfare or blowing of trumpets, Private Colletti was promoted to Private First Class. I have no recollection whatsoever of the promotion. The written proof of the great event was provided by the return address on a letter I wrote May 6, 1942. Obviously, I was getting ahead in the Army. Wow! One stripe!

There were many changes in mid May of 1942. People were being shipped out with some going to overseas destinations and others to bases here in the States. The departure of one of the x-ray technicians in that lab created a vacancy, and I was offered the opportunity to leave the isolation ward and go to work in the x-ray lab.

The lab was staffed by six enlisted men, with Sergeant Bob Bennett in charge. The other five men rotated in their duties which consisted of taking and then developing x-rays in the dark room and typing and filing reports. My typing was excellent, and I did have some dark room experience back home, developing my own pictures. Because of the cumulative effect of x-ray radiation, the five technicians were rotated every week going from the office to the dark room and to the lab itself. We also were required to have a blood test every month to check on the amount of radiation to which we had been exposed. The medical officer, a trained roentgenologist, would come in every day to read the pictures after which we prepared typewritten reports. I thoroughly enjoyed the change and I was allowed to assist in the lab wherever my limited experience permitted. On the first day of my new job, we had two gunshot patients to x-ray. Quoting from a letter to Carl dated May 26th:

"One had to do with a sergeant who was shot in the face with a load of buckshot. Fortunately, it wasn't

a direct hit, the lead had first struck a wall and then it splashed into his face. The x-ray showed nineteen pieces of lead, two in his eyelids and the rest in his cheeks and skull. In the other case, the patient had shot himself in the foot with his own 45 caliber gun."

The x-ray lab became very busy in the month of June 1942. Quoting once again from a letter written June 20th:

"I've really been working these days! As you might know, Uncle Sam is trying to get a large fleet of glider pilots trained in a hell of a hurry. For the past week, hundreds of men have applied for the training and that translates into a lot of extra work. On average, on a normal day, we would take about 25 or 30 plates. For the past week, we have been taking 85 to 90 per day and that is a very heavy workload. I've now learned enough to operate the machine and of course, I have the darkroom technique down to a "T." Needless to say, it is very hot and stuffy in a ten foot square room with only the darkroom light on while developing that many plates and then drying them. Also, fresh, unexposed film must be reloaded in the light tight cassettes.

After each plate is read and diagnosed by the medical officer, I write down the diagnosis and then type up the reports and distribute them to the doctors or wards that had requested them. Then we have to file our reports and keep our records straight. Of course, there are always inspections so things must be orderly at all times. Going back to the darkroom, new solutions must be mixed as required, file plates that have been read must be filed and supply needs must be anticipated and ordered before we run short. A half an hour has been added to our working day in an effort to keep things moving smoothly. It's a lot of work, but at least I feel that I am accomplishing something. I was a little bit apprehensive the first time I set up the machine and took the x-ray myself. The machine sells for about eight thousand dollars and the x-ray tube itself is worth about a hundred fifty dollars. Each individual exposure requires a different meter setting because of the various density of bone.

Overloading the machine might burn it out, and overexposure will damage the tube. It is quite complicated in that respect, but I'm on to it rather well."

About 20 June, much to my surprise, I was promoted to corporal -- wow -- two stripes! Progress was slow in the Army, but being in x-ray and doing work that is more meaningful did help.

The transfer of personnel created space in the regular barracks and finally we were moved into T66 which was behind the hospital. I was on the upper floor and it felt so good not to have to brave the elements to perform the much-needed daily rituals such as bathing and shaving.

One of the things I enjoyed doing was going to the flight line to get an up-close, first hand look at whatever aircraft were parked there. Two fighter planes were parked side by side, a P40 and the other a Bell Airacobra P39. The Bell was a radical departure from the conventional designs, its engine was behind the pilot and the driveshaft to drive the propeller passed between the pilot's legs. I got up on the wing and opened the door (yes, it had a door) to see into the cockpit. The cockpit was very small and cramped and it was obvious that only someone my size, one hundred forty pounds, five foot six could squeeze into it. The plane was used in the Pacific Theater in New Guinea and saw a lot of action.

While meandering around the flight line, I went over to the operations area and learned that we were eligible to go along as a passenger, on a space available basis, on departing flights. Of course, one had to be on leave or have a pass and be fortunate enough to latch onto a flight that was going where you wanted to go. I signed on for whatever was going north, got a three-day pass (which didn't start until I departed) and

Chapter 2

waited to be called. There was a flight going to Baltimore, and I didn't hesitate to accept. I knew that the trip from Baltimore to Newark, New Jersey, which was on the main line of the *Pennsylvania Railroad*, was fast and it would give me enough time home to make it worthwhile.

A few moments after becoming airborne, a thought occurred to me. Despite the years of building model planes and of living, breathing and thinking of aviation, this was the first time I had been off the ground, and I loved it! Being in the medical department was good duty, but I longed for the Air Corps. There was one sticky problem: I needed to have two years of college, or equivalent, to be accepted into the Aviation Cadet Program and I didn't have it.

Things were going well in the x-ray lab, but it was obvious that I had reached the limit of what I could do. Formal training was needed, and I was offered the opportunity to go to the Army Medical Center, Walter Reed Hospital, on the northern outskirts of Washington DC for the x-ray technician course. If successfully completed it would entitle me to promotion to staff sergeant. The other benefits were obvious; four and a half hours from home and a social situation in Washington where the women outnumbered the men about five to one! No more whistle blowing at the dances! A new speed record of acceptance was set by me that day. At 8:30 AM, Friday, July 31, 1942 I left Langley Field and boarded the train for Washington DC.

Promoted to T-5, July 1942

3

WALTER REED HOSPITAL, ARMY MEDICAL CENTER, WASHINGTON DC

The distance from Langley Field to Washington DC is about 250 miles, took twelve hours, and I finally arrived at 10:00 PM. When I went to claim my baggage (which was my barracks bag), I was instructed to go to a lower level of Union Station. What they didn't tell me was that mine would be one of hundreds of similar bags piled ten feet high. Fortunately, it was one of the last to be added to the pile.

The following morning I was able to see how truly beautiful the Army Medical Center was. There were trees, flowers and shrubs everywhere, super imposed upon green, manicured lawns. My barracks was a two story brick building set atop a slight hill. It had finished floors and I was delighted to see that each student had a wall locker, which was a great improvement over the standard footlocker. There was much more room between beds and for once I was not in an overcrowded environment.

Classes began the next day, Monday morning. The instructor was a tech sergeant, who extended a welcome and then proceeded to outline the course of study. There was much to learn beginning with the nomenclature of the x-ray machine, descriptions and functions of various parts, wiring diagrams, loading and handling film, and darkroom procedures were also briefly covered. I had taken mechanical drawing in junior and senior high school, and that training proved to be very helpful when reading diagrams and tracing electrical circuits. Students who had more of a classical background in high school seemed to have a more difficult time understanding it. Knowledge of physics was also important.

Toward the end of August, we began to study anatomy, a subject of which we knew nothing but in which we had to excel. Obviously, it would be impossible to carry out the doctor's x-ray requests if we did not have complete knowledge of the human body. The classroom had many pictures and charts which gave us a graphic description of the subject, but our attention was focused on the adult skeleton in one corner of the room. It had been reworked, using nuts and bolts, making it possible to remove an arm, hand, etc., for closer study. Certainly, it was a new experience for us, but also a very interesting one. To say that a few were squeamish would be an overstatement, but it did require some mental adjustment when we began to handle the bones.

You can rest assured that there would always be someone in the group who was a joker and who could be relied upon to dream up some gag. Our joker was named Benny and he pulled this stunt on one of the students who was uncomfortable working with the skeleton. As we exited the classroom for noontime mess, Benny removed the skeleton's hand, put it in his pocket and brought it to the mess hall. He waited until his *target* had selected a seat, put down his books and then got into line to get his food. Benny then put the hand on the table where the target would sit, and covered it with a napkin. All eyes were focused on the victim as they waited for him to return. When he picked up the napkin, the sight of the hand on the table was more than the poor guy could handle. He put his tray down, said he wasn't hungry after all, did an about face and walked out of the mess hall. After he left, we realized that the joke wasn't funny and left us with a guilty feeling.

Without doubt, the most important aspect of the anatomy course was the loose-leaf notebook which we started with the first class and which counted heavily toward a passing grade. It was our responsibility to make an ink drawing of the particular bone that was being studied, supplying the necessary medical

terminology which we would be using in actual practice. Tracing the bone from the textbook picture was permissible, and neatness and accuracy was a must. This was accomplished after school hours for it was a slow process. Incidentally, I still have the notebook!

Early in September, we finally began to use the machine. The class was divided into two man teams, alternating as patient or technician. The x-ray lab was a long room, partitioned into stalls about eight feet wide. There was lead shielding on the walls of each stall to reduce (hopefully) the amount of radiation we were being exposed to. Unfortunately, there was a great amount of radiation, due to our inexperience. If a mistake was made a retake was necessary. That wasn't bad on simple takes such as the hand, but the very difficult ones such as sinuses had to be repeated many times. As we progressed in our anatomy studies, the pictures we took became more difficult, but slowly, progress was made.

There was an exam every Saturday morning, at 8:00, which could be completed in half an hour if you had studied. Upon completion of the exam, we were free until reveille Monday morning. The great motivation for being prepared was the fact that it was only about four and a half hours from Washington to Newark and that trains departed just about every hour. Secondly, one of the students had a car, which was parked outside the classroom, ready for a mad dash down to Union Station, hoping to hit it right and not have to wait for the next train. Six of us booked passage for the entire school term chipping in to share expenses. If you weren't finished with the exam when he was ready to go, you missed out!

Coming back to Washington, however, was a lot different. Once again, the idea was to cram all one could into that little time. Family expected some time spent with them and going out seeing old friends (if they hadn't been drafted!) was a priority. Sleep, of course, was resorted to just before collapsing. When it was time to leave, a family member would drive me to the Linden railroad station where I would take the train to Newark and then catch the midnight train for Washington. Finding a seat was a joke because the train was very crowded. I would stand until we reached Baltimore, where many got off, giving others a

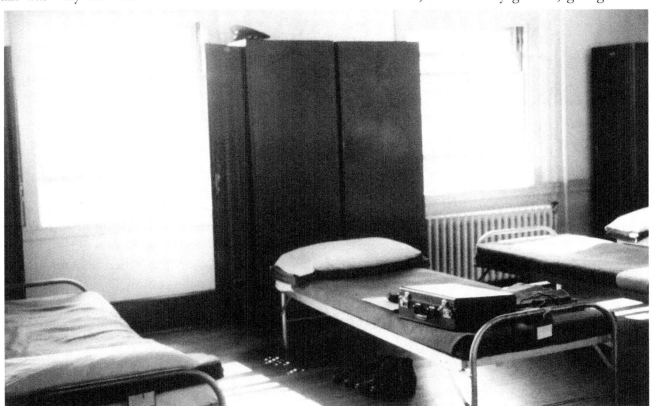

My bed.

chance to sit down. Much to my surprise, I learned how to sleep standing up! Transportation from Union Station to the Medical Center was very good with a stop at the very entrance I needed. Time and again, I could see that the lights were already on in the barracks and the men were falling out for roll call. I would join the group, answer "here" when my name was called and skip breakfast, choosing instead to lie down for a little while before classes began. I hoped, as I joined the others to go to class, that I had been scheduled to be the patient that day because I could then lie down on the table. It was quite a sight to see many of us stripped down to our shorts, sound asleep while the technician twisted arms, legs and body into position using sand bags to keep everything in place!

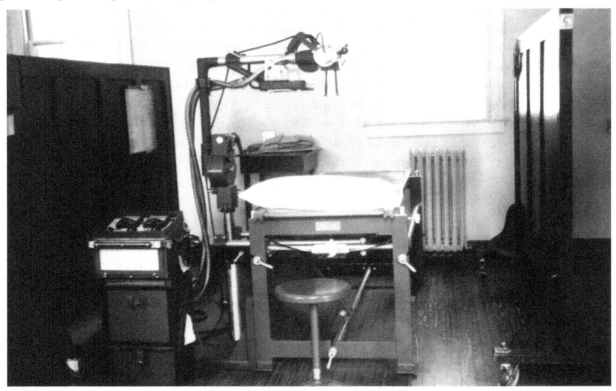

X-ray booth. Only place to sleep after a long weekend home.

One of the most useless duties we were given was air raid duty which required men so assigned to remain on post over the weekend. I don't know what we could have done about it if there had been a raid, since everyone in Washington would have known about it too. I got stuck with it a number of times, but I looked upon it as an opportunity to get some rest. The midnight train ride from Newark to Washington did take its toll. On one wasted weekend, I did what all the other air raid wardens did; I went into town. Tommy Dorsey was appearing live on stage and of course, the featured vocalist was Frank Sinatra. That I did not want to miss! At the completion of the movie, the lights dimmed for a moment and then brightened as the band began to play the Dorsey theme song, "Getting Sentimental Over You." Tommy Dorsey then greeted the audience and said,

"Ladies and gentlemen, Frank Sinatra." He strode onto the stage to the microphone and without any fanfare began to sing his first number which was "Take Me."[7]

> Take me, I'm yours if you'll take me, I want you to make me a part of your heart.
> And hold me, I dreamed you would hold me, now really enfold me, say we'll never part.
> All the love I have to give, I want to give to you,
> And as long as I shall live, I'll only live for you,
> Take me, and never forsake me, my darling, please take me and make me your own
> And make me your own.

He sang without a break for half an hour, one great song after another. The Sinatra of that era was the one I remembered best. It was a very memorable, enjoyable evening.

Socially speaking, wartime Washington DC was heaven on earth for servicemen, with women out numbering men. One Saturday night, in late August, I attended a dance at the YWCA in town. There were five floors of dancing with an orchestra on every floor. Cost at the door was twenty-five cents. The USO had denied entry to about 90 girls and many of those who had already been admitted were dancing with each other for lack of male partners. It was rather sad to see.

Musically speaking it seemed that every few days a new hit song could be heard. In the spring everyone was singing "Deep in the Heart of Texas", "Blues in the Night," "Zoot Suit", "Tangerine", and "Moonlight Cocktail." The summer months also had plenty of hits with many of them embracing a sort of *wait for me* theme which was understandable since so many men and women were separated from loved ones. "I Don't Want to Walk Without You", "Dear Mom", "Johnny Doughboy", "Don't Sit Under the Apple Tree", "Stage Door Canteen", "He Wears a Pair of Silver Wings", "A Boy in Khaki", "This is Worth Fighting For", "When the Lights Come on Again" and "Praise the Lord and Pass the Ammunition" were songs that I remember well. Harry James hit it big with "Sleepy Lagoon", and the juke boxes were kept busy playing, "One Dozen Roses", "Jersey Bounce", "I Remember You", "Jingle Jangle Jingle", "Amen", "Gal in Kalamazoo" and "Mr. Five by Five."

There was a Minsky's Burlesque in town and of course, we all went. While there, you could be certain to hear one of the big hit songs of the day which was called "Strip Polka."[8]

> "Strip Polka"
> There's a burlesque theater where the gang loves to go
> To see Queenie the cutie of the burlesque show
> And the thrill of the evening is when out Queenie skips
> And the band plays the polka while she strips
> "Take it off, take it off" cries a voice from the rear
> "Take it off, take it off" soon it's all you can hear
> But she's always a lady even in pantomime, so she stops and always just in time

During September and October more classroom time was devoted to the use of the portable x-ray equipment, since it was likely that many of us would be assigned to a combat unit. There, we would be working out in the field where working conditions would be a far cry from what we did indoors. The problems were many; heat, moisture, improvised darkroom, mud, etc. just to name a few.

The good times came to an end with completion of the course in late October. I received my diploma, was recommended for promotion to staff sergeant and was given orders to return to Langley Field. It had been a wonderful four months. Lots of work, but a lot of fun too, possibly the best time I would spend in uniform.

For the Duration *plus* Six Months

Army of the United States

To all who shall see these presents, greeting:

Know ye, that reposing special trust and confidence in the fidelity and abilities of Technician 5th Grade Silvio G. Colletti, 32185849, Med. Dept., I do hereby appoint him *Corporal (Temporary), Med. & Dental Service, ARMY OF THE UNITED STATES, to rank as such from the thirteenth day of October one thousand nine hundred and forty-two. He is therefore carefully and diligently to discharge the duty of † Corporal by doing and performing all manner of things thereunto belonging. And I do strictly charge and require all Noncommissioned Officers and Soldiers under his command to be obedient to his orders as Corporal And he is to observe and follow such orders and directions from time to time, as he shall receive from his Superior Officers and Noncommissioned Officers set over him, according to the rules and discipline of War.

Given under my hand at Station Hospital, Langley Field, Virginia this thirteenth day of October in the year of our Lord one thousand nine hundred and forty-two.

JOSEPH NAGLE, MAJOR, MEDICAL CORPS
ACTG. SURGEON

W. D., A. G. O. Form No. 58
March 25, 1924

* Insert grade, company, and regiment or branch; e. g., "Corporal, Company A, 1st Infantry," "Sergeant, Quartermaster Corps."
† Insert grade.

Medical Department Professional Service Schools
United States Army

Washington, D. C.

This is to certify that

TECHNICIAN FIFTH GRADE SILVEO G. COLLETTI, MEDICAL DEPARTMENT,

has satisfactorily completed the

Enlisted Specialist Course in Roentgenography

prescribed at

The Army Medical School

August 1, 1942 - October 24, 1942

Given at the Army Medical Center, Washington, D.C.   October 24, 1942.

_____
Lt. Colonel, Medical Corps,
Director.

Form 60b
Medical Department, U. S. Army
(Authorized May 3, 1939)

_____
Colonel, Medical Corps,
Acting Assistant Commandant.

GPO 16—19736

4

BACK TO LANGLEY FIELD

Upon returning to Langley Field, I experienced a sort of *coming home feeling* when I reported to the x-ray lab. There were two changes to speak of, I being one of them. When I had left for Walter Reed, I was just an assistant to the other technicians, helping out with whatever needed to be done. Now I was the man in charge when it was my week to be in the lab, taking those pictures which the doctor had ordered. For the sake of our health, we continued to rotate our duties, spending a week in the office, lab and darkroom. We were kept busy, Langley being a major base with many GI families living on the post. It was not unusual to have a pregnant women come in followed by some GI that had been hurt in training.

The other change probably would come under the heading of *isn't it a small world?* But first, it is necessary to backtrack to the late thirties. Twelfth Street, in Linden, was the scene of many touch football and softball games. Around the corner on Wood Avenue lived one of the regulars, Phil Gushin, who was a year or so younger than I. We were good friends, but our activities were primarily confined to the sports arena. Notice was received early in December, informing us that a new commanding officer would be

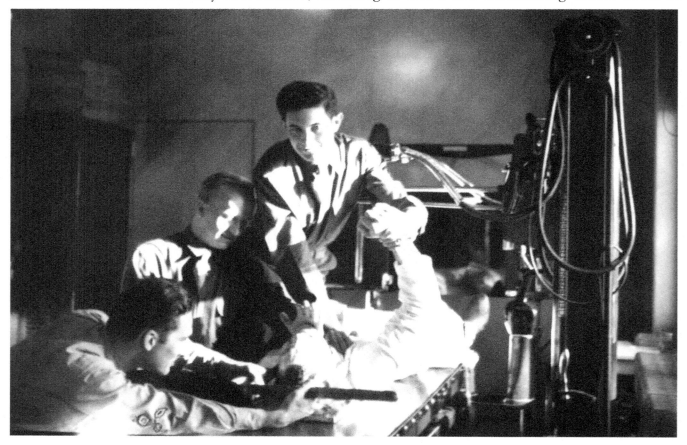

arriving and his name was 2nd Lt. Phillip Gushin, newly graduated from officer's candidate school. I had a few days to think about how I should react at our first meeting; but obviously, the only correct way was to observe proper military courtesy, salute, as you would any officer, and say sir. It all went well when we did meet face to face, with warm conversation when we recalled memories about Linden and the kids with whom we had played in our teens. Due to our busy daily routine, however, we had very few meetings and simply engaged in small talk when we did meet.

Always looking for a laugh, we had fun with one of our friends who required a routine chest x-ray. Each plate we exposed was identified through the use of alphabet letters made of solid lead, which are used to spell out the patients name, etc., and which are placed in the lower corner of the cassette that contained the film. Since the x-ray does not penetrate lead, the vital information is *printed* directly onto the film. Using some cunning and ingenuity, we managed to add our friends name to the x-ray of a very pregnant woman. Finally, the moment arrived when *our mark* came in to get the doctors report. With big smiles on our collective faces, we told him everything was fine, he was in perfect health and that he was pregnant and proved it when we showed him the plate with his name on it!

* * * * *

My ambition to someday become a commissioned officer remained, but realistically speaking, it did not seem to be an attainable goal. The memory of being on 24-hour KP the first day at Camp Lee, Virginia, however, was still very fresh in my mind. Graduating from Walter Reed, with the possibility of a promotion, gave rise to the thought that perhaps it would be wise to just make the best of my present situation and take it as it comes. The future was very uncertain in that month of November 1942. In all probability, I would follow in the steps of those before me, being shipped out to some base where x-ray technicians were needed. With the acceptance of that decision, I found that I could relax and concentrate on the job at hand. All went well for a few weeks, but two events upset the apple cart.

To this very day, I am of the opinion that the smartest, most beautiful uniform of any country was our own so called *pinks and green* worn by American officers at that time. It was conservative; not full of *scrambled eggs* and excessive embroidery, and it had class. Class A uniform consisted of the forest green blouse and so-called *pink* pants (which actually was beige,) khaki shirt and khaki tie. When not wearing the blouse it was permissible to wear all green, all pink or a combination of both for shirt and pants. On this particular day, I was typing reports when an officer entered. He was a colonel and his uniform consisted of pink shirt, pink pants with a forest green tie with highly polished mahogany brown shoes. I had seen this combination before, but he also had a pair of silver wings on his chest. I took one look at him and thought, *that's for me*. Just getting a commission was no longer enough; it had to be in the Air Corps and I had to have the wings. The desire to wear that uniform motivated me, but the old stumbling block remained, I didn't have the required two years of college or equivalent. Dead end.

The second event took place in the same office. I was concentrating on the report I was typing and looked up when an enlisted man entered the room. He handed me a paper which was a doctor's request for an x-ray for Sergeant William Holland. I was about to say something and stopped when I had this strange feeling that we knew each other. We both had puzzled expressions on our faces, feeling that we had met before, but the answer to the question of where and when eluded us. The standard questions came next when he asked, "Where are you from?"

My reply was "New Jersey."

"I'm from New Jersey too" he answered.

"What city are you from?"

Our replies were the same, "Linden."

He asked me my name and his next question was, "Do you have a brother named Sal?"

"Yes" was my reply and with that his face lit up.

"Now I remember" he stated. "He [Sal] had dated (and married) my neighbor, Helen, right?" All the facts were correct. Slowly I, too, began to recall those events in the thirties. I had gone with Sal on a few occasions, when he went to Helen's house on Blancke Street, and it was there that I was introduced to *Dutch* Holland.

His next question was, "What the hell are you doing in the medical department, why aren't you in the Air Corps?" I had made the local newspapers quite regularly winning model airplane competitions, and he was aware of it, so the question was understandable. Of course, my answer was that I did not have the required two years of college, so I never tried to get into the Air Corps flight training program. I really perked up, however, when he explained that he was with the 5th Material Unit, located on the flight line here at Langley, and that he supervised the taking of the aviation cadet exam. His job was to hand out the test instructing them of the most efficient way to answer the questions, that there was a time limit and to explain whatever other rules had to be observed. When time was up, he would collect the papers and turn them in to be graded. He urged me to take the test, emphasizing that I had nothing to lose if I failed. We talked for a while, and he advised me to take my time and think it over before I made a decision. Right then and there, I knew there was no need to think. This was the break that I had been hoping for but which I never knew existed. The next day I submitted my application and was promptly informed that I was to take my exam two days later. This was a very new situation for me, and while I waited, I wondered how difficult the questions would be.

What I do remember was that the test covered a wide range of subjects; math, hypothetical combat situations, common sense reasoning and bits of history and current events among others. We were advised not to get bogged down on any one question, but rather to concentrate on those which we felt confident of answering quickly and correctly keeping in mind that there was a time limit. The questions were of equal value so there was no advantage in wasting time to solve the difficult ones. When there were no more questions, the test papers were handed out and the clock was started. Finally, time was up, the test papers were collected and as we left the room, we were told that we would be notified of our grade. I couldn't decide if I had or had not done well since I had never before taken a test of that type. Time dragged on as I waited to receive the report. When it finally arrived, I was amazed to learn that I had passed! I couldn't believe it! I was too stunned to comprehend the full impact of the good news. The report also gave me the date for taking part two of the exam which consisted of appearing before a board of officers. I appeared on the scheduled date and was asked a number of innocuous questions, (or so I thought) such as my hobbies, do I play a musical instrument (of course, my uke, and I mentioned I had it with me from the first day of military service) and so on. To this day, I am of the opinion that they were simply trying to decide if I was officer material, or how I would look in uniform. It went well. I was approved by the board and my commanding officer was notified of my appointment as an aviation cadet subject to passing my physical exam. My head was spinning -- things were happening very fast. The physical was the next hurdle and of course, there were doubts in my mind. Here in the hospital, I had seen many men come through to take the physical exam for flight training and I was aware of it being much tougher to pass. I didn't have long to wait. I scheduled myself for the physical.

Needless to say, I experienced a strange feeling knowing that this time I was the one going through the mill rather than helping some one else complete their processing. I knew the routine by heart. First stop;

see the doctor for the usual exams, weight, height, etc. Then a chest x-ray, where the smart-aleck friends of mine made me the object of laughter, doing to me what we did to so many men we had x-rayed. This little bit of flippancy would take place when we took a chest x-ray. The routine was to tell the patient to push up tight against the machine, take a deep breath and *hold it* while we made the exposure. We would purposely take our time before informing him that it was okay to breathe, but we were mean. At long last, we would add, "Now blow it out your ass!" and we would all laugh!

The dental check was very important. We learned from those who had to have dental work re-done that there could be a problem with a faulty filling when you ascended to higher altitudes. A filling that was fine at sea level could give you a very bad toothache when air pressure was reduced.

The vision check was next, starting with the common eye chart and then becoming more comprehensive than any I had ever taken. The Ishihara test for color blindness and depth perception were also stressed.

Sergeant Dutton and I were in the same barracks back at Camp Lee and he was the man who conducted the hearing test. Memory fails me as to the particulars, but I do recall that I spoiled his day. He would partially turn his back and whisper various common words and you were to tell him what he said. His *ace in the hole*, and the word he loved to catch people with was *Cincinnati*. He seemed so unhappy when I answered correctly!

Perhaps the temptation to cheat on the physical was understandable. It would have been easy since these were all my friends, but it would have been utterly stupid to falsify the results. There was just too much at stake.

There was no waiting for the report because I was given the result at the completion of the various tests. I was physically qualified for flight training and the report was sent to the proper command.

It was the 17th of December when my unit was notified of my change of status. I was now an aviation cadet, was no longer a corporal, was relieved of my duties at the hospital and I would soon receive orders to leave for the Air Corps Classification Center, Nashville Army Air Base, Nashville, Tennessee. There was nothing to do but wait.

The ukulele was put to good use as I awaited my orders. Checking the book of song titles I had learned to play reveals that we were all singing, "Brazil", "Daybreak", "There Will Never Be Another You", "There Are Such Things", "I Had the Craziest Dream" and by far the biggest hit was Bing Crosby singing, "White Christmas." The holiday season was near and once again, our thoughts were of previous years when Christmas was spent at home with family and loved ones. The commanding officer instructed the cook to keep the mess hall open for Christmas Eve, to make a batch of cookies and to keep the coffee pot working. Those who were fortunate went home on leave, but for those remaining the best we could do was gather together and sing. I did the best I could on the uke, whether good or bad, and we did a pretty good job of singing. Certainly, it was better than just sitting around and moping about where we would rather be. (There was one fact I noticed: *everyone sang*, whether Gentile, Jew or whatever. The faraway look in everyone's eyes said more about what we were feeling or thought than words could ever express.) For me it was my second Christmas away from home, and it was also a nostalgic time for I realized that I would soon be leaving. I had made some good friends and I knew I would miss them, but I also knew sooner or later, in one way or another, we would all be sent to various parts of the world.

For the Duration *plus* Six Months

5

NASHVILLE, TENESSEE. WELCOME TO THE AIR CORPS

It was in late January when I said goodbye to friends and was provided with transportation to the railroad station in nearby Hampton. All I can remember is that I arrived in Nashville, Tennessee January 30, 1943 at 11:00 AM and that it was very cold. After the necessary paperwork was completed I was assigned to a barracks which, by comparison, made Langley Field seem like a first rate hotel. There were no toilet facilities in the barracks. To heed nature's call it was necessary to go outside to a separate building. The terrain was very hilly. The door end of the building sat on the ground, but the other end was up on stilts that were about eight feet high. The wooden floor had gaps in the planking and the wind would bounce off the hill underneath the floor and come up through the cracks. There probably was a heating system somewhere, but it did us little good. Each man was issued two blankets, but they proved to be inadequate. After two nights of freezing, someone had the bright idea of putting a layer of newspaper between the blankets and that helped. Some time was devoted to letter writing after evening mess, but when it got too cold, we got under our blankets and resorted to playing that old word game called Ghost. To boost morale a little we took comfort from the fact that this was just a classification center and that we would not be here very long. We also soon learned, much to our dismay, that we would be doing KP duty which for me brought back unpleasant memories of Camp Lee. The benefits that fourteen months of service had earned had been wiped out. To add insult to injury we were confined to the base, when we should have been permitted to go into Nashville, because of an outbreak of measles. Welcome to the Air Corps!

Included in our ranks were commissioned officers and many enlisted men who had ratings. Once they became aviation cadets, however, all evidence of previous rank was removed and was replaced by a wing insignia on our hat. (I never did learn if the previous held rank would be restored if the individual was removed from the cadet program.) From now on, we would be called *Mister*.

It was here that I first met Eugene Perry. He was proud of the fact that he came from Massachusetts and that he lived on the last house on the cape (Cape Cod.) Perry was only about five feet five, black hair, dark flashing eyes, dark complexioned and had a great sense of humor. It didn't take very long for someone to nickname him *Perry the Pimp* on the basis of the subject matter of most of his conversations. We quickly became friends and maintained that friendship virtually throughout our cadet days. He had his clarinet with him and I had the uke, so we combined to make some of the most ungodly music to which anyone had ever been exposed.

Despite the shortcomings of the living conditions, the testing experience at Nashville was a lot of fun similar to the tests of skill on the boardwalk when visiting the Jersey Shore. Unfortunately, I no longer remember many of the tests, but I do recall successfully completing one that made me feel good. A small group of cadets, perhaps six, were sitting at a table with the sergeant in charge. We were given a rectangular box, about fifteen inches long, six inches wide and four inches high. There were two rows of pegs, twelve in each row fitted into square holes. The top of the peg had been divided into two colors with all the pegs oriented with the same color at the top. It was a timed test and the object of the test was to pull the peg out of the hole, rotate it 180 degrees and then insert it back into the hole. When finished, the colors would be reversed. The start signal was given and we all went to work. With about half the time remaining, the Sgt. looked at me and said, "Why aren't you doing the test?" I said I had done it and that I was finished. He looked and indeed saw that it was so. Only half convinced, he repeated the test and once again, I beat the clock. What he didn't know was that I had had three years of watch repair experience before going into the service, and that the twirling movement needed to twist the screwdrivers was exactly the same as rotating the pegs. This was old hat for me! Also, fingering the chords on the uke helped make my left hand more versatile. My finger dexterity and sensitivity would be of great help to me in the months to come.

Carl Frank September 19, 1943

One other test comes to mind and this had to do with the ability to concentrate under difficult conditions. A metal plate, approximately fifteen inches square, having an inch diameter hole in its center, was hung vertically and was part of an electrical circuit. We were then given a metal stylus, about the size of a pencil, which had an attached wire. The object of the test was to keep the metal stylus in the hole without letting it touch the edge of the hole. If you failed, the circuit would be completed and a gong would ring. Additionally, we were told to remember an eight-digit number which we would have to recall, when asked, while holding the stylus steady. What they didn't tell us was that while you tried to keep the stylus centered and listen for the numbers, they would suddenly play recorded, ear blasting, crashing noises which were unexpected and resulted in a lot of gong ringing! They got their jollies on that one.

More physical testing was also in order concentrating on coordination and another involving a spinning chair to simulate problems with vertigo. At last, all tests had been completed and I had passed. It was at that moment that I thought that just passing the physical was a greater accomplishment than learning how to fly. Some time later, it occurred to me that those of us who had qualified for flight training could find great satisfaction and comfort in knowing that we were privileged to join a select group of young men, who physically and academically, comprised the top ten percent of the American male population.

With testing completed, and the measles quarantine lifted, we finally were given open post which simply meant that we were free to go to Nashville. Memory fails me completely, I can't remember a thing about the city or where I went.

Waiting for the verdict was difficult, second-guessing ourselves as to how we had done. Toward the end of the month, the report was posted on the bulletin board. I was elated to see that I had qualified for pilot, navigator and bombardier training. I chose pilot training and was assigned to class 43J. Preflight training was next on the agenda.

6

PREFLIGHT TRAINING, MAXWELL ARMY AIR BASE
MONTGOMERY, ALABAMA

It was the 1st of March of 1943 when we got off the train at Maxwell Field and were greeted by cadet officers who were adorned with white gloves and carrying a sword at their side. We were ordered to "Fall in" followed by "March" and with the second step, the verbal abuse began.

"Straighten up, chest out, chin in, don't look around, get in step, you men are a disgrace to the uniform," etc.

Most of my classmates had entered the cadet corps directly from civilian life and had no previous military experience. They knew nothing about dismounted drill and it was obvious to the upperclassmen that they were very *green*. By comparison, I had about 17 months of service and had learned the routines long ago. All in all, it was a very unfriendly, hostile welcome. We began to march at the standard 120 steps per minute and were immediately told that we were the *underclass* and as such had to increase it to 140 steps per minute. I had two heavy barracks bags and the uke and it was a struggle to move at the faster rate. Needless to say the criticism by the upperclass of how we marched, looked, etc. was unending since in their eyes we could do nothing right. Welcome to the West Point system of upper and lower class! The Honor Code was the backbone of the West Point System. Cheating was not tolerated and immediate dismissal was the result if so caught. Even worse was the stipulation that it was your responsibility to report any cadet that you knew was cheating and failure to do so could result in your dismissal. This of course was counter to what we were brought up to believe that you should not *snitch* on your friends. It was a very difficult concept to embrace.

At long last, we got to our living quarters which were not a barracks, but rather a long, one story building somewhat similar to today's motels. The door of each individual room opened upon a wide paved walk which ran the entire length of the building. Soon afterward, the orientation sessions began and it was made very clear that we, the underclass, had a prescribed set of rules to follow regarding the use of the walk. Number one: Upon opening the door of your room, you must first wait to see if there were any upperclassmen on the walk. This was easy to determine because only the upperclassmen could use its entire width. We, the underclass, had to walk straight out the door (if the way was clear) go to the very far edge of the walk which was designated as the *Rat Line*, and make a military left or right turn as needed. Quickly we had to get up to the mandatory 140 steps per minute, *always* walking at attention with eyes straight ahead and no head turning. If an upperclassman caught you moving your head or your eyes he would ask, "Are you spying, or do you want to buy this place?" (Someone very accurately commented that we didn't know what Maxwell field looked like until we became upperclassmen, because only then could we move our head and eyes!) This was the way it was done every time we moved from one area to another. To complete the dehumanization we were labeled *Zombies* and would remain so for the next thirty-two days when we would then become the upperclass.

Very soon, we learned what life would be like in the mess hall. An underclassman would be seated at the corner of the table and was called the *gunner*. When a food item was needed, the gunner stopped eating until he got the attention of the waitress who then supplied the needed item.

We were at attention while eating and had to sit on the very edge of the chair or bench, back ramrod straight, eyes straight ahead and eat the so-called *square meal*. The term square meal had nothing to do with nutrition; rather it entailed the ritual that had to be followed. Without looking down at our plate, we would somehow manage to spear something with our fork, bring it straight up from the dish to mouth level, and then horizontally to our mouth. Then the fork would be moved horizontally to a point above the dish, then vertically down to get another mouthful; the so-called square meal. After a bite or two, invariably one of the upperclassmen would ask you to recite the "Boidies Poem" which had to be done with proper vocal expression. This was the poem:

Spwing had spwung, the gwass has rizz, I wonder where the boidies is?
The boidies are on the wing.
But that's absoid, everybody knows the wing is on the boid!

We were lucky to be able to eat half our meal and usually left the mess hall hungry.

Certainly, the military could not function without inspections, and we had them constantly. The first time we assembled in the morning, an upperclassman would plant himself squarely in front of a Zombie and put his head within inches of his. Then a typical dialogue such as this would follow:

"Mister, did you shave today?"

"Yes Sir."

"Mister, did you use a razor?"

"Yes Sir."

"Did you put a blade in the razor?"

"Yes Sir."

"Did you take the blade out of the paper wrapping?"

"Yes Sir."

"Then why do I see some beard on your face?"

Being green, we at first would answer something like this:

"Since there were so many men shaving at the same time, I could not get close enough to the mirror to see." At that moment the upperclassman would ask,

"Mister, are you quibbling?"

Right then and there, we learned that regardless of the question, there were only three answers we were allowed to give and they were, "Yes Sir," "No Sir," "No excuse, Sir." To say anything else would be considered quibbling and that was not tolerated. It made no difference if you had a legitimate excuse for not doing something -- if you had a broken arm and couldn't shave the answer would still be the same, "No excuse, Sir."

Another ritual was the requirement to sing as we marched from one building or formation to another. What irked me was that it was never in my key so the best I could do was try to fit in wherever possible. One part of the lyric to "The Army Air Corps"[9] song was, "We live in fame or go down in flames but nothing can stop the Army Air Corps." Personally, I could not see the "go down in flames" part as accomplishing very much for the Air Corps or the country. Better for the enemy to go down in flames.

Saturday morning was the big day for inspections and parades. We would march to the parade grounds and have to stand at attention for very long periods of time. A curious aspect of prolonged standing was the fact that it caused people to faint and fall. Our first impulse was to assist the cadet, but that was forbidden since we were at attention. At most parades an ambulance would be positioned behind the standing ranks ready to assist anyone who had fainted. Failure to pass inspection would result in the awarding of demerits which would vary from one to as many as the inspecting officer thought the shortcoming merited. Every ten-demerit points would earn the cadet a one-hour walking duty tour which had to be walked at attention over a prescribed course, carrying a rifle (usually a wooden rifle,) and salute everything that passed. The unfortunate aspect of this was that the tour had to be walked when open post was granted which meant that we could not leave the post when otherwise free to do so. This was a tough rap when one considers how little leisure time we had.

Much to our dismay, we lost the very first weekend of open post due to an outbreak of measles which naturally resulted in a quarantine of the entire class. In view of the fact that the measles was becoming the bane of our existence (as was the case in Nashville), we decided to change the lyric of "The Army Air Corps Song"[9] just a little. Following the words "Nothing can stop the Army Air Corps" we added and sang, "Except the measles!" and then repeated, "Nothing can stop the Army Air Corps!" Very clever, we thought!

Just how much good the class system accomplished has always been a good topic for debate. Some thought it did little good, others took the position that it weeded out the hotheads, and those who could not maintain composure when provoked. I know that there were a few instances when I had to force myself to remain in control when listening to the vicious, verbal abuse I had to endure. It was difficult, but we managed to live with it. The key word here is *verbal*. Never was there any physical contact: words yes, but touching no!

Physical training (PT) was a daily ritual. Sit ups, chin ups, deep-knee bends, the obstacle course, shuttle runs and sprints were the order of the day with a cross-country run thrown in a few times a week. Once again, my model airplane experiences were a big help. Back then, we flew free flight models with the winner being the model which remained aloft the longest. Official timers were appointed and stopwatches were used to time the flights. The idea was to hook a thermal current which would keep the plane up for many minutes and carry it miles away from its launch point.

In an effort to not lose the plane, we would start running after it. I developed an uncanny ability to run without looking at the ground since it was vital to keep the plane in sight. Whether it was a plowed field, cornfield, woods or whatever, somehow or other I seemed to know where my feet were. That capability was put to good use on the cross-country runs. For me, this was second nature, no problem at all. I showed off a little by sprinting the last hundred yards, at the end of the run, so that I could be one of the first to hit the showers. With twelve people trying to do the same thing at the same time, this was important since in reality we were limited to a two-minute shower.

Preflight was a grueling time since the physical and academic demands were great. The subjects were many and varied; theory of flight, math, map reading, charts, aircraft and naval recognition (many good men were lost to so called *friendly fire*.) Learning how to send and receive Morse code and how to do it visually by watching a blinking bulb. Our instructors were former teachers or professors who had received special training in army schools. At the risk of being accused of bragging, I think I knew as much or more than the instructor did about theory of flight as a result of my model airplane experiences. I could have taught that class! There were sessions on the machine gun range and the pressure chamber where the pressure was reduced to the equivalent of 28,000 feet and how it felt to have insufficient oxygen to breathe when we removed our oxygen masks for a few moments. We welcomed lights out at 9:00 PM. We were tired and reveille at 5:00 AM would come much too soon.

Without a doubt, there was one event in our military life that no one enjoyed and which should have been mentioned much earlier. Going back to the first days of induction, we all were required to have our shots for tetanus, smallpox, etc. with follow up booster shots at prescribed intervals. The procedure was to line up single file, and keep moving up until it was your turn to be inoculated. What made it so difficult was to see all those ahead of you having that syringe stuck in them, with the obvious result of many men getting a little more lightheaded than they would admit. Ironically, more often than not, it was the big, macho, he-men who keeled over! Many times, in an attempt to speed things up, a shot was given in each arm simultaneously. The tetanus shot was the one that left you with a sore arm for a few days. Once again, my experience with giving shots back in the isolation ward of Langley Field was helpful since I wasn't a stranger to syringes. It was never a pleasant experience, but I never had the problems that some of the cadets had.

Speaking of health, the only time I had ever been on sick call in my entire military career was here at Maxwell Field. Whatever ailed me (temperature, elevation, cough, etc.,) required only a two-day stay in the hospital, much to my relief. A confinement of a week, with the subsequent loss of training, would have made it impossible to keep up with my classmates. In such cases, the cadet would be pushed back into the following class.

Once again, Eugene Perry and I were lucky to have been assigned to the same room. We got along very well and of course, our *music*, with practice, had improved a little. The big hit song of that month was "As Time Goes By." Naturally, we managed to stagger through that, much to our amazement. Regardless of the rendition, the guys did enjoy the sessions since we were very tired of singing "I've Got Sixpence" and the "Army Air Corps Song."

If we hadn't fouled up, we were finally permitted to enjoy open post, which gave us the opportunity to visit Montgomery, the capitol of Alabama. It was a very nice city and it had the typical servicemen's activities, which we did enjoy. The weather was warm and it felt good just to walk around and take in the sights and I welcomed the chance to get away from the daily grind.

We didn't realize how quickly time had passed until the date of the upperclass ball for class 43I was posted on the bulletin board. That meant that they would soon be moving on to the next phase of training and we, the Zombies of class 43J, would then become the upperclass. It would then be our responsibility to pass on to class 43K all that we had learned; how to eat square meals, recite poetry and learn how to walk the Rat Line! That memorable day was April 1, 1943. Just thirty more days of preflight training. I couldn't wait.

My recollection of those days as a member of the underclass at Maxwell Field is very clear and easily recalled, but strange as it might seem I remember very little of my upperclass days. The schoolwork continued as before changing only in the depth and scope of the subjects we were studying. Upon the completion of a particular course, another would be introduced; but learning Morse code never ceased, we hammered away on that for our entire stay.

As an upperclassman there was one thing I knew I would not do and that was to be as vicious to the underclass as some of the upperclassmen were to us. In my mind, there was a dividing line between *getting them on the ball* as compared to being mean spirited. I approved of the system; it served the intended purpose, but I didn't like to see it abused. Each member of the graduating class of preflight was given a 34-page cynosure complete with illustrations and text depicting our stay. We tried to get as many autographs of our 43J classmates as we possibly could, and I am proud to add that many members of 43K also signed my book. Reading it recently, for the first time in many years, was a revelation. Just about every state in the union was represented. I've often wondered what became of them and how many died in combat.

Left to Right: John Floyd, Ed Rawley, Ralph Saunders, Andy Stefano, Dan Hottler, Gene Perry

April 1943 was dwindling down to its final week, and we knew that we would soon be graduating. Naturally, our thoughts turned to where we would be sent for the next phase of training which would be primary flying school. Since we were in the Southeast Training Command, we could only speculate if it would be Florida, Georgia, Alabama, Mississippi or some other state. When the information was posted on the bulletin board, I was pleased to learn that I would be going to Carlstrom Field, Arcadia, Florida.

Many times, I found myself thinking about the day that Bill Holland came into the x-ray office at Langley Field, and urged me to take the aviation cadet exam. Many times, I have thought of how this would never have happened if it had been *my week to be in the darkroom instead of the front office*. If that had been the case, I would never have known of his existence at Langley Field and would have never taken the exam that changed my life. I could only wonder and speculate as to where I would have gone from there.

On the 29th of April, 1943 I departed Maxwell Field for Arcadia, Florida. I had been in the Air Corps for four months and had not even gotten close to an airplane. Finally, that would change.

"Preflight" Class of 43-J, April 1943[10]

7

PRIMARY FLIGHT TRAINING, CARLSTROM FIELD, ARCADIA, FLORIDA

Carlstrom Field, Arcadia, Florida

    Traveling by rail was not the fastest mode of transportation during those days of WWII for there were many delays en route. We had left Maxwell Field early in the day, and we seemed to feel that we were *on vacation* just sitting there looking out at the passing countryside as we moved along. It wasn't long before we began pulling down the window shades while trying to find a comfortable position in our coach seats. We traveled through the night; and what awakened us hours later, was the fact that it had become quiet, no clickity-clack because the train had stopped. It seems that we all had the idea at the same time; raise the shade and see where we were. To our surprise, what we saw were cows; lots of cows! Apparently, none of use realized that inland Florida was cattle country. A short time later, the train started to move and soon afterward, we could see that we were coming into Carlstrom Field. What came into view looked more like a country club than an airbase. It was laid out in a circle, perhaps only a sixth of a mile or so in diameter. The center of the circle was a large paved open area (which we later learned much to our delight) would be the scene of a weekly dance. The flight line, hangars and parked aircraft were visible on the tarmac on one side of the perimeter. As we got closer, we could see a swimming pool and buildings that were a lot different from the army barracks we had known in the past. This was an Embry Riddle School of Aeronautics with whom the government had contracted to provide flight training. It was a civilian school which explained the departure from army style barracks. The typical army routine came next; get off the train, fall in at attention and answer to your name when it was called. The commanding officer then spoke a few words of welcome and we marched off to our assigned rooms.

Our living quarters were long, white, two-story buildings with palm trees and green lawns. For a moment, my mind went back to classification center, Nashville, Tennessee and the memory of the wind coming through the cracks in the floor! What a change! There were six cadets to a room and once again, Gene Perry and I were roommates. The usual routine prevailed: select a bed, unpack, read all the printed rules and regulations regarding what to do, when to do it and how to do it. Each day, one of us would be in charge of having the room ready for inspection, but the entire room was given demerits if something did not pass. That put the burden on everyone, and it was clearly apparent that teamwork was paramount. It had been a long day, we were tired and hungry and chow time couldn't come too soon. The mess hall was very pleasant and for a little while, we could relax. Tomorrow would come soon enough.

Without doubt, the only unpleasant thing, we sadly discovered, was the water. When you turned on the shower, the water reeked of *rotten eggs*, the typical smell of sulfur water. It was just impossible to drink. Unfortunately, it didn't go away when it was used to brew coffee or tea and that the only escape was to get a drink out of the soda machine. We learned to live with it, but it was not easy to do the first week.

Flight training at primary flight school began in ground school with classes in meteorology, navigation and engine mechanics. We would be flying the Stearman PT17, a two place, open cockpit biplane, and the first session was devoted to making us familiar with its workings. It was important to know how to perform a preflight check of the plane, and it didn't hurt to know that you had fuel in the tank before taking off. Understanding how to read and interpret the information displayed by the cockpit instruments was also thoroughly covered. Another aspect of flying which we knew nothing of was the so-called *traffic pattern*. Certainly, it would be utter chaos to have planes leaving and landing, from many directions, with each jockeying for position in the vicinity of the airfield. The traffic pattern was a preset, orderly plan which allowed everyone to safely leave and enter traffic. Another important little item was the *windsock* (or any other device) that was positioned on the airfield to clearly indicate the direction of the wind since it was elementary to always takeoff into the wind. At long last, the morning session of ground school came to an end. The mess hall was the next stop on the schedule and from there we finally went to the flight line for our first close up look at an airplane. It had been a long time coming.

I'm quite sure that many of us had similar thoughts as we assembled and marched to the nearby airfield. Who is my instructor? Will I like him? Will I get airsick? Do I have the ability to learn how to fly? It was the first time in our respective lives that we had been confronted with questions such as these.

Upon our arrival, the commanding officer spoke a few words and wished us luck. The tactical officer then took over, called our names and assigned us to an instructor. When he had finished, we broke ranks and sought out the person who was going to teach us to fly.

My instructor's name was Roland Roelofs, a civilian (as were all the instructors), and I judged him to be about thirty-two years old. He was very pleasant, about five foot ten, a little bit heavier than our typical air corpsmen, and quiet spoken. Trusting to memory, I believe each instructor was assigned four cadets. We wore nametags and after a few minutes of greeting and small talk, we walked over to a nearby PT17 and listened intently as he began to introduce us to the important features of the plane. He got into the cockpit and we climbed up on the wing as he pointed out the various instruments and controls, while explaining the procedure for starting the engine, checking fuel, reading instruments and many other details. Later on, one of the first things we had to learn was the so-called *blindfold cockpit check* which required us to locate and touch each instrument or control when he called it out. The student sat in the front cockpit and the instructor occupied the rear cockpit. Communication between instructor and student was accomplished through the use of a *gosport tube* which was in essence a tube with a funnel-like device on one end, into which the instructor spoke, and with the other end of the tube connected to the student's helmet. It was rather primitive, but it did work if he shouted. Taxiing safely from one point to another, could not be done in a straight line due to the nose-high stance of the PT17, making it impossible to see anything ahead and close to the plane. This blind spot was overcome by taxiing diagonally to one side and then diagonally to the other as we moved across the field. There was a lot to learn and a lot to remember. Earlier, we had checked out our parachutes and received instructions as to their use and care. As I sat there waiting for my turn to go up, I tried to recall all the little details which were so important. There were many thoughts going through my head such as how long it had taken to get to this moment and how unbelievable it all seemed. We all probably had similar thoughts because it was a brand new experience.

As we walked toward the plane for my first flight, Mr. Roelofs explained that he wanted me to place my hands and feet lightly on the controls and follow through as he made his moves. At long last we were seated in the plane, the engine was started and we began to taxi to our takeoff position. After a short

Colletti, Saunders, Mr. Roelofs, Michner

hesitation for a safety check, he advanced the throttle and we quickly picked up speed and became airborne. It was wonderful! I could follow the movement of the control stick and the rudder pedals, as he made corrections, and he explained the need to coordinate both controls when making turns. Since this was basically an orientation flight, there was little flight instruction given. That would come next time.

Probably the most important aspect of that first flight was learning how to descend to the correct altitude when entering the traffic pattern, and reducing airspeed while aligning with the runway when coming in to land. It was a wonderful once in a lifetime experience. Much to my relief that first flight put to rest all the apprehension I had about getting airsick. I felt at home in the air.

Actual flight training began with the second flight. Once again, I was told to "follow through" as the instructor moved the controls, and I would then take over and try to duplicate what he had done. The need of making coordinated turns using the stick and rudder controls (and later the throttle) was repeated over and over. With practice, I began to get the feel and response of the controls. At this point great emphasis was placed upon being constantly aware of the features of the terrain over which we were flying and the direction of the wind. An alert pilot would always have some idea of where he could land in the event of engine failure or other emergency. Knowing the wind direction was very important and could be determined by looking for tell tale signs such as the direction of drifting smoke or the movement of trees. Back in preflight, one of the exercises which we did religiously was what I called the *head roll*. It began with putting your chin on your chest and slowly twisting your head to one side and then upward and then down again on the other side. The importance of all this was to develop flexibility of your neck muscles with the final result being the ability to just about see to the rear because of the greater range of movement of your head. This ability was utilized immediately in our flight training. The standing rule was, *keep your head moving. Don't just look straight ahead.* When the instructor did catch us getting careless we would hear,

"You've got your head up your ass and it's locked." Just about the time I thought I was doing great, the instructor would cut the throttle and shout,

"Emergency landing" into the gosport tube. Frantically I would look for signs of wind direction and any open field that might permit an emergency landing. Once I had committed myself to a site, the instructor would allow the plane to get down to about two hundred feet before taking control and gunning the engine. Later, I would be told how poorly I had done and how I would have never been able to land in that undersized field!

After the stress of our first week of actual flight training, most of us were looking forward to our first weekend of open post. Those who had accumulated demerit points had to remain on the post and spend their free time walking hour-long duty tours. For those who had permission to leave, Arcadia was the nearest town and it was our primary destination. In my 1958 encyclopedia, Arcadia had a population of 4760, so I would think back then in May and June of 1943, it was even less. Sad to say, there was little to do once we got there. I distinctly remember standing on the corner of the crossroads, in the heart of the city, where the street signs read, Zolfo Springs, (north), Nocatee and Punta Gorda (south), Okeechobee (east) and Sarasota, (west.) You would be out of town if you walked two blocks in any of these directions. I believe there was a theater, but memory fails me. The so-called *social life* consisted of walking up one street and down another and then deciding it was time for a coke or whatever might be available in the stores. If you were a lover of western music, you had it made, but there was next to nothing of the big band kind of music. In many ways, remaining on the post was a better choice, but it was important to get away from the barracks and mingle with people. It was boring, but it was a change.

The PT17 was a lot of fun to fly. The open cockpit and wind noise helped create a greater sensation of flying than one would have gotten in an enclosed canopy. As I recall, the best one on the flight line could attain a speed of one hundred five miles per hour, but the average probably was about ninety-five. One of the plane's characteristics was its tendency to *ground loop* which meant that a wing tip would drop very low when landing, and drag the ground. Fortunately, I had been spared that embarrassing experience.

Once again, the passing of time has dimmed many of the little details of the day I soloed, but I do remember that it went well. The customary procedure was followed. Mr. Roelofs was in the rear seat as an observer while I taxied out, took off, flew the pattern and landed. Satisfied with my performance, he got out and told me "it was all mine." My first solo flight, needless to say, was a memorable experience. Those of us who had accomplished that feat became fair game to, and at the mercy of, other cadets who were determined to maintain the existing tradition which was to throw the poor guy into the swimming pool fully dressed! Sort of like a *rite of passage*.

Having soloed, however, did not mean the end of dual time with the instructor. New techniques and maneuvers were introduced and performed with the instructor aboard. It was also very important for the student to learn to navigate by himself once up there and not get lost. It seemed elementary, but some cadets made the mistake of not learning how to identify natural landmarks such as lakes, rivers, water towers or structures that would help him find his way back to the base. There were a few occasions when a lost pilot

"Hot Pilot Colletti" Arcadia, Florida, June 22, 1943

had to be rescued. Very embarrassing! After being introduced to new maneuvers, we would be sent up solo, usually for an hour, to practice what had been learned. We were now well into our last few weeks of training. As we became *hot pilots*, Perry and I would seek each other out before takeoff, make note of our respective plane numbers and agree upon a rendezvous point somewhere away from the field. The first one there would wait for the other, and together we would climb up to the altitude needed for our maneuvers. We had worked out a routine where we would takeoff, fly away from the field, and then work our way back as we practiced stalls, spins or whatever aerobatics the instructor had wanted us to do. We timed it so that we would be just a few miles from the field in those last few minutes of our flying time, but with sufficient altitude to roll the plane over on its back, pull the stick back and perform the so called *Split S* maneuver (which was the bottom half of a loop.)

The loss of altitude would put us into position to enter the traffic pattern just a few miles away. We thought it was a neat way to finish! Unfortunately, not everyone was successful in their pilot training. If the instructor felt after sufficient dual instruction that the cadet had not progressed enough to solo, he would be sent up for a check ride with a check pilot. An unsatisfactory ride would usually result in the student being eliminated from flight training, and he would be reassigned. I think that the wash out rate was about fifteen percent of the class. During the 1930's just about every *air-minded* kid could be found reading "Flying Aces," "War Birds" or "Air Trails." These magazines had great World War I flying stories and we couldn't wait for each monthly issue to appear on the newsstands. We were completely swept away reading about "The Red Knight of Germany" or of our own Eddie Rickenbacker. Naturally, we managed to learn a few things about flying, and it was just one of those *few things* that got me in hot water with my instructor. To explain: In order to get the plane to turn to the left, for instance, the pilot would push the left rudder pedal and at the same time, move the control stick to the left in order to lower the left wing and make a coordinated turn. However, if the controls were crossed, using left rudder and moving the stick to the *right* the plane would *sideslip*, sort of move to the side while moving forward. It was a maneuver that could be used to make a last moment correction in order to line up with the touchdown point of the field when coming in to land. I had soloed quite some time ago, but this was a dual instruction day, and I was flying the plane as we came in to land. The problem was that I was slightly off course, not lined up with the runway and only about three hundred feet above the ground. I didn't want to make a turning correction at that low altitude, so I dropped the nose a little more, crossed controls and neatly side slipped and straightened out just before touching down. I was feeling very pleased with myself until we had parked the plane and turned the engine off. At that moment the instructor bellowed,

"Where the hell did you learn to do that?" He chewed my ass out and, in no uncertain terms, made it very clear that this was not in the Air Corps curriculum! So much for using the information I got out of Flying Aces. Incidentally, I clearly remember how negative the Air Corps was in regard to people who had had previous flight training and who were licensed pilots in civilian life. Their position was that they, the Air Corps, wanted students to learn to fly *their way*, and it was easier to train someone with no previous experience than to break experienced pilots of bad habits. Of course, the reaction of some of the cadets was to quote the old saying, "There is the right way, the wrong way and then there is the Army way!"

Navigation had become more important as we got into the final two weeks of training since our flying took us further from the field. Not paying attention to time, distance and direction could easily put a student in unfamiliar territory. Proper use of our instruments and relying on them was continually stressed.

The Link Trainer was the device that was used to teach us about instrument flying, and I will never forget my first experience in it. *Flight simulators* is the term used today to describe what we referred to as blind (or instrument) flight trainers. A simulator displays a picture of the situation outside the plane and the pilot can then see how the plane is affected by the corrections he makes. The Link Trainer, however, was just a mockup of a plane with a short, stubby wing and fuselage. The student would get in, the hood would be closed, and he would be sitting in the dark with just the glow of the instrument panel before him. Through the radio headset, he would receive instructions from the instructor, who was seated at a desk about ten feet away. If memory hasn't failed me, there were six basic instruments to monitor; the altimeter, airspeed indicator, artificial horizon, needle-ball indicator, compass and gyrocompass. A typical instruction flight might go something like this: Through the headset, I would hear:

"Cadet Colletti, takeoff on a heading of 90 degrees and climb to an altitude of 1500 feet at the rate of 800 feet per minute and level off. Maintain that altitude and heading for one minute and then make a 90-degree climbing turn to the right and level off at 2000 feet. Now make a 360-degree turn to the left and maintain your airspeed and altitude."

The instructor could monitor the progress of the mission to show us how well (or poorly) we had done. The session would last from 30 minutes to an hour, and it could be very tiring due to the deep concentration required. After about twenty minutes of my *first session,* this is what I heard from the instructor:

"Well Cadet Colletti, you are on a heading of 85 degrees, you are in a *dive* going 400 miles an hour and you are 900 feet *underground*. What do you want to do now?" Of course I had made the cardinal sin we all made the first time under the hood. I had allowed myself to concentrate too long and too much on one or two instruments instead of monitoring all six, with the unfortunate result that I was unaware that the plane had drifted from the prescribed flight path. In time, we learned that the trick was to sweep the entire instrument panel with our eyes without locking onto any one instrument. Also, in the beginning there was a tendency to overcorrect, which I finally solved by sliding my hand down on the control stick rather than holding it at the very end.

Probably the most important aspect of learning to fly *under the hood* was the need to be able to intersect a radio beam, identify it and follow it to the base. This was all done through radio signals which were received in our headset. The student had to tune in to the frequency of the radio station, identify it and then listen for the "A" or "N" Morse code signals which the station was transmitting. If the signal became louder, he would know that he was coming closer to the station, and of course, the opposite would be true. Also, the "A" or "N" signal would inform the pilot as to which side of the radio beam he was on as he gradually refined his position while *homing in on the beam.* (This is a very crude description of how it was done, but I hope, good enough to be understood.) Without doubt, we all felt wrung out after an hour of blind flying in the Link Trainer.

Physical training (PT) never eased up. The emphasis placed upon conditioning was constant and we took it in stride. I didn't waste any time in getting on one of the softball teams, and it felt wonderful just to be swinging a bat once again. Not all went well however. I was playing shortstop and I charged the ground ball that was hit to me. I bent down to field it and it was at that moment that I felt a sharp pain in my right knee. When I attempted to straighten up it seemed that there was something caught in the moving parts of the joint. In my mind, I could picture an object, jammed in the hinge of a door, which would prevent the door from closing. There was some pain and I knew that it would require attention. I reported to the physical training instructor and he applied an Ace type bandage and gave me permission to skip PT for a few days. My biggest concern was having to run the so-called *Shuttle Run* which required a sharp, 180-degree turn at the end of each leg. Trying to pivot and turn, I knew, would really make the problem worse. Luckily, the shuttle run was not scheduled and there was enough improvement after a few days, to allow me to participate in the exercises. In the deep recesses of my mind, however, I knew I had to be very careful in the way I moved.

Fortunately the knee problem happened at the very end of our primary training when the daily routine had been scaled back making it possible to rest it as much as possible.

Without doubt, the most important topic of conversation, during those last few days at Carlstrom Field, was the speculation as to where we would be sent for our Basic Flight Training. Of course, the *latrine rumors* were plentiful and had us going to just about every southern state. We were wondering which type of aircraft we would be flying and just how difficult it would be to make the transition from the primary trainer to the more powerful and sophisticated basic trainer. At last, the official announcement was made. We would be going to Bainbridge Army Air Base in Bainbridge, Georgia. We were happy to see, on our map, that Bainbridge had more to offer than Arcadia insofar as (or so we hoped) social life was concerned. We also knew that we would be flying the BT13, which someone had dubbed as the *Vultee Vibrator*.

Saying goodbye to Carlstrom was a little sad. It had been a great place to be (except for the sulfur water), but it was time to move on.

Class 43J, Arcadia, Florida. June 22, 1942 – Colletti, Michner, Mr. Roelofs, Saunders, Stone

8

BASIC FLIGHT TRAINING, BAINBRIDGE, GEORGIA

Bainbridge Army Air Base, July 1943

It was the 1st of July 1943 when I arrived at Bainbridge Army Air Base, Bainbridge, Georgia, after a long train trip from Arcadia. It was located about twelve miles from Bainbridge and bordered on US Highway 27, a fact that all of us were very happy to learn. It was a big improvement when compared to the remoteness of Carlstrom Field. This was an Army air base, unlike the civilian, Embry Riddle Flying School we had attended at Carlstrom Field, and a military atmosphere prevailed.

Our new home was the standard army barracks, nestled among pine and oak trees, which provided much welcomed shade. There was a centrally located large barracks type building which housed the bathing and toilet facilities. The usual routine, we soon learned, was to undress in the barracks, wrap a towel around us and carry the needed toilet articles when attending to life's daily needs. It was refreshing to walk around practically nude, enjoying a few minutes of relief from the July heat.

Once again our thoughts were similar to those which we had the first day of primary training. Who was my instructor? Would he be *all brass*? (He would be a commissioned officer and *not* a civilian.) How difficult will it be to fly a much more sophisticated plane or will it be more than I can handle? Those and many other questions filled our heads the night before the first day of training.

Instructor 2nd Lt. Vernon B. Simpson

It was a five-minute march to the flight line, where we assembled to meet our instructors. I was introduced to 2nd Lt. Vernon B. Simpson, who was about twenty-three years old and from Hampton, Virginia. (Would you believe that is where Langley Field is located?) My first thought upon seeing him was, "This isn't Lt. Simpson, it is movie star Tyrone Power!" Not only was there a very great physical resemblance, but his manner, attitude and personality was much the same. It wasn't that he was cocky, but he had that devil-may-care manner and very little use for the Army way of doing things. He was easy going and relaxed and I was happy to have him as my instructor. There were five students assigned to him, and after introductions were made, we asked and answered questions, such as where we were from, military service, etc., as we tried to learn a little more about each other.

The BT13A was made by Consolidated Vultee and someone had nicknamed it the Vultee Vibrator because it shook so much when performing certain maneuvers and, I must admit, was aptly named. The upperclass tried to frighten us when we first arrived, warning us *not* to put the plane in a tailspin because it was a killer plane and would not come out of it when it was supposed to. I guess everyone needs to have their fun! Cadets and instructor walked over to one of the aircraft and Lt. Simpson got in the back seat while we clambered up on the wing and fuselage as he explained the cockpit layout. The plane had features that were completely new to us, such as a variable pitch propeller, wing flaps, radio communication between pilot and student and with the control tower. In addition, we were in an enclosed canopy as compared to the open-air primary trainer. Questions were asked and answered and then we took turns sitting in the cockpit and made mental notes of the instrument panel. Once again, it was our responsibility to be able to pass a blindfold cockpit check before we went up for our first flight.

Every plane has its own peculiarities and this was apparent when we taxied out and took off on my first hour of dual instruction. Simpson told me to keep my feet and hands on the controls and to "follow through" as we took off. The plane had a tendency to pull to the left on takeoff, due to torque, and it was necessary to anticipate this and apply corrective right rudder immediately as the throttle

Back: Cadets Cole, Chase, Chandler; Front: Unknown, Lt. Simpson, Cadet Colletti

was advanced. Once airborne, he went through the standard maneuvers; power on and power off stalls, turns, spins, etc., and the Vultee Vibrator really did vibrate, but there was no problem recovering from a tailspin. Obviously, the upperclass was pulling our leg! That first hour of dual instruction was a real eye-opener for it exposed us to what needed to be learned. Correct flap and propeller position during takeoffs and landings, and how to contact the tower before making any moves were all new to us. The radio headset had to be worn constantly, and it was difficult at first to understand what we were hearing because of the constant background static. Knowing how to tune to the proper radio frequency and how to monitor radio transmissions also took time to master. Some of the BT13 trainers were equipped with the Curtis Wright engines and some had Pratt and Whitney engines and we quickly learned the difference. For some reason, the planes with the Curtis Wright engines seemed to leak a little oil which accumulated on the inside, bottom of the fuselage. When flying inverted, the oil would drip through the open floor of the cockpit and make a mess. Happy were we when we were assigned to a plane with the Pratt and Whitney engine. Once again, Eugene Perry and I were together. We had become close friends and our *music* had improved. We went into Bainbridge on our first open post, walked around, went to the movies and checked out the USO Club. Bainbridge was typical of many southern cities. There was a large, park-like square in the center of town, with crosswalks, trees, benches and very pretty flowerbeds. The busses from the base would discharge their passengers on the north side of the park. As silly as it might seem, we had a good time just going to the 5&10 store and looking at things that were so reminiscent of life back home. We liked Bainbridge. The people were friendly and we felt welcomed.

Colletti with the Vultee BT-13A

The cadet flight training program never eased up on the ritual of daily inspections, standing at attention for long periods of time and parades. Probably the one thing we thoroughly disliked about the base was the ever-present gnats. I do not know why they were so great in number, but they drove us crazy especially when standing at attention. They would crawl across our lips, eyes or our nose and we could do nothing but stand there, staring straight ahead, unable to shoo them off or scratch. It was maddening, but moving when at attention, would usually reward you with demerits and the automatic duty tours which would be walked when everyone else was free to leave the base.

Though more demanding than the PT17 of primary training, I seemed to adjust well to flying the BT13. A typical hour of dual instruction might involve practicing power on and power off stalls, loops, barrel rolls, Immelman turns, spins and procedures such as finding an emergency landing field in the event of engine failure. Now, however, just performing different maneuvers was not enough.

Precision was being stressed more and maintaining required airspeed, altitude and compass heading were monitored closely. Wing flap position, correct propeller pitch and throttle position also had to be set correctly in order to prevent a deadly stall during those critical moments during takeoff and landing.

Four auxiliary fields were available for our use. Faceville was eighteen miles south of the base, Reynoldsville fifteen miles southwest, Vada eighteen miles northeast, and Babcock Field eight miles north. Bainbridge was easy to find for it was located between the Flint and Chattahoochee Rivers. Getting lost was embarrassing and easier to do than one might think. Should that happen, we were told to follow the *iron compass* which was the term used to describe railroad tracks. Following them would surely bring you to some landmark that could be identified.

The daily routine began when we reported to the ready room, on the flight line, at 6:30 AM to meet with our instructors. There would be a short briefing, the flying schedule would be announced, the first student to fly would check out a parachute and he and the instructor would be starting engines by 7:00 AM. Those waiting for their turn to fly would not be just sitting around, since there was no such thing as *idle time*. There was much to be learned and every cadet had better be deeply engrossed in reading the many manuals that were available. Our *Bible* was "The Pilots Information File" which we read religiously.

I recall one incident which was typical of Lt. Simpson. We were in the ready room waiting for a light fog to lift. A horseshoe pit had been set up outside of the ready room and Simpson and I had started a game. I was his first student and there was little we could do but wait for the fog to lift. The game was almost over when the word came to head for the planes. Simpson, however, wanted to finish the game and we kept pitching horseshoes after the others had left. At that moment, Capt. Jorgenson, the squadron commander, noticed our delay and asked Simpson if he would like to join us today?

Simpson replied, "Just a few more points, Cap." and continued to pitch!

After eight or ten hours of dual instruction, the instructor would decide if the student was ready to solo. Fortunately, Simpson thought I was ready and I have no trouble whatsoever remembering that most eventful day. I was at the controls when we left Bainbridge and headed for Reynoldsville. He told me to shoot two touch-and-go landings and all went well. After the second one I parked the plane, he got out and told me to takeoff, fly the pattern and land. I taxied back to takeoff position, advanced the throttle and took off. As I made my first 90-degree turn to the right, the sky opened up and it began to rain very hard. I flew the down wind leg, made the 90-degree turn to the right and then the final 90-degree turn to line up with the runway. The rain, however, had gotten heavier and I could hardly see where I was going, having almost no forward vision. I somehow managed to land, much to my relief.

It is difficult for me to accept the fact that the events I am writing about had taken place almost seventy-three years ago. Though much has been forgotten, many details are still sharply etched in my mind. The excitement of my solo flight was still with me the next day when we assembled in the ready room. Lt. Simpson had scheduled me for an hour of solo flying and I was to practice all the maneuvers we had been taught. I looked for the number of the plane assigned to me, found it, climbed in and made a mental observation that the rear cockpit looked so very empty! After starting the engine, radio contact was made with the tower and I was cleared to taxi and takeoff. While climbing up to the required altitude I had time to think of which maneuver I should practice first. It was an easy decision. What came to mind was the warning the upperclass gave us regarding the inability to recover from a spin; that the BT13 was a killer plane. Of course, this had been disproved, time and time again, while flying with the instructor, but now I was on my own. Leveling off I checked the sky around me for traffic, satisfied that there was none and throttled the engine back while pulling the stick back to keep the nose up. This of course eventually causes the plane to stall. At that moment the control stick is pulled all the way back and the rudder is pushed hard to the left or right and the plane begins to spin. What I so clearly remember is what was going through my head at that very moment. It was part of the lyric from the song "That Old Black Magic,"[11] and the line that goes, "Darling down and down I go, round and round I go, in a spin, I'm loving the spin that I'm in." The words were so appropriate!

Dead reckoning navigation, based upon known factors such as time, distance, speed and course, had now become much more important in our flying. Quite simply, if the distance between two points is known and if we flew at a constant speed and heading, then it would be easy to compute the flying time. The wind factor, its strength and direction, must also be taken into consideration since it would greatly affect our computations. (Accuracy was very important since, if I remember correctly, an error of one degree in our compass heading would put us one mile off course after flying sixty miles.) The schedule called for us to go on our first dual cross-county flight from Bainbridge to Valdosta, Moultrie and back to Bainbridge and that we were responsible for doing all the map work. Prominent landmarks such as lakes, rivers, water towers, railroad stations, etc. were noted and marked. We would use these landmarks as checkpoints to pinpoint our position as we proceeded toward our destination. The landmarks, close to the base, were now gone from view and it felt so very different to look down and not see a familiar road or lake. Getting away from the base made me realize that we were learning the true meaning of flying.

Soon afterward we were informed that our first daylight solo cross-county flight would be to Crestview, Florida which was almost due west of Bainbridge. Once again, it was our responsibility to lay out the course, identify prominent landmarks and compute flying time. This was double checked by the instructors, given the okay and sent us out to the planes. We memorized just about everything that was important and I felt quite a thrill as I took off. This was a first. A few minutes from Bainbridge, I found myself being escorted by two AT6's, single seat advanced trainers from nearby Dothan who flew alongside for a minute just to impress me with the fact that they were in advanced flight training and would soon be getting their wings. Hot pilots! The weather was good, I didn't drift off course and I was very satisfied with myself when I returned to the base. Another milestone successfully passed.

A new dimension would soon be added to our training when the schedule called for solo night flying to the auxiliary field at Vada. We would leave Bainbridge, fly to Vada where we would make a *touch-and-go landing* which meant that we would make contact with the runway, roll for a short distance and then takeoff to return to Bainbridge. Walking out to the flight line, alone at night, certainly was a new experience. I found the plane assigned to me, made my preflight checks, got in, started the engine, made radio contact with the tower and was cleared to takeoff. As I climbed up to altitude, I realized how easy it was to make a navigational mistake at night. Visibility was very good and I mistakenly identified the lights of Donaldsonville, which was about thirty miles away, for a smaller, nearby city. Judging distance at night was very deceptive, distant places seemed to be closer than they actually were. All went well as I neared the strip at Vada. I called in, was cleared to enter the traffic pattern and completed the touch-and-go landing without any problems. As I gained altitude, I turned to the correct compass course to return to Bainbridge. A moment later, I noticed a plane high above me in a spin with its landing lights on. It was so weird to see these two lights twisting around out of the darkness. Sure enough, it was Lt. Simpson who knew who I was (when I reported in at Vada) and he was just doing his thing!

There was a very bright, full moon that reflected off the unpainted wings of the plane and the instrument panel glowed beautifully under the ultra violet (I think) lamp that did not reduce my ability to see in the darkness. I felt very comfortable flying at night.

Perhaps my preoccupation with the beauty of the moment contributed to the near miss which happened a few minutes later. Approaching Bainbridge, I entered traffic and proceeded with the touch-and-go landing. Somehow, the right wheel went off the pavement and was dragging in the softer grass. I first tried to ease the wheel back, but to no avail. In a few moments, I would be at the point on the runway where I should be taking off, so in desperation, I yanked the controls very hard and managed to bring the wheel onto the pavement.

Instructor 2nd Lt. Vernon B. Simpson

There was a problem, however. When coming in to land the wing flaps are set to a greater angle, allowing the plane to come in slower and at a sharper angle. For the takeoff, much less flap is used. I had reached the point on the runway where I was committed to takeoff, so I advanced the throttle. With my left hand, I frantically cranked the flaps up, but not quickly enough. The plane mushed into the air and the control stick became almost limp. I had this sickening feeling in the pit of my stomach as I thought I would stall out and crack up onto the runway. Slowly the plane recovered as the flaps were brought up and I picked up airspeed. There was an additional worry. Capt. Jorgensen, the squadron commander, was in the tower and I couldn't tell if he had seen my goof. I waited for the tower to call, but heard nothing. Fortunately, he was not aware of my mistake. Night flying once again was scheduled as class 43J entered the last few weeks of training. It would be our first night solo cross-county flight going from Bainbridge, down to Quincy, Florida eastward to Perry, Florida, north to Valdosta, Georgia and back to Bainbridge. Instructors would be circling above these cities and we were to check in with them when in their area. There was quite a bit of excitement among us knowing that we had never done anything like this before. We were responsible for navigation, plotting courses and becoming acquainted with checkpoints along the way. The instructors had checked our work and we were set to go.

The takeoff from Bainbridge was uneventful and I settled back looking for reference points along the way. As I neared Quincy, I reported in, identified myself, gave my plane number and waited for confirmation. I knew that Lt. Simpson was "Quincy Control," but there was no acknowledgement of my call. I tried again but there was only silence. I had made my turn for Perry, but I was uncertain if I should wait or proceed. It was at that moment that I heard in my radio headset, someone singing, "All or nothing at all, half a love never appealed to me,"[12] the lyric from the Frank Sinatra/Harry James hit song. This was followed a moment later by bright lights reflecting off my propeller from the plane that had come up very close behind me, making it very difficult for me to see in the darkness. Then the lights went off, Simpson acknowledged my call and cleared me to proceed to Perry! This first solo, night cross-county flight had not gone *according to the book*.

The remaining legs of the flight posed no problems. As I made my final approach to land at Bainbridge, the bonehead thing I had previously done was still fresh in my mind. This time I made all the right moves.

At this point in our training, I felt quite confident about successfully completing basic flight training. Now I had to decide if I wanted to go to single-engine or twin-engine advanced flight training. I pondered this decision for quite some time, finally deciding for twin-engine. Ever the optimist, I felt that I would survive the war and use my twin-engine experience to get into commercial airline flying when I reverted to civilian status. Experience in flying single-engine planes would be of little help. Simpson was not pleased when I told him of my choice. He felt that I was better qualified for single engine advanced, but to me that seemed to be the wrong move if I wanted to improve my chances of becoming an airline pilot. A short time later, a notice went up on the bulletin board. Those who had chosen twin-engine advanced pilot training would be sent to Moody Air Force Base, Valdosta, Georgia. This time it would be a much shorter trip than the move from Arcadia to Bainbridge.

It seemed that the training program had been greatly accelerated as we neared the end of basic training. Solo day and night cross-county flying and night landings at a field other than *home* had been successfully accomplished. There was a great sense of satisfaction in knowing that we had done well, but the last, and perhaps the best challenge, was next on the agenda.

* * * * *

From the very first day at primary, we were constantly drilled to keep our head moving while in the air. Avoid close encounters with other aircraft and be alert to their presence. These last few training flights, however, would be the exact opposite for we were going to practice solo formation flying. The briefing before takeoff explained the technique involved and the need for utmost concentration. There would be three planes; the instructor in the lead, I was number one on his left wing and the other student on his right wing. We were to line up that way on the ground with the student's wingtip about forty feet away from the fuselage of the instructor's plane. Our eyes were never to leave the lead plane whether taking off, flying or landing. Simpson was quite empathic when he said if we were doing it properly, our eyes would never leave the lead ship and we would follow him into the side of a mountain. That seemed to say it all! Finally, all questions had been answered and we proceeded out to the flight line, got into our assigned planes and started the engines. Simpson made radio contact and then started his takeoff roll and we did the same. The temptation to look out ahead was very great, but I fought it off as we started to climb. As strange as it might seem, we were instructed to keep our hand on the throttle at all times and that it would be necessary to constantly make throttle movements in order to maintain our position relative to the lead plane. Slowly we began to get the knack of it as we followed the leader as he turned, climbed or descended. We had been working our way north, toward Babcock Field, to practice formation landings and takeoffs when Simpson told us to break formation and follow him single file because we were going to *buzz the house* of someone he knew. We followed him as he lost altitude and let down above a road intersection about half a mile from the house. We were very low; barely clearing the fence that bordered the farmland. Squarely in front of the house was a very tall sycamore tree and Simpson instructed us to head toward the tree, pull back on the stick at the last moment in order to clear the tree, and change propeller pitch simultaneously which would produce a very loud engine roar. As Simpson zoomed up, he *waggled his wings* as a signal for someone to meet us at Babcock Field. We reassembled, got into formation, headed toward the auxiliary field and made our first formation landing. Once again, we positioned ourselves for takeoff, got airborne, shot another landing and then waited for further instructions. We were at the most distant point from the road that bordered the field, and Simpson told us to keep our engines running and monitor the radio while he taxied away. Babcock Field was not flat. It had a bulge in the middle of it and when he moved off, he was lost from view. A minute later, he instructed us to come to where he was and cut our engines. As I recall, it was about 6:00 PM and we probably were the last planes flying. Drawing closer, I could see him talking to a very pretty young girl who obviously, was a natural redhead, perhaps seventeen years old and about one hundred ten pounds. She was dressed in riding breeches and shirt and parked nearby was the pickup truck she had driven to the field. There was a large paper bag placed before them and we were invited to come over and have some fried chicken! Introductions followed. Her name was Red, and she lived in the house we had buzzed. I reached into the bag and came up with a piece of dark meat, sad to say, having always preferred the breast. Regardless, I did like the chicken and I thanked her, remarking that the dining atmosphere sure was a lot better than the mess hall back at the base.

Despite the passing of many years, I can clearly remember that my first thought was, "This is really wild! There are three planes parked on an auxiliary field, whose pilots should be practicing formation flying but who are eating fried chicken and having a social event with a young civilian girl!" Very un-military, but then again, that was Simpson at his best. The entire incident could not have lasted more than fifteen or twenty minutes.

Looking at Red, the thought that came to mind was that she was my type and that it sure would be nice to see her again and get to know her better. Then in the middle of those thoughts, the reality of the situation sank in. Very soon, I would be leaving Bainbridge for advanced training and there would not be any chance of seeing her again. This was the way life was during the war years. You met someone you found appealing, but soon you would be shipped out and that would be the end of it. I kept thinking, as we flew back to the base, how great it would have been to date her and resurrect a social life that had ceased to exist from the moment I entered the cadet program.

That fried chicken incident and Red (mostly Red) were still in my thoughts as we flew back to the base. I wanted to know more about her and wondered if she and Simpson were dating or if they were just friends. After landing, and as we walked back to the ready room, I had a few minutes to carefully and *diplomatically* bombard Simpson with questions. I learned that her name was Verna Atkinson, that he had met her at one of the dances at the officer's club and that he was not dating her. Many of the local girls were invited and attended with chaperones in tow. She was a great dancer, didn't drink or smoke and was greatly liked by everyone who had met her. Although I had seen her for just a short while, it was clearly evident that everyone responded to her warmth, friendliness and ready smile. In addition, what I saw was a very pretty girl, with long, natural red hair, great figure and personality to match. What a package! The mental image didn't fade and I admitted to myself, I didn't want it to fade! She certainly was my type.

Soon afterward, we buzzed her house again coming in very low, almost clipping the corn tops. Hearing the sounds of our engines, she and her visiting sisters, Christine, Laverne and Elizabeth (Fritz) went outside to wave to us. Her sisters, thinking we were going to crash into the house, hit the dirt. After collecting themselves, they drove over to the field to say hello. This time Red was wearing shorts and a halter-top.

Class 43J was finished with basic flight training about the 27th of August, allowing us a few days to relax before moving to Moody Field for the final phase of pilot training. It felt great to be able to catch up on letter writing or just do nothing. I chose to go to town for the last time and just walk around or perhaps see a movie. The bus was fully loaded as it left the base, and the ride into town afforded us the opportunity to compare notes with friends who would be going to single engine advanced training. As we came into Bainbridge, the driver followed the traffic pattern to the designated bus stop on the north side of the square. I was one of the first to get off, and as I stepped down, I could see two people coming toward me who had walked through the square. They were a few steps away when I noticed that one was an older woman, but the other was young, wearing a blue linen dress, high heels and an eye-catching upsweep hair-do and she was a knockout. The young girl said,

"Hey!"

And I replied "Hi-there," having not a clue as to who she was. A moment later it hit me, it was Red! What I said next qualifies me to receive the gold medal for the most stupid remark ever uttered by man. With recognition, all I could think to say was, "I didn't recognize you with your clothes on!" Many of the cadets were close enough to hear what I had said and tried to keep a straight face, but slowly the little grins turned into outright laughter. Of course, what I was attempting to explain was that I had never seen her in anything except riding clothes or shorts, and only for a short time at that. I almost died; feeling stupid and embarrassed hoping the ground would open up and swallow me. What an ass I had made of myself! She introduced me to her mother and all I could think of was what her mother might be thinking: "How does this person know what my seventeen year old daughter looks like without her clothes and where and when did it happen?" It was humiliating. Tactfully, Red started a conversation and explained that she had been to the dentist and would soon be leaving for Georgia State Women's College to begin her freshman year. I asked,

"Where was the college located?" and her reply staggered me;

"Valdosta, Georgia." Quickly I added that it sure was a great coincidence since I too would be going to Valdosta for advanced flight training! We said our goodbyes and a moment later, they got into their car and drove off.

Walking through town, I was completely absorbed thinking of what had happened. A few days ago, I was resigned to the fact that we would be going our separate ways and that I would never see her again, but now all had been changed. Although there would be little leisure time, we did have open post days and it was only about ten miles from Moody Field to Valdosta. I looked forward with great anticipation to my next duty station.

After an hour or two, I came to the conclusion that there was nothing in town that interested me. What did interest me, however, was the new student at Georgia State Women's College.

Verna "Red" Atkinson, 1943

9

TWIN ENGINE ADVANCED PILOT TRAINING
MOODY FIELD, VALDOSTA, GEORGIA

It was September 1, 1943 when I arrived at Moody Field and my first impression was very encouraging. The typical welcome speech was made by the commanding officer, who wished us good luck and success, followed by introductions to the various personnel who would see to our everyday needs. Our housing was not the *country club* layout of Carlstrom Field, but better than the bare bones, typical army barracks of Bainbridge. The food was very good and very plentiful. The temptation to overindulge was not lost on the people in charge. I distinctly remember the sign above the exit door of the mess hall which read, "Take all you can eat, but eat all that you take." A sergeant was posted at the door whose job was to see how much food you were throwing away. Quickly we learned that the sign was enforced. If you put it on your tray, you had better eat it.

At long last, I had a little free time, found a phone booth and placed a call to Red. I can't remember a word we said, but it was exciting just talking to her. She informed me that Saturday night was dance night at the college and she invited me as her guest. I was careful, during the coming week, not to goof up inspections or get demerits which would have cancelled my open post. Upon leaving the phone booth, it occurred to me that we hardly knew each other, our only contact being the few minutes at Babcock Field and at the bus stop in Bainbridge. Saturday night could not come soon enough.

Marching down to the flight line, that first day, I wondered what type of person my new instructor would be: stern, easy going, very military or none of the above. I concluded that no one could compare to the unique Lt. Vernon B. Simpson, and I was right. All the speculation soon ceased when the assignments were read. My instructor was Lt. Wilkinson, handsome, about five feet ten inches tall and in his mid twenties. Introductions were made, followed by a little bit of small talk, *where are you from, how long have you been in the service*, etc. We would be flying the AT10, made by Cessna, which had been dubbed the *Bamboo Bomber*. It had two engines, retractable landing gear and side-by-side seating, a radical departure from what we had previously flown. When not flying, we were expected to study the material available in the ready room regarding the AT10. There was also one other book that occupied a great deal of our time and with which I was already familiar: the "Pilot's Information File." (Very informative reading, but sad to say, there was no plot!) In addition, classes in weather, code, link trainer, engine mechanics, navigation and other subjects were on the curriculum. Spare time was conspicuous by its absence. One other item of note took place that very first day. Lt. Wilkinson made little effort to conceal his displeasure with the workload assigned to him. He thought five students were too many and he grumbled about it.

A check of my pilot's logbook shows that my introductory flight was on September 5th, and was an hour and twelve minutes in duration. The AT10, with the side-by-side seating arrangement made it a lot easier for the instructor to chew out the student when he screwed up.

Once again, I was told to follow through on the controls as he performed various maneuvers, to get the feel of the plane's response. Learning the traffic pattern quickly was paramount, since the AT10 required more airspace.

Two facts became obvious on that first flight: Twin-engine flying would not be as much fun as single engine, and there was a lot to learn, but all went well.

A day after my introductory flight, Lt. Wilkinson was granted an emergency leave. My logbook shows that I did not fly from the 5th to the 13th of September (which happened to be my twenty-fourth birthday.) When not attending ground school classes, I sat in the ready room reading the "Pilot's Information File" and trying to remember what I had learned in my first session. Finally, on the 14th I was assigned to fly with a temporary replacement instructor. The walk to the flight line was uneventful until I saw that this next session of dual instruction would be in a completely different plane; the Curtiss Wright AT9. What little I had learned on my first session was of little or no use. There was no similarity to the AT10; being completely different in every respect, and by comparison, the AT9 was considered to be a much *hotter* plane. When we landed, another hour and thirty minutes of dual flying time was entered into my log. In essence, I had been given two introductory dual sessions. On the 15th, I had another training flight in the AT9, with the temporary instructor, which added another hour and eighteen minutes to my total time. I was relieved to see that I was not scheduled the next day. Totally confused, I felt that perhaps I could mentally sort out what I had supposedly learned.

Open post could not have come at a better time for it had been a difficult two weeks. The bus trip to Valdosta seemed to take forever before I arrived at my stop. I walked the last few blocks to the college and upon seeing it thought that it was a very pretty campus. Following the crowd, I made my way to the dance and when on the floor, looked not at faces but for a mop of red hair which was easier to spot. Dodging dancers, I walked to where she was standing; we each said "hi" and I remember thinking that at last I was with her. This time it was not on a flying field, with my instructor, or at a bus stop in town with her mother at her side. Soon afterward, the music started and as we danced, it occurred to me that it was the first time I had actually touched her. Unfortunately, the moment didn't last too long because other cadets began to cut in, bringing back memories of dances in the past when there were many more men than women. Despite all the cutting in, we managed to spend a good part of the evening together, dancing, talking and getting to know a little more about each other. Strange as it might seem, and what I couldn't understand, was why it bothered me to see her being held by another man while dancing. I had been with her just a few hours, but I could not deny that I had become strongly attracted to her in that short length of time. When the dance was over and it was time to leave, I asked her for a date for the next dance and she agreed.

There were two thoughts running through my head on the return trip to the base. One was very comforting and the other very disturbing. What bothered me was what was happening on the flight line. I just could not seem to get a handle on why things were not going well. The comforting thought, obviously, was Verna Atkinson. I kept thinking of how good it was to be with her and that it would be a long week before I could see her again.

Lt. Wilkinson had returned from emergency leave when I arrived on the flight line on the morning of September 17th. Checking the schedule, I saw that I was scheduled to fly and this time it would be in the AT10. Once again, I was faced with the problem of trying to remember which plane I was flying and vital information such as engine rpm, flap position for takeoff and landings, stall speeds, etc. of the AT10. I had but four hours dual instruction time, which was less than the other students. At the end of the flight, an additional two hours and twenty-four minutes of dual time was entered into my logbook. This was unusual because most sessions were for an hour or an hour and a half. (Perhaps he thought he was doing the right thing by cramming additional flying time into one training period, but it was a mistake. I felt that I would have been much better off with two shorter periods which would have given me the opportunity to assimilate what I had learned.) I now had a total of six hours and twenty-four minutes of dual instruction time. On the 19th of September, I was informed that I had been scheduled for a check ride with a check pilot since Lt. Wilkinson was of the opinion that I was not making progress. The check ride was a failure. Two days later, I had a check ride with the assistant squadron commander and he also was not impressed. About the 24th, I appeared before the board for disposition with the opportunity to speak on my behalf. After hearing my story, they allowed me to have a little more time, but from the experience of others, we all knew that it was almost impossible to get the decision reversed. Logical thinking indicates that check pilot number two doesn't want to reverse check pilot number one, who does not want to make the instructor look bad. The final report said, "Official reason for elimination was unsatisfactory flying, *poor coordination* and judgment." Previous classes had a washout rate of about five. By comparison about 25 cadets were eliminated from class 43J, all having 150 hours or more. We all couldn't have been that bad. Evidently, *they* couldn't determine that I had poor coordination and judgment until I had logged that many hours. Apparently, the Air Corps projections indicated that they had more people than they needed, keeping the best and eliminating those, such as myself, who had lagged behind regardless of the reason.

Although I had qualified for pilot, navigator and bombardier training at Nashville, it was necessary to wait for the official report from Maxwell Field before I could be reassigned. I did want to remain in the aviation cadet program and when interviewed, I chose bombardier training. Soon afterward, I was notified that my choice had been granted, but I first had to complete the aerial gunnery training course at Tyndall Field, Panama City, Florida.

Certainly, the failure to succeed in pilot training was a severe blow to my pride and morale. It hurt and it was bewildering. I could have accepted failure, if it had happened in primary or basic, but to have come so close and then being eliminated was demoralizing. A few days later, I began to put things into perspective. Thinking more clearly, I found comfort in the thought that I had done my best, even if it wasn't good enough. Perhaps it wasn't meant to be. Recalling my so-called *philosophy* I asked myself, "How can you now say that everything happens for the best?" A moment later I had a follow up thought, "How can you say that it *didn't* happen for the best?"

Despite my disappointment, there was one unforeseen, positive aspect to being eliminated. I had no duty assignment to speak of and was given open post every evening. Although the college prohibited dating off campus, Red and I found a way to be together when she did not have a class. Fortunately, there was a public phone in the entrance hall of her dorm and we made great use of it. We pre-arranged going to the movies being careful to enter separately, a minute apart, making certain that there was an adjacent empty seat. Speaking for myself, I couldn't care less about the action on the screen, being happy just to be sitting beside her.

On Sunday afternoons, the students were allowed to have guests on campus, listening to music in the so-called *cabin in the woods* or meeting with other students in the Rotunda. My camera was put to good use taking pictures of her as we walked around the campus. When I received the processed film, I wasted no time in putting her pictures in my wallet.

Much to my surprise, I was granted a furlough and I accepted. I left on Tuesday the 17th of October, finally arriving home in New Jersey about four in the afternoon the following day. Seeing everyone again was wonderful for it had been nine months since I had last been home. In a way, however, it was strange to be with the family and among familiar surroundings. Strange because it was quite confusing, not knowing where I belonged. This was home, but it wasn't home. Home was Moody Field and wherever I would go from there. The thought occurred to me that it would be easier *not* to come home for the simple reason that furloughs had become an emotional roller coaster. (I would imagine that most servicemen had similar reactions when they came home on leave.) Carl Frank, stationed in Maryland, was able to get a three-day pass knowing that I would be home. For whatever reason, it turned out to be a very quiet, subdued reunion, which was very uncharacteristic of us. Hopefully, there would better times in the future.

The trip back to Moody Field was very uncomfortable. I could not get a reservation and had to settle for a seat on the so-called *Havana Special*. I had left at 9:30 PM on Wednesday, October 26th, finally arriving 11:30 AM, Friday the 28th. After checking in, I was informed that my orders had not come through, so I was still *on vacation*. My request for a three-day pass was approved, which was great news, making it possible to attend the dance on Saturday night. A phone call to Red was next and I was happy to learn that she would be there.

Red was very amused at an incident that took place at the dance Saturday night. I was well aware that I could be leaving at any time, so I naturally wanted to be with her as much as possible. What rankled me was that one of my classmates kept cutting in on me. I have long since forgotten his name, but I still retain the image of his face when I told him "to buzz off, she was *my* girl and I didn't want him cutting in any more." What tickled her was my pugnacious

Verna and Colletti, October 17, 1943, Georgia State Women's College

attitude toward a man who probably out weighed me by forty pounds, was about six feet tall and could reduce me to pulpwood if he so desired. Apparently, he got the message. He found another target, much to my relief.

We said goodbye on Tuesday November 2nd. I left Moody Field on the 3rd. The memories of that last date were all that I would have for a long time.

10

AERIAL GUNNERY SCHOOL, TYNDALL FIELD
PANAMA CITY, FLORIDA

I left Moody Field on November 3, 1943, the very day that class 43J graduated. Looking out the window of the bus I could see the men who were yesterday's cadets, now wearing their brand new officer's uniforms. I wondered how it felt to be standing there, taking the oath of office, receiving their commission as 2nd lieutenants, the subject of countless photographs and congratulations as family members or loved ones pinned on their bars and wings. I envied them. They had worked very hard to achieve their goal.

After an all night train ride, we finally arrived at Tyndall Field, Panama City, Florida, on Thursday, November 4th. The usual well-known routine followed: Fall out, answer to your name at roll call and listen for any special instructions. Our barracks turned out to be a long, low building with concrete floors, filled with upper and lower bunk beds with barely sufficient aisle space between them. We were not too far from the Gulf of Mexico and I noticed that it was sandy where there was no pavement. Much to my surprise, it was very cold in the morning when we fell out for the first assembly of the day.

Judging from conversation as we became acquainted, I concluded that most of the men in the class were people, such as me, who had been eliminated from other schools. For some, however, gunnery school was their first choice. Upon successful completion of the course we would become aerial gunners and probably be recommended for a staff sergeant's rank to go with it.

* * * * *

Aerial gunnery training began on the ground on the skeet shooting range which was laid out in the shape of a half a circle with a 25-yard radius. There were two target houses, one on the left and one on the right, spaced about forty yards apart. On command, a clay target would be thrown from one house across the open end of the circle, and at different angles, in order to simulate the flight of a moving target. There were eight designated shooting stations on the circle corresponding to half the face of a clock. Using a shotgun, the shooter would begin at the first position, take his shots and proceed to next position until he completed the round. The object of all this was to teach the gunner to aim not where the target was, but where it would be a moment later. The descriptive term for this was *leading the target*. Skeet shooting was a lot of fun, a great relief from the stress of pilot training.

Very soon I learned that the enlisted men on the base had a hostile attitude toward cadets and rightly so. Some time in the past, it seems that the first cadet classes had an attitude problem with the GI's. They made it clear that they, the cadets, thought that they were superior to the GI's and the enlisted men resented it. Having come from the enlisted ranks made it easy for me to understand how they felt.

I was not impressed with Panama City. The town was dull and the people appeared to be cold and unfriendly. There were hundreds of well-paid shipyard workers living there and the local merchants took advantage of their newfound wealth by setting their prices sky high. Richmond, Virginia or Valdosta, Georgia, it was not.

Gradually we proceeded to other types of guns and targets, firing just about every type weapon the service was using at the time. Included were the 45-caliber pistol, (aim low and to the right and the bullet will hit high and to the left!) the Thompson sub-machine gun, 30-caliber rifle, the 30-caliber machine gun, and the most important of all, the 50-caliber machine gun. There might have been others, but I cannot remember what they were. For a gun lover, this would have been the realization of a dream. I wasn't, but I did enjoy the experience.

Although only a few weeks had passed since I had said goodbye to Red, I quickly began to miss her. Thinking back, it occurred to me that she was the athletic type, but very feminine in manner and speech. Despite the heat, she wore gloves and a hat just for a simple trip into town. We danced very well together, and surprisingly, I learned that she liked to do the rumba which was my favorite dance. No one had better cut in when we were dancing to "Siboney!" Had anyone tried, I would not have given her up because that number was reserved for us! Quoting her very own words, she told me "I had found a rebel who disliked country music and who preferred Latin music."

Valdosta was about one hundred and eighty miles from Panama City, but there was no possibility of leave. Letter writing was the only practical solution and happy was I indeed, when she responded so quickly. That there was little of importance to write about was immaterial. What mattered most was that there was a letter from her at mail call. Our letters conveyed the thoughts which we could not say in person.

* * * * *

The 50-caliber machine gun was probably the most important weapon in which we had to become proficient, since it was used in all our planes. Proof of our knowledge of the gun was the so-called *blindfold check* where we were required to dismantle and reassemble it just by feel. What I remember so clearly was that I was given a brand new gun, covered with a rust preventing grease, which made it much more difficult to identify the parts. As I started the test, I again thought how my watch making experience helped me. My fingers were sensitive to the shape and feel of the various parts, in spite of the grease. Passing that test was mandatory. What I had learned about the 50-caliber gun would be put to good use many months later.

Soon afterward, we learned how to operate an electrically powered gun turret, which was large enough to accommodate the gunner and two 50-caliber machine guns. There were two controls, one for each hand that resembled the handle of a pistol. Pushing one or the other would move the guns horizontally and moving them up or down would change the elevation of the guns. Obviously, it was essential to be able to coordinate our hands in order to simultaneously move the guns left or right or up and down while firing at a moving target. Additionally, the speed of the movements could be controlled by varying the distance the control handles were displaced. This took place outdoors where turrets were set up to fire at targets that were thrown from towers. In a sense, it was like skeet shooting, but this time we were using machine guns. It took a while before we could hit the targets with any consistency.

Another training device which we liked was located in a large building. Inside, the ceiling and wall were curved from left to right and from the floor to the ceiling. The student gunner was seated in a turret directly in front of the wall which in essence was a giant, curved movie screen. When the projector was turned on the *movie* showed enemy aircraft coming in for the kill from every possible angle. The gunner would attempt to track the moving fighter planes and his hits could be recorded electronically. There was a sound track that simulated the roar of the attacking planes, which made it very realistic. The gunner had to be very alert, since there was no warning of the direction of the *attack*. In our haste we screwed up many times. Poor coordination, or being too slow to fire, often resulted in a kill for the bandit. Eventually, we got the hang of it.

Outdoors once again, a new challenge awaited us. Imagine a hula-hoop, about waist high, mounted on legs on a flat bed truck. The gunner positioned himself in the hoop, holding a shotgun, and the truck then proceeded down a sandy, bumpy, winding, rut-filled road which had been cut through the pine trees. The road was very narrow and at times, some of the tree branches would scrape the truck. Hidden in the trees were towers which would fire skeet targets as we came bumping along. We, of course, were supposed to have multiple sets of eyes since there were no clues as to where to look for the incoming target. In addition, the lurching and bumping practically knocked us off our feet until we learned that it helped a little to stand with our knees slightly bent. As we passed the hidden towers, a *bird* would come flying out giving us a few seconds to bring the gun up, decide where and how much to lead it and then fire. By far the most interesting target was the one that was positioned at the closed end of a U-turn. They told us about that one for safety reasons. The reason was simple: the bird was fired from close range and directly at us. If we missed, the damn thing would probably hit us in the head. I congratulated myself when I hit it!

Socially, there was little to do. I attended a dance or two at the USO Club, but it just wasn't much fun. There was a music room off the dance floor, which had a record player and records. Looking through the pile, about the only one worth playing was named "Pavanne" by Glenn Miller. It was a good number but had never achieved great popularity. Out of desperation, I played it over and over.

Without question, the hit song which could be found in most jukeboxes was "Paper Doll"[13] by the Mills Brothers. The melody and lyrics were easy to remember making it the kind of song everyone could sing. Perhaps some of the men who had received *Dear John* letters could identify with that part of the lyric which went, "I'm gonna buy a paper doll that I can call my own, a doll that other fellows cannot steal." So much for love life during the war years! In that respect, I felt quite lucky. Though we were miles apart, the letters I received from my Rebel Redhead helped to bridge the gap.

* * * * *

Apalachicola, Florida is about fifty miles east of Tyndall Field, on the shoreline, with US 98 nearby. We were now in our fifth week of training which consisted of air-to-water and air-to-air firing. Since this could not be done in the congested Panama City area, we made a temporary move to a small auxiliary field in Apalachicola. There was a mess hall, operations shack, tents for housing and not much more. Still, I enjoyed the change to the less crowded and easygoing environment. I recall, thinking to myself, what a great place this would be to have a cottage on the beach. (My foresight was right on target, for I recently read that after all these years, people had finally discovered the area and were moving in. The *old-timers* had managed to keep it a secret for many years, but no longer.)

The first two sessions were flown in a Lockheed Hudson and were called *splash missions*. We were firing at a floating, wooden target and we could easily judge our marksmanship by the splashes made by our bullets when they hit the water. Being able to see our mistakes made it a lot easier to make corrections. In addition, we spent a good part of the week tracking and firing (empty) guns at attacking AT6's as they made passes from many directions. We learned a lot in the simulated classroom training, but it was quite a different experience when you were in flight.

The final week of training was the most important. We would be airborne, firing at a towed target. Our rounds were color-coded, which made it possible to count the number of hits each student registered. Failure to achieve a certain percentage of hits would be reason for elimination. How well I scored has long since been forgotten, but I did qualify. Quoting from my letter to Carl of December 29th:

"On December 21st I graduated from gunnery school and got my silver gunner's wings, which made me feel so much worse for washing out of pilot training."

I didn't minimize the achievement, for I was happy in thinking that this was the first step in my comeback, but the desire to wear the beautiful *pinks and green* uniform never lessened.

Pandelis Camesas, Robert Coakley, John Cole and Andrew Courvoisier, among others, were new friends that I had made at Tyndall Field. I was very pleased to learn that we would be together again, in the same barracks at our next station.

The very next day, December 22, 1943, we departed Tyndall Field for Victorville, California, to begin bombardier training.

11

BOMBARDIER SCOOL, VICTORVILLE ARMY AIR BASE
VICTORVILLE, CALIFORNIA

I'm certain that no one will ever forget that memorable trip from Panama City to Victorville, California. For starters, we were put aboard converted boxcars which had bunk beds stacked about five or six high and positioned across the car. There was no wasted space, the only clear area being in the vicinity of the sliding doors. With each lurch, the *lucky men up top* thought they were on one of those rides at an amusement park. We were in complete agreement in thinking that they were entitled to flying pay. The train was following the southern route, meandering slowly across the country, being shunted aside to allow more important traffic to proceed. We took advantage of one of those down times someplace in Alabama. We came to a halt right in the middle of a very small town. Looking out the door, we could plainly see that we were blocking the main road and that there was a store about three blocks away. Someone asked the trainman how long we would be stopped and he replied "at least twenty minutes." That comment gave birth to an idea that occurred to all of us at the very same moment, for we began to jump off the train and head for the store. The storekeeper probably never knew what hit him, because we bought all we could carry. For once, we all had a little extra to satisfy our cravings!

One thing still bothers me after all these years: Try as I might, I cannot remember how the sanitation problem was solved, because there were no toilet facilities in the boxcar. Perhaps those long delays en route were intentionally scheduled just to provide an opportunity to heed the call of nature.

Another memorable event took place when we arrived in New Orleans one morning. The officer in charge of the group informed us that we were free to go into town, but had to be back on the train by 7:00 PM without fail. The last syllable of the word "dismissed" was barely out of his mouth when the exodus began. Regardless of where I walked through town, I was sure to meet one of my classmates prowling the streets. Needless to say, the French Quarter and its female inhabitants got a lot of attention. I can't say I blame the guys who were trying to make up for lost time. I did my share of walking and looking and finally went to a movie. The decision was easy because I still had vivid memories of the suffering of the men who came down with venereal disease back at Langley Field. I could still see the expression on their faces as I gave them their weekly injection with that big syringe! Happy with my decision, I lucked out, because it was a good movie.

Of course, some of the men were late in returning and missed the train. They had enough presence of mind to check with the civilian in charge of operations. He managed to get them aboard a passenger train which, hopefully, would allow them to catch up with the troop train. As it turned out, they arrived in Houston, Texas before we did! We did have a stopover in Houston, but it was a short one and we had to remain on board. The officer in charge probably came to the conclusion that one such escapade was enough and wasn't going to push his luck. When we left, we were well aware that there was a long way to go before we got to California. Fortunately, some of us still had some canned food that we bought in the *Alabama Raid* and now was a good time to eat it.

We finally arrived in Victorville on the 28th of December, a mere six days of Class A boxcar travel. On Christmas Eve, one of the very few of us who knew what day it was, made a very big mistake. Very cheerfully, he wished one and all a "Merry Christmas." This was a very unwise statement when you consider the circumstances we were in. What kind of a merry Christmas can this be, far from home, tired, jammed in a boxcar and thinking of where we wanted to be? The curses and venom which were dispatched in his direction were nothing compared to the final insult which would have required him to perform a sexual maneuver which was anatomically impossible. Poor guy! So much for observing the holiday.

At the station, we were greeted by a cadet officer who would be in charge at all our formations. He was perhaps an inch shorter than I was, about one hundred forty pounds with very short blond hair. We have all heard of the saying, "love at first sight," but how can you *dislike* someone at first sight? Immediately I realized that he reminded me of the typical Prussian officer depicted in fictional stories in "Flying Aces Magazine." He fit the description perfectly; coldly efficient and, we soon learned, with little or no sense of humor. Making his mark in the military was his goal. Taking on the chore of being a cadet officer would certainly showcase his leadership qualities (or so he hoped.)

Perhaps I should digress a bit and describe the people who were on that train. From what I could determine, we were in the bombardier pool because we had been eliminated from some other training. We had been through the mill, so to speak, and knew the ropes. We weren't new recruits who didn't know their ass from page twelve (or any other page) in the Sears catalog. Maybe *cynical* would be a better choice of words. We had seen and been exposed to enough army life to be able to quickly evaluate

Lt. Longley with the "Prussian General" to his left. Colletti far left in front.

people. Later, when there was some spare time to compare notes, most of us were of the same opinion. We had him pegged right. This guy was *chicken shit*.

Barracks assignments came next and I was pleased to see that most of us who had become friends would still be together. Walter John Chilsen (Merril, WI); Pandelis Camesas (Astoria, Long Island, NY), Robert C. Coakley (Flandreau, SD) and Everett E. Cobb, Jr. (Portland, OR) were across the aisle from me. Next to me was John Howard Cole (Jackson, TN.) On the other side were Andy Courvoisier (Huguenot Park, Staten Island, NY); Anthony F. Cubre (Fresno, CA); Raymond DeBlasis (Philadelphia, PA); Serge S. Davison (Long Island City, NY) and James T. Delaney (Brooklyn, NY.)

Chapter 11

At our first class, we learned that there would be eighteen weeks of training, with the first six weeks devoted to dead reckoning navigation. Quite logically, the bombardier must first locate the target before he could hit it! There would be many hours of navigation study daily and there would be two, four-hour exams every week. Each cadet had to fly nine missions as a navigator which called for making regular, timed entries in a flight log. Without doubt, what I had learned in pilot training would certainly be very helpful. The first class would begin at 7:00 AM and the day would end at 5:30 PM. Sandwiched in between were the ever-present physical training, code, weather and miscellaneous ground school courses.

Saturday morning was probably the worst day of the week for there was always an inspection. At the very first one, the inspection officer was in the barracks for almost forty-five minutes, checking on just about everything we owned. Then we had to undergo a personal inspection outside, standing at attention in ranks, while he looked for properly shined brass and shoes, creased pants, etc. He had a block of wood two or three inches long, which he used to measure the space from the ground to the cuff of our pants. Of course, receiving demerits for failing a test would lead to walking duty tours when everyone else had time off. When that session of fun and games was over, we usually went to the drill field for a military revue which was a fancy name for a parade. Our schedule was very tight, with hardly enough free time for letter writing.

Most of us went into Victorville when we finally were granted open post. We usually congregated at the Green Spot with good reason: It was the only place in town! Two of the most popular songs on the jukebox were "Star Eyes" and "Besame Mucho" by Jimmy Dorsey's Orchestra with Bob Eberly doing the vocals. Soon afterward, they had another hit, "My Ideal." Another very popular number was "Shoo-Shoo Baby" but I don't remember the artist. Not being a drinking person, I soon tired of the Green Spot. The next time, I went to the local USO and was delighted to discover that they had a good, live orchestra and a nice crowd of dancing partners. I had not had a date since I said goodbye to Verna on November 2nd (that's not to say that going to a USO dance was going out on a date!) It felt good to hear a live band and dance once again.

Looking forward to mail call was the highlight of the day since Red had been writing three or four times a week. Slowly, we began to know each other better and the better I knew her, the more I liked her. It occurred to me that this was becoming a *romance via correspondence*, but it was the only way to go. Of one thing I was sure: I didn't want it to stop.

L to R: Cadets Serge Davidson, Ray DeBlasis, Silveo Colletti, Pandelis Camesas, Robert Coakley, Jack Cole, Walter John Chilsen
Green Spot Café, Victorville, California

One of the very first things I learned on a training navigation flight was not to trust the pilot! Dead reckoning navigation is a method used to keep track of your geographic position based upon speed and distance calculations. Example: If your speed is one hundred miles an hour and you have been flying for two hours, then you know that you have covered two hundred miles. Looking at the course plotted on the map, you can easily calculate your position. All would be fine except for one thing: the wind. Obviously, depending on its direction and speed, it could slow you down, speed you up, push you to the left or right or diagonally. The instrument used to help solve this problem was called a drift meter. It was an optical device which had a line etched on the lens and the entire unit was mounted on a rotating base. Looking through the meter, the navigator would select a distinctive object on the ground and track its movement relative to the line on the lens. By rotating the meter, the ground object could then be made to move parallel to the line. Reading the calibrations at the base of the meter would tell him the number of degrees the plane was drifting off course. This information was then transferred to a hand held, so-called *E6B computer* which was a specialized type of slide rule. From this, he could then determine the wind's speed and direction and the all-important actual ground speed of the plane. All pertinent information such as elapsed time, compass course, indicated air speed, etc., would be entered in his flight log at five-minute intervals. On this particular mission, the pilot seeing that I was completely absorbed with the drift meter began a very slow turn. Being *green*, I assumed that he would do his job and maintain constant speed and direction. Soon we were way off course and it was then that he very innocently asked, "Where are we?" When I gave him a wrong position report, he asked me why hadn't I noticed the change in course. I started to explain that I was busy with the drift meter, but I knew that there was no excuse. He proved his point very well when he said that I had my head up my ass and it was locked! It was then that he informed me that we were nearing Barstow, California. (I was sure glad that he knew where we were because I didn't have a clue.) All this gave birth to a joke which we all could identify with since many of us had been victims of the same experience. Regardless, we were able to laugh at ourselves when we repeated this imagined conversation that supposedly took place over the plane's intercom:

"Navigator to pilot, over."

"Pilot to navigator, go ahead."

"Navigator to pilot, where are we, I've got a *right to know!*"

Although that particular mission was a disaster, it proved the point that you learn more from your mistakes than you do from your successes. Certainly, I now was fully aware of where my head should *not* be. I would not make that mistake again. During the month of January, I had flown four missions with five more to go.

* * * * *

Bob Coakley and I had both washed out of pilot training. With that failure in mind, we made it a point to never anticipate success, in any of our classes, regardless of how good our grades were. At the conclusion of a good mission, we would ask each other, "Do you think we'll make it?" Our answers were always, "Well maybe, perhaps," or "time will tell" or whatever imprecise responses we could think of, but never "yes." It had become a kind of defense mechanism and the back and forth banter continued throughout out stay at Victorville.

Without doubt, one of the most closely guarded secrets of the United States, sometime around 1942, was the Norden bombsight. At that time, extreme measures were taken to prevent it from falling into enemy hands. It was kept under lock and key until it was needed for a mission and then, under armed guard, was brought to the flight line and installed in the nose of the plane. The bombardier was responsible for its safekeeping and was under orders to destroy it should a breach of security exist. By the time I began my training it was assumed that the Germans had probably learned many of its secrets by examining downed aircraft. Still, it was a classified item. Ask any young person today if he knew what the Norden sight was, and he probably would have no idea what you were talking about. So much for one of the wonders of WWII. Although there were more navigation missions to be flown, classes soon began on the Norden. I knew little about the sight, but what I did know aroused my curiosity and I was impatient to get started. In that first class the instructor made a rather simple statement when he said:

"The bombing problem can be summed up in a few words. What you, the bombardier must do, is find the exact point in the sky where the bomb must be released in order to hit the target." How to do it, of course, was the problem. Today, I would imagine that the sight would be classified as a computer, but designed to only do a specific job. It had two main parts, the base which contained the automatic pilot mechanism, and the head which contained the optics, gyroscope and the mechanism that did the work. The section that held all the *works* was known as the rate end. The optics, located in the center of the head, consisted of a telescope, which had a magnification of slightly more than two, and a crosshair superimposed on the lens. There were two knobs, slightly below and at the right end of the head, which were known as the *course knobs*. They were operated by the bombardier's left hand and could be turned as one or separately. They were coupled to the autopilot making it possible for the bombardier, by turning the knob, to make corrections to the plane's course without the pilot's assistance. Turning one knob would make large course corrections while the second knob was used to *fine tune* what had previously been done. There was an index window about an inch or so wide, extending from the top down to the bottom of the sight directly in front of the bombardier. Under the window, two electrical contact points and a numbered scale were visible. One contact was adjustable and it was set on the scale based on information in the bombing tables that were given to the bombardiers. The tables also supplied information about the ballistic characteristics of the bomb we were dropping and those values were programmed into the sight. The right hand, of course, had a very important job to do. It was used to operate the rate knob, which determined if the bomb would hit short or over the target. Soon, what we had learned in ground school would be put to use.

* * * * *

Marching down to the flight line to the training range, that first day, I began to think about the bombing instructor that I would soon meet. (It seems that I had done this before.) The sad memories I had of my experiences at Moody Field with Lt. Wilkinson, were still very fresh in my mind. There

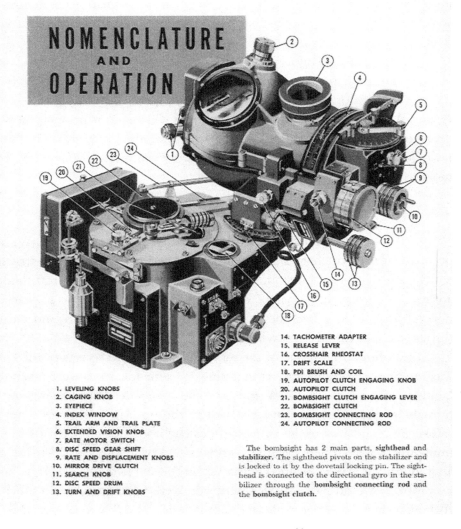

"Bombardiers' Information File"[14]

was no denying that the so-called *chemistry* between instructor and student certainly made a great difference. Simpson at Bainbridge chewed us out, but there was no malice in what he said. When we screwed up he called us "stupid ass" etc. but it was just a teaching technique. Wilkinson, however, was determined to reduce his workload one way or another.

Lt. Ericcson was my new instructor and regardless of how hard I try, I remember very little of him. He was in his mid twenties, tall and businesslike. I did like him. What I did remember was the fact that the names of three of my instructors ended in *son*. I began to wonder if there was some message being sent to me, and if so, what it meant.

The classroom bombing range was a large, hangar type building with a very smooth, level cement floor. Across the floor were a number of towers, about seven feet tall, made of steel tubing, with a base about seven feet square. There was a platform at the top, large enough for the student, instructor and the bombsight. The tower was mounted on wheels, which were steerable and an electric motor provided the thrust needed to roll it across the floor. The sight was coupled to the steering mechanism of the tower, permitting the student to change its direction by turning the course knob. The last item of equipment was the *Bug*. It was about twenty inches long, fifteen inches wide and eight inches high. It was electrically driven and it had a printed, paper target attached on top. When switched on, it would begin to roll across the floor and the bombardier would begin his bomb run. The bombsight could be swiveled in the direction of the bug and the student, looking through the telescope, would pick up the target and attempt to place the crosshairs in the telescope over the target on the bug. If the target drifted to one side, he would make a course correction. If it seemed to go down or up, he would make a rate correction. What he was attempting to do, was to synchronize on the target even though it was moving. (What was required here, obviously, was the ability to coordinate hand and eye, an ability which I did not have according to the Washout Board at Moody Field.) When the bug passed under the sight, a plunger would be activated and it would stamp a mark on the target. (That is, if the bug had not been completely missed, as was the case in the very beginning!) With each bomb run, the bug's direction would be changed making each run a different synchronization problem. There were other, very important tasks that the bombardier had to accomplish, which are difficult to describe.

Up on the tower, student and instructor would be sitting side-by-side making bomb runs on the mechanical bug. Hitting the target was important, but probably more important was the need for the student to develop proper procedure, such as remembering to open the bomb bay doors before dropping your bomb load! It was felt that, with practice, accuracy would be achieved.

I can't remember how much time we spent on the training towers, but it is probably safe to say that we had to attain an acceptable level of proficiency before we began flying missions.

* * * * *

Fortunately, most of the people in my barracks were friendly and easygoing. There were those who had been eliminated from other training schools and others who were entering the aviation cadet program directly from civilian life. Some were high school graduates and some were college students, but I do not know what the percentages were. One thing was certain; it was a challenge to keep up with them.

Regardless of the situation, you could rest assured that someone would come up with a joke or comment that would have everyone laughing. This happened after evening mess when we had a few hours of spare time before lights went out at 9:00. There were only a dozen or so people in the barracks, some reading, writing letters or getting things ready for inspection. Across the isle from me and to my left, Walter John Chilsen was standing near his bed and, a few beds over stood Pandelis Camesas. It was very quiet so normal conversation was possible. It was then that Walter John called out;

"Pandelis?"

He replied "Yes Walter John, what is it?"

"Pandelis, don't you think that *Silveo* has a very odd name?" He said it with a straight face, with no humor in his voice, the same voice he might have used if he was reciting Lincoln's Gettysburg address. Incredible! It was the best laugh we had had in weeks. (Walter John and I would go on to share another experience not too long afterward.)

Another memorable event took place in the classroom. The subject that day was the study and identification of clouds and how important it was to know which were dangerous and should be avoided. There were pictures of various cloud formations and the instructor called upon one of the students to identify each cloud. Standing before the class, he began;

"Let's see... This one is a stratus cloud, and this one is a nimbus and this is a cumulo-nimbus and to me this one looks like a nimble penis." The poor instructor couldn't decide if he should *gig* him with a dozen demerits or congratulate him for using his imagination. He had a sense of humor, however, and he enjoyed the gag along with the entire class.

Life in the barracks was always hectic usually with insufficient time to do even the simple things. At reveille, there would be a mad scramble to claim a sink and be the first to shave. A typical scenario would find three people at the same sink; the shortest in front (me) and the taller men to the rear, thereby making it possible for all to use the mirror at the same time. Showering was a two or three-minute affair, depending upon how many were waiting, and most of the time we would have to start dressing before we were dry. Somewhere, somehow I

The crowd at the sink explains why I needed the "clock in my head."

developed the unique ability to wake up about ten minutes before reveille. While everyone was still asleep, I could shower and finish shaving just about the time the lights were snapped on, which was quickly followed by a stampeding horde of griping, half-asleep men. Someone remarked that "I had a clock in my head." Perhaps. Strangely, I have retained that ability to this day.

* * * * *

We had now reached the point where little more could be learned by sitting atop a training platform and making simulated bombing runs on a mechanical bug. Soon we would begin flying training missions.

I believe it would be safe to say that most of us had similar thoughts as we marched down to the flight line. What would it be like? Will I get the hang of it or will I mess it up with some stupid, bonehead mistake? We would know soon enough.

The aircraft being used to train bombardiers was the Beech AT11. It was a twin-engine, stubby-nosed plane, with retractable landing gear and twin rudders. The nose looked like a big, curved window with excellent vision in all directions, and was large enough to accommodate student, instructor and the bombsight.

Beech AT11

There was a trap door on the floor of the nose, and to one side, which opened downward. From the ground, the sight would be handed to the student in the plane who would mount it on the base.

The first thing we learned was that there was a great amount of heavy work involved in dropping bombs: they first had to be loaded into the plane! They were filled with sand, each weighing a hundred pounds and had a small powder charge in the nose. Upon contact with the ground, the flash of the exploding charge would be visible and bright enough to be photographed. Ten bombs had been delivered to each plane and were lying on the ground. One cadet would pick up a bomb, hand it to the next man standing on the wing near the open door of the fuselage who would then hand it to the two cadets in the plane. Together, they would hang the bomb on the bomb racks. Taking into consideration that I weighed only one hundred forty pounds, I concluded that I need not look for any bodybuilding, weight lifting training program. I was getting all the exercise I could ever want or need just loading one hundred pound bombs. I sure envied the bigger, taller men who found it easier than I did. Much to my surprise, I realized in the months to come, that my smaller stature would prove to be an asset.

Once airborne, we could see that our bombing ranges had been laid out in a rough, circular pattern across the Mojave Desert. They were typical targets, of which we are all familiar, made up of circles painted on the ground.

The bull's eye, however, was a six-foot square affair which was known as the *shack,* and this was our aiming point as we attempted to synchronize on the target. Memory fails me regarding the distance between the painted circles, which might have been fifty or one hundred feet. There were about six targets in all, and we would make bombing runs on all of them from an altitude of eleven thousand feet. Our studies in the weather classroom taught us that the sun would quickly heat up the desert sand, which in turn, would create vertical air currents and turbulence. This was not just bumpy air such as we experience today when flying in a commercial jet. On some days, we were constantly tossed around as we circled the range. This became even worse when we dropped down to about a thousand feet to make low altitude runs. There the turbulence was greater because we were closer to the hot, desert sand. If we didn't get airsick then, we probably could rest assured that it would never be a problem.

Two methods were used when flying bombing missions, one being a manual mission and the other automatic. In the manual mode the pilot would concentrate on a simple instrument, called the "PDI" that was positioned directly before him and which had a needle pointing to zero. When the bombardier made a course correction, the needle would move to the left or right depending upon the direction he turned the knob. Seeing this, the pilot would turn the plane until he had the needle back to zero. At all times the pilot would be in control of the plane. In the automatic mode, however, the plane would be flying on autopilot. The bombsight, being coupled to the autopilot, now gave control to the bombardier who could make course corrections by simply turning the knob. In the automatic mode, the pilot was responsible only for maintaining proper altitude and airspeed. With a green bombardier, you can be certain that the manual mode was used because cranking in large, erratic course corrections, when on autopilot, would have the plane standing on a wingtip.

I soon learned, on my very first mission, that using the bombsight in the air was a far cry from tracking a mechanical bug across a hangar floor. Although the pilot was responsible for flying from one target to the next, it was up to the bombardier to locate it as quickly as possible and begin his run. My first attempt at bombing from eleven thousand feet was quite an adventure. I had picked up the target through the sight and began to make corrections. Coming closer, I could see both the course and rate crosshairs drifting off my aiming point, proof that I was not synchronized. Frantically, I began to make corrections with both hands, and of course, I over corrected. Now the crosshairs were drifting off in another direction with the need for more knob twisting. Much too soon, we reached the bomb release point so all I could do was to look down to see where it had hit. I believe I was given credit for knocking down a couple of cactus trees and maybe a wild rabbit on that first run. Fortunately, I was still in the county!

In a Hollywood movie, you would see the bombardier squeeze a button when he wanted to drop his bombs. This was fine if you wanted to dump them all at once, ("salvo") or one at a time whenever he felt the urge to get rid of one. In actual use, however, it was quite different. The bombsight was an electrical device. On half the circuit was the contact point the bombardier positioned (properly, he hoped) based upon information in the ballistic tables. Once programmed into the sight, it did not move. The other half of the electrical circuit, however, was controlled by the rate knob and it was moving constantly. Starting from a low, six o'clock position, it would travel upward until it reached the other contact point. When they came together, the circuit would be completed and the bomb would be released. Built into the sight was a short lever called the trigger, which allowed the bombardier to abort the release of the bombs if he was not satisfied with the bomb run. The technique we were taught was to leave the trigger in the off position until a few seconds before the contact points came together. Failure to engage the trigger would cancel the bomb drop. Obviously, many of us wondered why the bomb was still hanging on the rack in the bomb bay when it should have been falling toward the target. It was at that moment that the instructor would repeat the familiar expression that I first heard in pilot training: "You've got your head up your ass and it's locked!"

As always, mail call was the highlight of the day. Receiving mail from friends and family members was great, but what I looked for most eagerly were the letters from the Georgia Redhead. I would read them first, put them aside, read my other mail and then slowly and carefully re-read her letters. She was a very popular girl, and I knew she was corresponding with others in uniform. What she wrote to me, however, was more than "today was a pretty day and then it changed to rain," or "I had corn flakes for breakfast and tomorrow I'll probably just have toast." Quite simply, what she wrote was what I wanted to read about, *us*. Everyone needed a morale booster, and she certainly had become mine, but what I was feeling, when I read her letters, was far more than just a boost to morale. I could not help wonder where this relationship was going, but I was certain of one thing: I didn't want it to stop. Time would tell.

San Bernardino was a popular destination for many when there was enough time to make the trip. Usually those who went would end up in a bar, but I, being a nondrinker, would soon become bored and chose instead to remain on the base. With most everyone out of the barracks, it was a good time to get out the uke and play for a little while. I did not have a radio, so I had no idea of what was being played or what the hit song of the day might be. The jukeboxes were great, but the noise level in most of the places where they were located, drowned out the melody and the lyrics making it difficult to remember what I had heard. I enjoyed going to the movies whenever possible, which usually began a short time after evening mess. One thing I learned way back in 1941: if you wanted to get a decent seat, don't go in a group with a bunch of guys who insisted on having "just one more" before heading for the theater. I got burned twice that way. We got there late and had to settle for seats in the very first row. Perhaps some of them, after having one too many, didn't care where they sat, but I did.

The highlight of the week for me and a few close friends, would take place on Sunday morning, when we would forgo the mess hall and go to the commissary for a leisurely breakfast. Bacon and eggs was the popular choice and it would be served hot, which was a big improvement over what we usually received. For a little while, we did not have to contend with crowds or long lines, making it a nice change from the hassle of the every day routine. I recall this one particular Sunday, late in January, when Ray DeBlasis, Serge Davison, James DeLaney and I invited the two WACS, who worked in the photo lab, to join us for breakfast. One was Sue Lively, from Alton, Alabama, but I cannot recall the other girl's name.

After breakfast, the walk back to our squadron area took us past the empty swimming pool which had been drained for the winter. Everyone seemed to be in a silly mood, especially DeBlasis, who climbed up the ladder to the high diving board with a life preserver around his neck. At the top, he called out to the *drowning* Sue Lively,

"Don't worry, I'll save you!" We were acting silly, but we sure enjoyed these few moments when we could relax. We needed more of them.

Class 44-6 was now well into the month of February. We had been flying missions just about every day, with a great deal of improvement in the results, when the weather got too bad to fly. I wrote the following in a letter to Carl dated Sunday, February 27, 1944:

"My head feels as though I am still up at fourteen thousand feet, squinting through a bombsight at the targets on the ground. This is Sunday, but I've put in a full, tough day of flying. During the past week, "Liquid California Sunshine" has kept the entire class grounded and as a result, everyone is behind schedule. In an attempt to make up for lost time, we have been scheduled to fly on Sundays, which means we lose our open post on Saturday night. Too many of the guys would get drunk on Saturday night, making them unfit to fly the next day, so we all have to remain on the post.

> *I was under a great deal of pressure today because I was dropping both practice and record bombs. All told, we drop only about thirty record bombs, but they are the bombs that count. Our average circular error is computed on the basis of those few drops. Today, I had ten of them and I had a lump in my throat with each release. I did well, ending up with an average circular error of one hundred twenty feet. The maximum permissible circular error that a cadet can have and still graduate is two hundred and thirty feet and he probably would be given a check ride as he approached that figure."*

The method used to measure these record bombs was to photograph them with a hand held, thirty-five mm movie camera. There was a rather large hatch on the floor and to the rear of the plane. A second cadet was aboard as the photographer, and it was his job to remove the hatch cover and lie down on his stomach with his head extended over the hole. Ballistic tables informed us of the time it would take for the bomb to reach the ground, so he would begin to count off the seconds and start filming before the bomb hit the ground and for a few seconds afterward. The flash of the small powder charge in the nose of the bomb would indicate where it hit relative to the target circles. The accuracy of the drop could then be measured and recorded.

This sort of scary maneuver of lying on your stomach over an open hatch became even worse when we tried low altitude bombing. For the student bombardier, the target would seem to be upon you before there was time to synchronize. For the photographer, he had all he could do to keep from getting airsick. The sun, heating the desert sand, created a lot of turbulence which tossed the plane all over the sky. Being far back in the fuselage, every up or and down movement was more pronounced. It was difficult to hold the camera to your eye and remember to start the count. Of course, it was also important not fall out of the plane! Surely, we were all happy when we were finished with the low altitude stuff.

* * * * *

Being so busy, it was easy to forget how much time had passed since we first arrived at Victorville. I realized this when I checked the bulletin board and saw that all of us had been given a scheduled time to report to the base tailor for the purpose of being measured for our officer's uniform. This did not mean we had it made. What it did mean was that the tailors needed that much time to take measurements and check the uniform for proper fit. On my way to the tailor shop, I had a rather sad recollection: I had done this before at Moody Field, and for a moment, knew once again how excited I felt when I put the forest green blouse on for the first time. My next thought was "I wonder what had become of *my* uniform?"

A new month, March, brought a new experience: we would begin three weeks of night training missions. Up until now, every thing we had done had been done in daylight, giving us reason to wonder if it would be more difficult to use the sight in the dark. Although the dials of the instruments would glow under the light we used, a good sense of feel would be needed to manipulate the knobs and switches that were involved in the bomb run. In addition, being on the night shift would necessitate a complete change in our life style which meant going to bed just a few hours before our usual 5:00 AM reveille. Of course, we were allowed to sleep to a later hour, but those first few night sessions turned our *body clock* upside down.

Much to my surprise, I had no problems in making those night bomb runs. I remembered how much at home I had felt, back in pilot training at Bainbridge, when flying those night solo missions to auxiliary fields. Picking up the target was not difficult because the *shack* was illuminated, but it was harder to synchronize because it took me longer to see that the crosshairs were drifting off the target.

I have a fond memory of an incident which took place on one of the first night missions. Things were going rather smoothly, so the pilot switched the radio to a regular broadcast station which was playing popular music. A few minutes later, I heard a song being played on an alto sax. I had never heard it before and I hated the announcer for not identifying it when it was over. Not knowing the name, I decided to call it "Night Hawk" since I was flying at night. I was able to remember the melody, but there were no lyrics since it was an instrumental. One of the first things I did, when I got back to the barracks, was to get out the uke and pick out the melody and a few chords which, I hoped, I would remember. It wasn't until about a year later when I heard it again, and this time the DJ did his job. The song was "Poinciana" and the artist was Benny Carter, one of the best in the business. I must have about ten versions of that song in my record collection (including Benny's), Percy Faith, James Last and singer Catherina Valente are great, but the version I like the best was done by Glenn Miller and the band he led when in the service. Johnny Desmond does the vocal, but at the end, the band takes over and finishes up with that wonderful Miller sound. I am sure that most of us will identify with a person, place or event when they hear a particular song. Every time I hear "Poinciana," I find myself transported back to that night bombing mission over the Mojave Desert in March of 1944.

Another great memory of those night bombing sessions has nothing to do with music, but with an individual: Walter John Chilsen, he of the famous "Don't you think Silveo has an odd name" remark.

At this point in our training, we had become skilled enough to fly our missions without the need of our instructor. It was not unusual, however, to have another cadet go along as a *student instructor* with a fellow classmate who was getting too close to a check ride. On this particular night, I was Chilsen's instructor. My job, I was told, was to carefully monitor his procedure and advise him of any mistakes I thought he was making. I do not remember how many bombs he had to drop, but they were all for the record and it was important for him to do well. He seemed calm and relaxed, but I was in a deep sweat worrying about him. We finally reached the target area and he began his first bomb run. I was watching him like a hawk, hoping he would have a good release, but for some unexplainable reason, I couldn't help think that it was I who was on the hot seat instead of him. What he did next left me with my mouth agape. At the crucial point of his bomb run, when he should have been completely absorbed in synchronizing on the target, when his commission and wings were in jeopardy, is the moment he chose to raise his head up from the sight, look at me, give me a silly little grin, a little finger wave and then utter,

"Hi Silveo!" For a long few seconds, I gave serious thought to inflict bodily pain upon Cadet Chilsen. Under the circumstances, I felt that no jury would ever convict Cadet Colletti of the charge that my actions constituted cruel and unusual punishment. Simultaneously, a second thought emerged; my commanding officer would probably frown upon such behavior, and it would be I, who would find himself up the proverbial creek without the paddle. Then, in a quick moment, I began to laugh. How could you be angry with a guy who can make you laugh when you have knots in your stomach? Someone up there must have been watching over him that night, for he did well, much to my relief.

Our little "Prussian General" cadet officer was still in charge of our platoon when this incident took place. Looking back, I guess we didn't like him because he was always playing up to the commissioned officers, putting his *leadership qualities* on display, but I think his image became somewhat tarnished on this particular day. We were marching, four abreast, down an alleyway which led to the side entrance of the mess hall. At that moment, a delivery truck turned into the alleyway from the far end and was slowly approaching us. It was obvious that there was insufficient space for the platoon to get by, so thinking quickly the *General* sized up the situation and felt that we could get by if we squeezed together. To accomplish this he gave the order, "Incline to the right." Unfortunately, there was no such order in the drill book. Certainly, we knew what he was trying to do, but we, smart-asses that we were, were not going to make it easy for him. I believe it was Ray DeBlasis, he being first in line, who decided to obey the order to the letter. He dropped his right shoulder about forty-five degrees, and then moved closer to the man on his right. Seeing this, everyone in the platoon followed suit, so now you have about forty men, *who were supposed to be marching at attention* shuffling along with their right shoulders in this grotesque position. We squeezed by the truck just in time for our tactical officer, Lt. John Longley, standing on the mess hall step, to witness something I am sure he had never seen before. The General was livid with rage (not that I blame him.) He had lost face and there was nothing he could do about it, since we were doing what good soldiers do, *follow orders*. It would have been very interesting to learn what Lt. Longley might have said to our sterling cadet officer in the private meeting that took place.

* * * * *

Helendale, California was a small city about fifteen miles north of Victorville, and that was where we would be for a week. The object of the move was to expose us to the problems of working under field conditions, as would be the case in some combat zones. At the briefing, we learned that we would be living in tents; there were no permanent buildings; all our activities would be outdoors and to pack only the bare necessities, but be sure to bring our summer shorts, canteen belt and canteens.

The "Ritz Carleton" in the Mojave Desert.
Chimney of the central heating system is the pipe sticking out of the top of the tent.
We were led to believe we would have room service, but they lied.

It was already hot when the truck convoy pulled up the following morning and I was happy to get a seat toward the open, cooler end. Fortunately, it was a short trip. Sure enough, the camp area lived up to the Spartan description that had been given us. The tents looked seedy and beat up with little attention paid to precision in the way they were laid out. There were a number of large tables, which would have multiple uses, set out under the

broiling sun. Welcome to the fringe of the Mojave Desert! A non-cadet sergeant was in charge and led us to the tent area, and told us to pick any tent or tent mates. Four of us chose one, and upon entering, began to laugh at the sight of a potbelly stove. We asked each other and the sergeant,

"Why do we need a stove?" He only grinned as he turned to leave, but he did advise us to select a fireman before we went to bed. Man, this guy is really trying to pull our leg, was our reaction. How stupid does he think we are?

We were dressed in our regular long sleeve khaki shirts and within minutes, they came off. Next went the undershirt, soon to be followed by the pants and then the donning of shorts. We probably would have also taken them off if allowed. Now we knew why we were told to bring our web belts and canteens. Water was being consumed at a great rate, and it was a lot easier to fill up a canteen and hook it onto the web belt than to hike back to the water tank every time we needed a drink. Soon, I would have first hand experience with something I had learned about way back at Camp Lee in 1941: my old friend the slit trench. Oh well, who needed toilets? It was hot. Lunch mess was eaten under the broiling sun. There were no trees or shade and the heat in the tents was stifling. The remainder of the day was spent on the so-called *flight line* where we loaded hundred pound bombs for tomorrow's missions, being thankful when that job was finally done.

Once again, someone rose to the occasion with a comment that gave us a good laugh. This time is was Bob Coakley, clad in shorts, web belt and canteen who posed the question," Has anybody seen 'The Desert Fox', General Rommel?" As hot as we were, we could have easily thought that we were in the Sahara Desert fighting Rommel instead of in the Mojave Desert!

Mohave Desert March 26, 1944. Learning how to operate "in the field." Couldn't cool off during the day and froze at night. Loading 100 pound, sand-filled bombs under the scorching sun worked miracles for the waistline.

Finally, we breathed a sigh of relief as the sun slowly began to set and soon afterward, a few men decided that a shirt would now be comfortable, put their shirts on and buttoned them to the very top. It didn't take long to realize that it was time for the shorts to go, so they were exchanged for pants.

After evening mess, we headed back to our tents which were now quite comfortable. Of course, we, wise guys that we were, had not selected a fireman and lived to regret our mistake. We awoke the next morning with our asses freezing! No one would volunteer to start a fire in the stove, so cold or not, it was time to get up. We put on all the clothing we had knowing full well that before long we would begin the disrobing process once again. We had learned a lesson: the desert gets very cold at night!

Our bombing missions were being flown over the same target areas, but now we were doing more low altitude bombing. The weather had become hotter, resulting in more turbulence, which made it more difficult to make bomb runs and to photograph the hits.

The week in Helendale, though physically demanding, was good training. It certainly made us realize that many of us could find ourselves living under very difficult conditions in the not too distant future and it would not be for just a week.

There was much rejoicing when we returned to Victorville where we would be sheltered in a barracks with showers, sinks and toilets. One week of eating out of mess kits under a broiling sun, sleeping in tents and using a slit trench had proved to be quite enough.

This is "Sergeant York Colletti" of Class 44-6. I must have hit some of the targets because I am rated as "marksman" on my service record. Obviously, a mistake had been made.

Back: Andy Courvosier, Bob Coakley, Colletti; Front: Mel Cohen, Paul Clifford, Everett Cobb, March 26, 1944. This was the day when Bob Coakley asked "Has anyone seen The Desert Fox, General Rommel?" We replied "To the best of our knowledge, he was still in Africa using camels to tow his broken down tanks."

Chapter 11

Saturday Night
"The Victorville Way"
April 8, 1944

Zom:

I whish (sort of a new way to spell "wish", isn't it?) that I could give you some definite information regarding my graduations, possibility of a furlough and all that, but damn it every day it becomes only more confused. For the past thirteen weeks, the graduating classes have been getting their bars right on shcedule, were given leaves and egeryone was happy, that is, up until two weeks ago. Class 44-5 was <u>supposed</u> to graduate today, but a letter from Gen. Arnold, requesting 75 bombardiers immediately, made them change their plans, graduated the class two weeks early, and no one got a leave. There is a strong possibility that the same thing will happen to me and my bunch, so what can I tell you Zom? Graduation day, to the best of my knowledge, is still April 29, but who knows where I'll be at that time. Everything is so messed up. Even if I got a leave, I would go nuts trying to see everyone who I wanted to, and that includes little Verna down

Apr 8, 1944

in Georgia. I've got to see her, but how? I've been trying to figure that little problem out for a hell of a long time. I want to see her, and yet I know that if there is anyplace that I have to go, it's home, and I do want to go home too. Boy, sometimes I wish that I was twins!

I've got three weeks to go, and the worst is over, but I'm too damn scared, afraid, superstituous and half jinxed to try to say anything more about it. I'm really sweating this one out, in no uncertqin manner, so I'm not going to say another word about it.

So much for now U-Boat, I've got a few more letters to answer. I brought them along to the U.S.O. where I could use this typewriter and bat them out in half the time/

 Keep me posted/

  Look out for the barrels in the road-
   Your old pal,

Chapter 11

Class 44-6 was scheduled to graduate April 29, 1944, if everything went according to plan. Class 44-5 was supposed to have graduated April 8th, but General Arnold had requested seventy bombardiers immediately so they left two weeks early. It possibly could happen to us.

Try as I might I could not stop thinking about being eliminated from pilot training, with only a month to go before graduating, for that disappointment was still very fresh in my mind. I was becoming apprehensive and a little jittery, afraid that some last minute, stupid mistake would wash me out. I decided the best thing to do was just try harder these last few weeks, and hope for the best. This was my frame of mind, as April was ushered in, bringing with it the following, unforgettable event:

The class was returning to the barracks and as we drew closer, I could see Lt. Longley waiting near the front entrance. I was near the end of the line and I heard him calling my name as he walked toward me. Together we turned toward the entrance and I followed closely behind. He began to speak and his first words were,

"You are excused from all classes for the remainder of the day." I never heard what he said after that. In my mind, what I kept hearing over and over, were these very same words that I had heard when I was eliminated from pilot training: *You are excused from all classes for the remainder of the day*. I couldn't utter a sound, but in my head, I was screaming to myself, "This can't be happening again! Something is not right. What had gone wrong?" It was a gut-wrenching moment, with many questions and no answers. Lt. Longley opened the door and I followed in a dazed condition. My bed was the second one on the left and it was then that I noticed that there was a camera crew with lights, reflectors and cameras pointed at my bed. He went on to explain that after checking the entire class of 44-6, they had selected my bed, footlocker and clothes arrangement to be the model for the new cadet manual, soon to be published. The photographers would be there for some time and I would not be able to get my books or clothes until they had finished. The entire episode probably did not last more than half a minute, but in that short space of time I had taken a wild ride on that all too familiar emotional roller coaster. An hour later, I still felt the after effects of that sickening moment. When the new manual was published, I was given the printed page with the picture of my bed area.

Shortly thereafter, we received our class book which had pictures of all the cadets in 44-6. I couldn't help but smile when I read the caption under my picture: "If he could only cook. Always on the ball. Always received compliments at inspections while the rest of us received gigs." It sure made my day.

"Bombs Away"[15] Class 44-6, April 1944

For the Duration plus Six Months

NO. 17 CADET REGULATION

ROOM AND BARRACKS DISPLAY

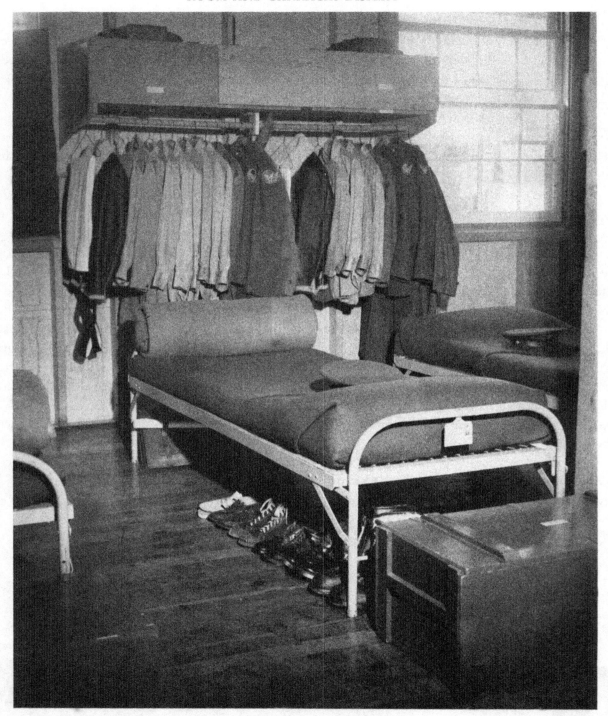

Check this picture with part II of this Regulation. In barracks of the open bay type, your area should look like this. Note particularly the arrangement of clothing.

Page from the new Cadet Manual[16] with the picture of my bed area. April 1944

The photographer was finished about the time everyone returned to the barracks after the last class of the day. John Cole had the first bed on the left, as you entered through the front door, and I had the second. A small group had converged around me, making comments about my newfound notoriety; "May I have your autograph," etc. It was John Cole, from Jackson, Tennessee, however, who took center stage. In his classic southern drawl he remarked,

"Gaw-damn, I just don't stand a chance. When the inspecting officer comes in the front door, he sees my bed first. Everything seems to be to his satisfaction, so he moves on to Colletti's bed area. After seeing his, he comes back to me, turns to the sergeant walking behind and tells him to gig me for some dammed thing he was completely satisfied with in the first place. I end up walking tours while you guys are on open post."

I could think of nothing to say except, "Jack, give me your T.S. Card and I'll punch it," but that would have been cruel, so I kept my mouth shut.

John Cole was a very handsome man. He was six feet tall, weighed about one hundred eighty-five pounds and had a great physique. Socially speaking, he was the kind of man who didn't have any problems making time with

Jack Cole (writing)

most any girl. Against this backdrop, the following remark he made seemed to be completely in character:

"When this damn war is over and I get back to Jackson, Tennessee, I'm going to hang out my shingle which will say, *Jack Cole, At Stud*," and he meant it! Much to my regret, months later I received a letter informing me that he had been killed on his first mission over Europe.

* * * * *

Graduation day, April 29th was but three weeks away, but there was one last hurdle that had to be crossed, and that was the final exam. The ground school instructor informed us that regardless of how well we had done in our bombing, no one would graduate if they failed the final exam. From memory, we had to make a decent, reasonable, free hand drawing of the rate end of the bombsight. It did not need to be a work of art, but it had to be accurate, all parts had to be identified and labeled with a description of their function.

Perhaps it was my three years of experience with watch repair which led me to appreciate the beauty and precision which was evident in a watch movement. For the same reason, I was intrigued by the Norden bombsight, for it also required great precision in manufacture and I marveled at how the inventor managed to solve the bombing problem. Most, if not all of my classmates, were satisfied to commit to memory only what they needed to know, but my curiosity led me to learn more than the course required. The exam held no problem for me, for the six years of mechanical drawing classes I had taken in junior and senior high school was very helpful. Little did I realize how important that extra little bit of knowledge would prove to be in the not too distant future.

After the exam, I went over to Bob Coakley and asked him, "Do you think we'll make it?" Sure enough, his answer was beautifully ambiguous,

"Maybe, maybe not."

He asked me the same question and I replied, "Check with me on April 30th."

* * * * *

"*Saturday, April 22, 1944*

Dear Carl,

The big day is only 7 days away and still it seems like a year. I have been flying simulated bombing missions over Los Angeles and the surrounding countryside and have "bombed" just about everything of value. So far, I've hit the railroad station, Grand Central Airport in Glendale, the water works main dam and the Rose Bowl in Pasadena. It was a lot of fun, having to do the navigating out, finding the pinpoint target and making a run on it. This time, I took pictures of the crosshairs in the sight, superimposed on the target. I did quite well, nothing spectacular, but at least I didn't get lost as a few of the guys did. Regarding leave, there are lots of rumors floating around, but nothing for certain. We will have to wait until next Saturday, for our special orders, before we know if we will be given leave time.

There is something else to sweat out. Monday morning, we will be told whether we graduate as second lieutenants or flight officers. I don't know how much you know about either, but although they both get the same pay, a flight officer becomes a 2nd Lt. upon promotion, whereas a 2nd Lt. becomes a 1st. Lt. About twenty in the class will be given the flight officer rank, but no one seems to know how they make the decision. All this uncertainty sure is making many of us very nervous.

We got our officer's uniforms Thursday night and you should have seen what went on in the barracks. Nine o'clock lights out was cancelled, and most of us were up until midnight trying on everything. First, we would put on a pink shirt with green pants, to see if we liked the way that looked. Quickly we'd switch to a combination of green shirt and pink pants which was soon followed by all pinks and then all green. We saved the best for the last, when we put on the blouse with our new "crushed look" hat. It was a riot. We carried on like a bunch of little girls playing "dress-up" with their mother's clothes!

Friday the 28th is the date of our graduation dance and reveille will be at 4:00 AM in order to be ready for graduation ceremonies at ten in the morning. I don't see any of us getting much sleep that night!

I'm keeping my fingers crossed, hoping all goes well. It sure would be nice to get to see everyone once again.

Your pal,
Sil

P.S. I received a great, 8 x 10 picture from Red today. She is wearing a black, low cut gown and an upsweep hair do."

Chapter 11

"Red" 1943

With the *dress-up orgy* successfully completed, most of us had finally decided which combination of pants/shirt we liked the best. For me, it was a rather easy decision. I had never forgotten how I felt that day, in the x-ray office at Langley Field, when I saw those silver wings on the colonel who was dressed in pinks with a green tie. I also remembered thinking "That's for me" and how I would have loved to wear that uniform and the wings. Then my head came down out of the clouds with the realization that it was an unattainable dream. That was a year and a half ago. What a difference a year and a half has made!

Class 44-6 had finished. There were no more classes to attend, we knew that we would graduate, but that did not translate into leisure time. We still had to fall out for physical training and whatever else the commanding officer could think of to keep us busy. Solution: let them go out to the parade ground and do close order drill for a few hours, with the men taking turns as the drill instructor. Out we went to the parade ground with one of us counting the very familiar, *hup, two, three, four*. About fifteen minutes later, someone else took over and we cranked it up again. DeBlasis was the drill instructor when we all started to gripe about how boring it was, but the forward march command had been given and off we went. Forward march, column left, column right, to the rear march, hup two three four, but now, there seemed to be a change in the count. It sounded more like "one, two, three FOUR, one, two, three, FOUR." Aha! That was the conga beat! One, two, three KICK, one, two, three KICK! Someone picked it up and quickly the others took their cue from him, making sure to execute *the kick*. Forty men were supposed to be marching at attention, but for a few, hysterical minutes we were letting off steam and it felt wonderful! Later, back in the barracks, we grouped together and began to speculate as to what the consequences would have been if the commanding officer had seen forty lunatics doing the conga on the drill field. Personally, I didn't want to know.

It was the 27th of April when the long awaited, final rating for class 44-6 was posted on the bulletin board. Just about everyone in the barracks was planted there, in front of me, each wanting to find his name to see what his final academic average was. There were some mutterings and some sounds of glee as I elbowed my way to the bulletin board. Philip R. Currin, of Los Angeles, was top man with a 93.4 average. In second place was Everett E. Cobb of Portland Oregon, with a 92.8 average. In third place, with an average of 92.1 was Silveo G. Colletti, of Linden, New Jersey. I stared at the board and had to read it three or four times before it sank in. Even I was amazed! As I turned and walked away, I couldn't help but think of how satisfying it was to be ranked that high. It was an exciting moment; a feeling that I had done better than I thought I could. From the very beginning, I knew that most of the class had had more formal education than I, but that made the accomplishment all the sweeter.

Coincidentally, we three were in the same barracks, had the same last initial, and our pictures are on the same line in the Class Book. A few days ago, I felt pleased when my bed area had been chosen as the model for the Cadet Manual. Finishing third, academically, really put the icing on the cake. Now I couldn't wait to talk to Coakley and tell him that there was a slim, outside chance that we might make it knowing that graduation day was tomorrow, April 29, 1944 at 10:00 AM.

April 28, 1944 would prove to be a hectic, unusual, exciting, very busy, eventful, happy and, in a way, sad day. We had made some very good friends, but now it was time to say goodbye and wish each other luck. Much needed to be done. We had to pack all our belongings, except for toilet articles and our new uniforms which we would wear for the first time tomorrow. Then it was back to the orderly room to get our orders. A big cheer went up when we read that we would be getting seven days leave, *plus travel time*. Part two instructed me to report to the air base, at Fresno, California at the end of my leave. I groaned when I thought about making two trips across the country, but regardless of the wear and tear, I knew it would be worth it. A second cheer went up when learned that the Red Cross had secured reservations for the large group who would be making the long trip to the east coast. Busses would be waiting in the squadron area to take us to our waiting train in Victorville, and we were free to leave the base immediately after the graduation ceremonies.

Suddenly, it became necessary to notify friends and family, resulting in a mad dash by all to send telegrams to those we could not phone. Confusion reigned supreme.

After evening mess, the entire class reported to the orderly room. We were completely surprised to learn that the paper we were signing was a formal discharge from the Army. Upon signing it, we became *civilians* and would remain so until the next morning when we would take the oath of office as officers. A second paper informed us that we (not all) were hereby appointed to the rank of second lieutenant in the Air Corps. In addition, it stated that we were "Officers and Gentlemen," and that my new serial number was 0776632.

Upon returning to the barracks, we began to compare orders to see where each of us had been instructed to report. Except for the few minutes after graduation, it would be our last chance to say goodbye. Home addresses were exchanged, so that we could contact each other's family and through them, learn where they were stationed.

Though tired, I doubt that many of us slept well that night. I know I couldn't relax for thinking about tomorrow and how much I was looking forward to the swearing in ceremony, when it all would become official. Until then, there was nothing more to do except wait. Another thought came to mind: I had been waiting for this moment for almost seventeen long months, going back to classification center in Nashville, Tennessee. It occurred to me that I had come to passionately hate that four-letter word: *wait*. I began to think how wonderful it would have been if P38, the Georgia Redhead, could have been here to pin on my bars and wings. I knew I would envy those who would have their girlfriends there to perform that all-important ritual, but she was almost three thousand miles away. Maybe, someday, it would be different, but for now, I would just have to wait. Once again, that much despised word had to be used. It was then that I groaned when I remembered that reveille would be at 4:00 AM.

When the lights were snapped on at 4:00 AM, I realized how different this morning would be. There was no need to do things at the frantic pace we had known for the past eighteen weeks. No need to push and shove in order to be able to look in the mirror while shaving. No need to make up the bed or have everything ready for the daily inspection. To the contrary, the mattress had to be rolled up and put at the foot of the bed. There was litter on the floor, but it didn't matter, for this was graduation day.

* * * * *

We had calmed down a little from yesterday's emotional high, but there was no denying that we were excited as we went to breakfast for the last time. We didn't stay there any longer than necessary, being anxious to get back to the barracks to dress for our next formation.

Looking around, I could see Chilsen, Camesas, Coakley, DeBlasis, Cole and all the others slowly putting on their new uniforms. It was a *dream come true* feeling for me, as I began to dress. I put my shirt on first. When I put my pants on, I became aware of how soft and different the cloth felt, compared to what I was accustomed to wearing. Next came the tie, socks and dress shoes. Fully dressed, we began to check each other out.

"Straighten your tie a bit; you missed a button," etc. were the typical comments, as we stood around admiring how gorgeous we all looked. About 9:30 AM, I put on that beautiful, forest green blouse, and shortly afterward, the order came to fall out. As we marched to the parade ground, Coakley asked me,

"Do you think we'll make it?"

I replied, "What do you think?" I began to laugh when I remembered the *conga line incident* of a few days ago, on this very field. A grandstand had been set up for those who had come to witness the graduation. We marched to a point directly in front of the stand and were put at ease while the commanding officer made a very short, congratulatory speech.

At 10:00 AM, we snapped to attention and were told to raise our right hand and repeat the oath of office. I put my hand up, and before I could repeat the first word, Coakley sneaked in one last "Do you think we'll make it?"

I couldn't reply, because I was too busy saying, "I do solemnly swear that I, Silveo G. Colletti, etc." Quickly, before the last word was uttered, I replied to Coakley, "I'm not a hundred percent sure, but I think so."

A loud cheer went up a moment later when the oath was completed and the commanding officer dismissed the class for the last time. With that, friends, family, girlfriends and wives charged onto the field, eager to perform the ritual of pinning on wings and gold bars which, by an act of Congress, made us Officers and Gentlemen. I envied them as they shared that wonderful moment with the most important people in their lives, wishing that Red could have been there, for that would have really made it perfect. Friend Sue Lively did the honors for me, and using my camera, recorded the moment for posterity.

When the final goodbyes were said, those of us who were going to the east coast made a dash for the barracks, picked up our bags and headed for the parked busses. They departed carrying a bunch of hyped up, glowing, exuberant, noisy puffed up flyboys who savored, to the fullest, that once in a lifetime moment. I couldn't help but think how beautiful the train looked, just sitting there waiting for us. That the three thousand mile trip would be made in coaches was unimportant. Considering our frame of mind, we were all on our own personal magic carpet which would be taking us home.

Sue Lively pinning bars and wings on 2nd Lt. Silveo G. Colletti. At last I had achieved three of four goals: The commission, the uniform and the wings. Number four, the Georgia Redhead, was next on the list, but "another matter" had first priority.

Chapter 11

Graduation ceremony April 29, 1944

Second Lieutenant Silveo G. Colletti

Chapter 11

Army Air Forces Bombardier School
VICTORVILLE ARMY AIR FIELD

Upon the recommendation of the Commandant of Aviation Cadets I hereby appoint

Aviation Cadet _Silveo G. Colletti_, a _Sergeant_ in the Aviation Cadet Wing, Victorville, California, to rank as such from the _Third_ day of _April_, 19_44_. He is therefore carefully and diligently to discharge his duties as _Supply Sergeant_, and all cadets coming under his command are strictly charged and required to be obedient to his orders as such. And he is to observe and follow such orders and directions as he shall receive from his military superiors, according to the rules and discipline of War.

Given under my hand at Victorville, California, this _3rd_ day of _April_ in the year of Our Lord one thousand nine hundred and _Forty-Four_.

Harold M. Skaggs
Major Air Corps,
Commandant of Aviation Cadets

Earl C. Robbins
Colonel, Air Corps,
Commanding Officer
Army Air Forces Bombardier School
Victorville Army Air Field

2nd Lt. Robert Coakley (left) and 2nd Lt. Silveo G. Colletti

103

For the Duration plus Six Months

ENLISTED RECORD OF

COLLETTI, SILVEO G., 32 185 829, Avn Cadet
(Last name) (First name) (Middle initial) (Army serial number) (Grade)

Born in New York City, in the State of New York
Enlisted or inducted 20 October, 19 41, at Fort Dix, New Jersey
When enlisted or inducted he was Twenty-two years of age and by occupation a Jewelry Salesman

He had Brown eyes, Brown hair, Ruddy complexion, and was Five feet Six inches in height.
Completed Two months, Eight days service for longevity pay.
Prior service: None

FINANCE OFFICE
VAAF, VICTORVILLE, CALIFORNIA
28 APR 1944

FOR CONVENIENCE, A CERTIFICATE OF ELIGIBILITY NO. _____ HAS BEEN ISSUED BY THE VETERANS ADMINISTRATION TO BE USED FOR THE FUTURE REQUEST OF ANY GUARANTY OR INSURANCE BENEFIT UNDER TITLE III OF THE SERVICEMEN'S READJUSTMENT ACT OF 1944, AS AMENDED, THAT MAY BE AVAILABLE TO THE PERSON TO WHOM THIS SEPARATION PAPER WAS ISSUED.

Final Statement paid in full $ 53.16

BENSON ALLEN, 1st LT., FD
Finance Officer

Noncommissioned officer _____ Virginia
Military qualifications: Marksman .45 Cal Pistol score 72.1% 1 April 44
Army specialty Bombardier
Attendance at Grad. Aerial Gunnery, AAFFGS, Tyndall Field, Florida, 21 Dec 43.
(Name of noncommissioned officers' or special service school)

Battles, engagements, skirmishes, expeditions None

Decorations, service medals, citations Awarded American Defense Ribbon, 11 Apr 44; Good Conduct, 4/11/44
Wounds received in service None
Date and result of smallpox vaccination 10/28/42 Vaccinia
Date of completion of all typhoid-paratyphoid vaccinations 11/11/42, 2/2/44 (B)
Date and result of diphtheria immunity test (Schick) None
Date of other vaccinations (specify vaccine used) Tet 1/23/42, 2/2/44 (B). Yel Fvr 1/13/42. Cocc 2/14/44 Neg
Physical condition when discharged Good Married or single Single
Honorably discharged by reason of Cony of Govt, Sec X AR 615-360 to accept commission AUS
Character Excellent Periods of active duty None
Remarks: No time lost under AW 107. Not entitled to travel pay. Qualified mentally and physically for reenlistment.

Print of Right Thumb

Signature of soldier *Silveo G. Colletti*

Harold M. Skaggs
HAROLD M. SKAGGS, JR., Major, Air Corps
Commandant of Students

INSTRUCTIONS FOR ENLISTED RECORD

1 Enter date of induction only in case of trainee inducted under Selective Training and Service Act of 1940 (Bull. 25, W. D., 1940) all other cases enter date of enlistment. Eliminate word not applicable.
2 For each enlistment give company, regiment, or arm or service with inclusive dates of service, grade, cause of discharge, number of days lost under AW 107 (if none, so state), and number of days retained and cause of retention in service for convenience of the Government, if any.
3 Enter qualifications in arms, horsemanship, etc. Show the qualification, date thereof; and number, date, and source of order announcing same.
4 See paragraph 12, AR 40-210.
5 If discharged prior to expiration of service, give number, date, and source of order or full description of authority therefor.
6 Enter periods of active duty of enlisted men of the Regular Army Reserve and the Enlisted Reserve Corps and dates of induction into Federal Service in the cases of members of the National Guard.
7 In all cases of men who are entitled to receive Certificates of Service under AR 345-500, enter here appointments and ratings held and all other items of special proficiency or merit other than those shown above.

INSTRUCTIONS FOR CERTIFICATE OF DISCHARGE
AR 345-470.
Insert name; as, "John J. Doe," in center of form.
Insert Army serial number, grade, company, regiment, or arm or service; as "1620302"; "Corporal, Company A, 1st Infantry"; "Sergeant, Quartermaster Corps."
The name and grade of the officer signing the certificate will be typewritten or printed below the signature.

U. S. GOVERNMENT PRINTING OFFICE : 1943 O - 530071

Honorable Discharge

This is to certify that

SILVEO G. COLLETTI, 32 185 829

Army of the United States

is hereby Honorably Discharged from the military service of the United States of America.

This certificate is awarded as a testimonial of Honest and Faithful Service to his country.

Given at VICTORVILLE ARMY AIR FIELD, VICTORVILLE, CALIFORNIA

Date 28 APRIL 1944

EARL C. ROBBINS, Colonel, Air Corps
Commanding

W. D., A. G. O. Form No. 55
January 22, 1943

For the Duration plus Six Months

HEADQUARTERS
ARMY AIR FORCES WESTERN FLYING TRAINING COMMAND
1104 WEST EIGHTH STREET, SANTA ANA, CALIFORNIA

AGA 30E-CK

29 APR 1944

201
COLLETTI Silveo G
44-6 Bomb (3-27-44)

SUBJECT: Temporary Appointment.

TO : Second Lieutenant SILVEO GAETANO COLLETTI
Army of the United States
(Linden, New Jersey)
VAAF, Victorville, California

A 0-776632

1. The Secretary of War has directed me to inform you that the President has appointed and commissioned you a temporary Second Lieutenant, Army of the United States, effective this date. Your serial number is shown after A above.

2. This commission will continue in force during the pleasure of the President of the United States for the time being, and for the duration of the war and six months thereafter unless sooner terminated.

3. There is inclosed herewith a form for oath of office which you are requested to execute and return. The execution and return of the required oath of office constitute an acceptance of your appointment. No other evidence of acceptance is required.

4. This letter should be retained by you as evidence of your appointment as no commission will be issued during the war.

By command of Major General COUSINS:

CHARLES S. RICKER,
Captain, Air Corps,
Actg. Asst. Adjutant General

1 Inclosure:
Form for oath of office.

Appointment accepted, Oath administered 29 April 1944

Ordered to active duty:

At VAAF, Victorville, California

On 29 April 1944

3370—Santa Ana—2-11-44—6,000 sets of 6

12

CROSS-COUNTRY TO NEW JERSEY AND BACK

A loud cheer went up when the train finally left the station for the three (or was it four?) day ride across the country. Everyone was still flying on cloud nine, walking through the cars we occupied and just having a great time, but then we began to settle down. It had been a long day, with very little sleep the night before, and it was beginning to take its toll. Now the most important thing was to find a comfortable position and try to get some rest. Riding in coaches isn't bad on a short trip, but unfortunately, it doesn't provide much comfort on a long haul. For a while, sleeping sitting up for a few hours was possible, but you couldn't stretch out. (I had quick flashbacks of the trips in 1942; going back to Washington DC from Newark when I had learned how to fall asleep standing up.) There were no vacant seats in our cars, so lying down on the seat was only possible if your seatmate took a walk. Then someone got a bright idea. He noticed that the seat backs could be removed and could be put on the floor, making it possible to lie down and stretch our legs. The conductor had no need to come through our cars, since we had been checked through to Chicago. In short order, everyone managed to *get horizontal* one way or another. Regardless, I marveled at how much physical abuse we were able to absorb and quickly bounce back. It sure was great to be young.

Sitting in that train, I was finally able to just look out the window and think about Miss P38. She, more than anyone, was the person I wanted to have been present at the graduation ceremony, but sad to say, that wasn't possible. I couldn't help but smile as I remembered why I nicknamed her *P38*. It was an easy choice, because at that time, the P38 was the best, most beautiful plane in the sky. It was #1 and I had known for quite some time that she was *my number one*.

P38

There was one nagging problem that I grappled with as the hours passed. I was racking my brain trying to figure out how I could go home, stay for a while and then go to see her in Georgia. We had said goodbye back on November 2, 1943, but it seemed much longer. I had seven days at home. It would take at least twenty-four hours to get to Georgia by train, if all went well. Once there, I would be able to see her for only a few odd hours because she would be in class. She wasn't allowed to leave the campus, which meant I would be sitting for hours, wasting time, until she was free. At best, I could stay for only a day or so and then I would have to return to New Jersey. Train schedules were not dependable, and I dared not risk cutting it too close and missing my train back to California. Common sense dictated that it just wasn't possible. There was nothing to do but *wait* until we had the opportunity to be together. More than ever, I detested that word.

Coming into Chicago, I vaguely remembered that I would have to change stations to complete the trip to Newark. I had done enough commuting going to New York, to know that to be a minute late could cost you a few hours when trying to make a connection. With that in mind, I got together with three others, explained the situation, and we decided to hit the ground running when the train pulled into Chicago. We hailed a cab, told him where we wanted to go and off we went. We lucked out. The New York bound train left Chicago a few short minutes after we got aboard. I congratulated myself for being so clever, or to use the Air Corps expression, "for being on the ball." Now we were on the last lap, but it seemed to take forever to cover those last few hundred miles.

Our senses had been dulled by those long hours on the train, but we all began to perk up as we pulled into Philadelphia. It was impossible to walk down the aisle, so the next order of business was to return all the seat backs to their proper places and take inventory of our belongings. I let out a cheer when we crossed the state line into New Jersey for that last hour or so of travel. All of us were looking out the windows, reading the names of the cities that were written on every train station. It was then that I told everyone to be alert for the Linden station, my home station, as the train whizzed past it for the last ten or twelve minute trip to Newark. I said goodbye to everyone, picked up my bags and walked to the end of the car, not wanting to waste a minute. The train began to slow down and I saw, once again, that old familiar train station. At last, it came to a stop and I bolted onto the platform, not wanting to get stuck behind a slow moving, time wasting crowd. There was no need to wonder where to go or what to do, for I had done it so many times before. I went down the stairway to the main concourse level and hustled over to the information desk and asked for the departure time of the next train to Linden. It was due to leave in a few minutes. I walked to the back of the station, where I knew I could easily find a telephone, and called home to let them know I was on my way. It was a very short call because time was running out and there was one more thing to do. I went over to the ticket window and bought a round trip ticket from Newark to Linden, knowing I would need it when I had to return to Fresno. I quickly put that ugly thought out of my mind. This was the time to dwell upon arriving, not leaving.

Being aboard the train for that brief 13-minute trip had produced this strange feeling that the calendar had been pushed back. That I was once again commuting from New York, and that this was May of 1941, not May of 1944. Looking at the uniform I was wearing was all I needed to bring me back to the present.

When the train pulled into the station, I looked up and saw Linden and remembered that I had departed for Fort Dix from this very same platform on that memorable day October 20, 1941. Nothing had changed. I walked down the stairs to the street level and hesitated, not knowing if I should walk or seek transportation. While trying to decide, I saw a bus about a block away and boarded it when it pulled up to the bus stop. A few minutes later I got off at 12th Street, walked the length of the street, past all the houses I had known since 1925, and felt a warm glow when I saw the familiar number 45 on the front porch. I was home! I vaulted the steps two at a time, rang the doorbell and took one-step into the living room and then the deluge hit me.

Anyone who had ever been around Italian families would have first hand knowledge of the greeting I received. This was not the time for handshakes or casual words of welcome. This was a time for hugging and kissing and a great display of emotion. For this was not a *laid back family*. To say that they were demonstrative would be an understatement. I will be the first to admit that it was an ego trip for me. I was very proud of the uniform and the wings and thankful for the opportunity to hold center stage and show off.

I was in all my glory, but there was one person who relished the moment more than I, and that was Pop. He was a great storyteller and his stories were always about things that happened back in Italy. Perhaps some were fact and some were fiction, but it did not matter. That we knew them all by heart was immaterial, for we would begin to laugh as he began with that very familiar first word. It was not fiction, however, when he told us of what a "big man" (his very words) a sergeant was back in the old country. To have a sergeant in the family was just cause for bragging and feeling superior to all others. I remember how proud he was when I made corporal, back at Langley Field, but it was evident from the look on his face, that this also was a once in a lifetime moment for him. He was glowing with pride as he looked at his son, standing before him, an *officer* in the Army Air Corps.

After supper (not mess), I finally got a chance to phone Miss P38, but I didn't call from home. I got a handful of coins and walked a few blocks to the nearest pay phone to make my call. This was one time that I did not want or need an audience listening in to what I had to say. Hearing her warm voice and laughter started me wondering, once again, if I could somehow make that trip to Georgia, but I knew that was just wishful thinking. I also knew that it could be quite some time before there would be another opportunity to be together, and unfortunately, I was right. There was nothing we could do except make phone calls, write letters and *wait*.

In all other respects, those few days at home were a lot of fun. Both Carl Frank and old friend Frank Dickert managed to get a furlough, and we three enjoyed being together once again. I had known Frank from the first grade and so we had a lot in common.

Furloughs are wonderful for the first few days, but when the mid point is reached, I would find myself counting down and saying, "Four days left, three days left…" and finally, "There are no days left" and it is time to pack your bag and go. My orders were to report to Hammer Field, Fresno, California where I would be assigned to a combat crew and then proceed to a designated base for the next and final phase of training before going overseas. Knowing that I would be going to a combat zone, made this farewell completely different than those in the past, realizing that the future was very uncertain.

It was time to leave. I felt into my pocket to make sure I had my ticket to Newark, kissed everyone goodbye and got into the car for one more ride to the Linden station and then on to Newark.

I got lucky once again being able to get a reservation, forty minutes before departure time, due to a cancellation. Although I was riding in coach, it was a much more comfortable train than the one from Victorville. As I sat there looking out the window at the passing countryside I couldn't help but think that I was getting to see a lot of the United States. The first time I was on the southern route and now, twice via the northern route.

During those endless hours, my thoughts ranged far and wide, but in the end, they always ended up with Verna and what I wanted where she was concerned. It didn't seem possible that we could care as much as we did, considering how little time we had actually spent together. Then I remembered how it bothered me to see some other man holding her while on the dance floor. More and more I realized that I wanted her in my life, but for now, all I could do was *wait.*

The train ride across the country was tiring and I was happy when we finally arrived at Hammer Field in Fresno. What I wasn't prepared for, however, was the shock of being saluted by enlisted men! I was still thinking like a cadet: *Salute anything that moves and looks like an officer and wait to be saluted in return.* Now, it was the other way around. I was the one who had to be saluted (by enlisted men). Obviously, there were adjustments that I needed to make since I was now an Officer and a Gentleman, by an act of Congress.

Much to my relief, the workload was light, requiring little more than filling out forms. We all had to take a physical, which was standard operating procedure for personnel who were on flying status.

Time dragged on, after the first few days with little to do, so I perked up when fellow bombardier, *John Boy*, came to me and mumbled something about going out. After beating around the bush, he finally got to the point and asked me if I would go out on a blind date. It seems that he knew this woman officer and had asked her out, but she agreed only on the condition that her girlfriend, a Naval officer, could go along. She had a car, so all that stood between him and happiness was the need to find her a date. My first answer was no, but his argument had merit; that there wasn't a thing to do on the base, so I concluded that a blind date certainly was an improvement over what I was doing, which was nothing. When the grand moment arrived, John Boy took over as the driver and the Naval officer and I shared the back seat. Try as I might, I cannot remember if she was tall or short, blonde or brunette or even her name. It is as though it never happened. We went out to dinner, but it was what happened afterward that I can clearly recall. He started to drive and soon afterward, I noticed that we had left Fresno and were now going down some dark, lonely road. We all managed to keep the conversation going while discussing the Navy, Air Corps and even singing some of the hit songs of the day. One of the big hits was called, "They're Either Too Young or Too Old."[17] The title, of course, alluded to the fact that with all the desirable, young men gone, all that was left were those who were too young or too old and who felt that all women should be *thankful* that *they* were still around to *comfort them*. We were all singing, "They're either too young or too old, they're either too gray or too grassy green, the pickings are poor and the crop is lean, what's good is in the Army, what's left will never harm me…" with the final line that went, "She's looked the field over and lo and behold, they're either too young or too old." We were in mid-song when John Boy pulled into this secluded, dark parking area, turned off the engine and then the lights. Instantly, we all stopped singing and the silence became deafening. In my mind, I could imagine what the girls might be thinking: "What kind of girl does this flyboy think I am? I'm as patriotic as anyone, but I'm not *that* patriotic." As we sat in the darkness, without a word being said, I remembered that there was a second ending to the song and began to sing, "The battle is on, but the fortress will hold, they're either too young or too old." That did it! Everyone laughed, John Boy started the car, turned on the lights and from that moment on, we had a pleasant, tension free, sociable evening. Music to the rescue!

Chapter 12

May 10, 1944, Linden. Home on leave after graduating from Victorville.
I sent this picture to Verna and wrote on the back: "I think you would look terrific sitting next to me."
Sure enough, that was where she sat for this is the car I used when I drove to Tifton, Georgia in November 1945.

111

13

B24 TRAINING, MARCH FIELD, RIVERSIDE, CALIFORNIA

The fun and games came to an end on May 25, 1944, when we received orders transferring us to March Field, Riverside, California for the purpose of training as a crew in the B24, a four-engine bomber. Prior to boarding the train, we were given orders which listed the names of the men on the newly formed flight crews. I found my name and saw that I had been assigned to crew number 251. We had all boarded the train as individuals, not as crews, which meant that we were scattered throughout the cars. I waited until we were under way, and with my orders in hand, began to walk through the train asking if there was anyone from crew 251. One by one, I located the seven of my crew members, two names were missing, the navigator and one of the enlisted men, who were assigned later. One name caught my eye, a gunner on crew 254; Sabu Dastagir, who was a very popular movie star. Little did I know how well I would get to know him a few weeks later.

Fresno, California May 25, 1944. A few minutes before leaving Fresno for March Field.

March Field was an old, well-established base, not too far from San Bernardino or Riverside and we took advantage of what the cities had to offer. One, The Mission Inn, in Riverside, was known far and wide. Two, transportation was good and it was easy to rent a car if someone had the urge to travel into Los Angeles or Hollywood. We got lucky when we were sent there.

Soon afterward I met Cliff Risley, our navigator, and Rex Reno the ball turret gunner. There was one more change. George Hynes replaced Donald Bowen as the flight engineer. The crew was now complete.

Very soon, I realized what a great difference there was in being a commissioned officer, even if only a lowly 2nd lieutenant. The officers were assigned two to a *room*, not in the barracks. Risley and I teamed up and shared a room, being free to come and go as we pleased. We could hang up our clothes and make ourselves comfortable. Another big difference was the fact that there would be no one blowing a whistle to wake you up. Now you, the officer, bore the responsibility of getting your butt out of bed and being on time for the daily formations. This was a piece of cake for me, for I still had the *clock in my head*.

The next day we were briefed by the operations officer who informed us that we would begin flying training missions on the 28th of May, and at best, we could expect only one off day in ten. Some days, it might be a navigation mission and another day it could be gunnery or bombing. Regardless of the type of mission, the entire crew would be aboard. There was a lot to learn.

* * * * *

The B24 was the biggest bomber in the Air Corps at that time. Its wingspan was one hundred and ten feet and, for the bombardier, represented a radical change from the much smaller plane I was accustomed to in Victorville. Obviously, the larger B24 would take longer to respond to course changes and I realized at the very beginning that it would require a less abrupt, lighter, smoother touch when I was turning the course knob. This was not an aircraft that you could *stand on a wingtip*. All those hours spent practicing formation flying, back in my pilot training days, was also an asset, for I had a better understanding of the pilot's task when he was following the lead ship in formation flying.

B24 Liberator

The first few days at March Field were devoted to making the transition from training aircraft to the B24 Liberator. It sat low to the ground, had a tricycle landing gear, wing positioned high on the fuselage and a newly designed, efficient wing shape known as the Davis Airfoil. The pilots had been checked out in the plane, but it would be a new experience for the navigator, bombardier and gunners.

To enter the plane it was necessary to double up and duck under the open bomb bay doors which rolled up *into* the fuselage and were radically different from the orthodox, downward opening doors. Standing in the open bomb bay and looking forward revealed that the fuselage had been divided in half, horizontally, by the flight deck which was the floor for the pilots and radio operator seats. Access to the nose was achieved by getting down on hands and knees, ducking under the flight deck and *crawling* the length of a narrow passageway to the right of the nose wheel. I labeled this maneuver *the Colletti Crawl* and it became an adventure when I was wearing a chest-pack parachute, metal oxygen walk-around bottle and a *Mae West* inflatable vest. (This was one of the few times in my life when I was happy to be five feet, six inches tall and weighing one hundred forty-five pounds.) The bombsight was on the floor in the nose, and the ceiling above it was actually the bottom of the nose turret. (I had to kneel when using the bombsight, but later models of the plane had a low seat for the bombardier.) There was an on-board electrical generator forward of the bomb bay, which supplied power when the engines were not running. Well before takeoff time, our engineer, George Hynes, would get it running, making it possible for crew members to perform pre-flight checks on their equipment. After completing my check, and satisfied that all was in order, I would program the sight using information from the ballistic table that was relevant to the one hundred pound, sand filled bombs we used in practice.

Flight Deck on B24

We began with night navigation missions with bombing limited to daylight runs. Initially, proper procedure and not accuracy was stressed as I became familiar with the instruments in the bombardier's compartment. It was very important to learn how the plane responded when I made course corrections using the course knob on the sight. When bombing with the plane flying on autopilot, I, not the pilot, was in control of the plane's direction. Much to my satisfaction, the first bombing mission went well.

When I first arrived at March Field, I found it to be necessary to read the notices on the bulletin board (regarding the officer's club activities,) two or three times before I realized that it applied to me. All that time I had spent as an enlisted man was still affecting my thinking. One notice had extended an invitation to *all officers* to attend a reception for a visiting bigwig. We, the *greenest of the green 2nd lieutenants*. were discussing whether or not we should *bother* to go since we were looking for fun, not speeches. The entire discussion became moot when one of the base regulars overheard our conversation and set us straight when he said,

"You damn fools, when the commanding officers says 'You are invited' what he is actually telling you is that he wants a big turnout, a lot of warm bodies in the seats and you had better get your asses there on time. You don't have a choice." We went.

At my first opportunity, I went to the USO dance in Riverside and was happy to see that there was a good ratio of men to women. Cutting in was permitted, but with a little luck, it was possible to dance the entire dance without losing your partner. There also was a weekly dance, at the officer's club, but this was limited to people with their own date.

Ground school took up a good part of the day when we were not scheduled to fly, for there was much to learn about the plane we would be flying in combat. Although the ground bomb crew would be doing the actual bomb loading, the bombardier was responsible for everything that went into the bomb bay. In combat, bombs of various sizes would be used, depending upon the mission, and I was introduced to something new: fuses. Depending upon the target, fuses with different characteristics would be screwed into the nose of the bomb. One type was a delayed action, which would penetrate more deeply into the target before exploding. Another was a proximity fuse, which would cause the bomb to detonate before reaching the ground and the instantaneous fuse which would operate on contact.

I liked my crewmembers and most of all, Wade Schroeder, my co-pilot. He was six feet tall, slim, with light hair, had a great sense of humor, a very easygoing manner and self-deprecating in speech. He was all of twenty years old, married to Fran, who was younger than he. Married men were permitted to live off the post, and much to my delight, they had invited me to dinner a few times. Regardless of how good the food might have been on the base, it was so much nicer to sit at a table set for three and have pleasant conversation while eating. We became very good friends; a friendship that lasted until his death in 2010.

During my training days at Victorville, we usually bombed from about eleven thousand feet, but that would soon change. Now I would learn how much more difficult it would be to bomb from higher altitudes which required the use of oxygen. In addition, a small mistake in synchronization would result in larger misses on the ground. At Victorville, I was not what one would call, a *hotshot bombardier*. I had done well, finishing slightly better than the class average insofar as accuracy was concerned. Therefore, I

Bomb instrument panel

had no explanation for the results I was now getting. I was completely surprised with the small circular error I was achieving, but the best was yet to come. For the first time, we were going to do high altitude night bombing from an altitude of twenty-four thousand feet. I had a ball! I dropped six bombs and managed to put them all within two hundred feet of the shack. Had the error been two thousand feet, it would still have been accepted as good bombing.

Perhaps it was the fact that the B24 was a more stable, steadier bombing platform, but whatever it was, I was ecstatic when the results were confirmed by the pictures. As excited as I was, the squadron bombardier was completely carried away. There was no doubt that I thoroughly enjoyed my few minutes of glory that night!

There was one mission which scared everyone on board. It was a night navigation mission, in which the gunners and bombardier had little to do and just went along for the ride. We became airborne just as it had gotten dark and were heading west out over the Pacific Ocean. Frank McCullough, the pilot, engaged the autopilot and relaxed as the plane began a slow climb to the prescribed altitude. The gunners and I were stretched out in the waist area of the plane, trying to find a comfortable spot on the hard metal floor and utilizing anything we could find to use as a pillow. Our altitude was about eleven thousand feet when Mac reached over and turned the autopilot course correction knob to make a climbing turn. That little loss of lift, as we began to turn, was enough to cause the plane to stall and go into a dive. Those of us who were asleep found ourselves flying through the air with ammunition belts swirling around our heads. We held our breath, wondering if we were going to pull out. Fortunately, Mac got it under control but not until we lost about six thousand feet of altitude. What added to the confusion was that we were in total darkness when it happened. We were lucky that night.

In my letter to Carl , June 26, 1944, I had written the following:

"We took off from March Field last night at 8:00 PM for a night navigation mission. We flew westward, about 90 miles over the ocean, and then turned northward and continued on until we came abreast of San Francisco. There, we turned 180 degrees to retrace our course back to base, only to find that it was completely hidden from view due to a solid overcast. The tower instructed us to head inland to the field at Blythe, Cal., finally landing there at 2:30 AM. We didn't get to sleep until 3:00 AM and were up at 6:00 AM. The plane had been serviced and we were airborne at 9:00 AM finally touching down at March Field at 11:30 AM. There were ten zombies walking around that day."

Another incident of note occurred when we went on an air to ground gunnery mission. One of the gunners from crew 254 had missed his day of firing and was assigned to fly with us to make up the missed mission. His name was Sabu Dastagir, the movie star and who was better known as "Sabu, the Elephant Boy." We proceeded to the target area, where he got into the nose turret and completed his firing schedule. Since there was no bombing that day, I had remained in the roomier waist area of the plane. After landing, everyone got out of the plane and returned to the ready room, but I remained aboard. The bombardier was also the armaments officer, and it was my responsibility to check the weapons and judge that they were in a safe mode before leaving the plane on the flight line. All was well until I got to the nose turret and noticed that the two small doors, through which entry to the turret is gained, where improperly positioned. The doors were designed to open into the plane, and could only open completely if the guns in the turret were pointed straight ahead. If the turret was turned slightly off center, either left or right, it would be possible to open only one door and have barely enough room to squeeze out. For his own safety, the very first thing a nose gunner was taught was to be certain to check the emergency turret cable which was stowed above and to the right of the bombsight. Pulling the cable would disengage the gear track, making it possible to manually rotate the turret until the doors were properly aligned to the inside of the plane. This was the only way a dysfunctional, injured man could be removed. Unfortunately, what Sabu had overlooked, was that the cable was not stowed in its proper place; but instead was hanging down and had become entangled with and hooked onto the metal ammunition belt which fed into the right gun in the turret. When the gun was fired, the belt moved forward, dragging the cable with it until it was taut. When there was no slack left in the cable, the belt could no longer move and the gun jammed. I was now faced with a problem which had never come up in gunnery school. The belt could not move forward, and I could not pull it out because it was being held there by the "belt holding pawl" which was doing the job it was designed to do. The gun had a live round in it and was pointing at congested areas and planes on the flight line. I struggled for over an hour before I managed to clear it. In addition, I missed out on one of my classes which I would somehow have to make up. What enraged me was that he had left the plane without revealing that we had an armed, malfunctioning gun on board. It would have played out differently if he had been on our crew. Much to my surprise, Sabu invited our respective crews to his home in Hollywood a few days before leaving March Field. Perhaps he was trying to atone for the unfortunate gun incident, but whatever the reason, we did have a nice time. I did not broach the subject while there, having had time to cool off. To the best of my knowledge, he went to the 13th Air Force.

* * * * *

Thanks to P38, mail call was never a disappointment for she wrote very often. Included in her last letter were pictures of her in shorts and in a bathing suit. The pictures went into my wallet and the letters were carefully saved to be read many more times.

We were finished with transition training at March Field, and were getting ready to move on, but there was one more very important thing I had to do. I got five dollars worth of quarters, found a phone booth and placed a call to P38. Making long distance calls, during the war years, was a time consuming experience. Hours of spare time were something I did not have, so I just stopped trying to phone her. It had been eight months since I had last seen her and four months since the last phone call. My call finally went through and hearing her voice when she said "hello" was enough to make all the memories come alive. I was too excited to remember the exact words that were spoken, but she told me everything I had wanted to hear. After we said goodbye and hung up, there were two thoughts foremost in my mind: One: I was in love with her and hoped that some day we would marry. The second thought had to do with the fact that it might never happen because I would soon be going into combat, where men were being killed every day and there was no guarantee that I would be coming back.

On August 11, 1944, we received orders to depart March Field for Hamilton Field, California. We were now identified as crew FQ 229-AB3 and we would be flying a brand new B24, airplane serial number 44-41356. This would be our last stop before going overseas.

Thinking back to those last few days of transition in the B24 at March Field, I was well aware of the fact that the sole purpose of the weeks of training had been to prepare us for combat duty somewhere in the world. If this was a worrisome thought, then I should have never gone into the Air Corps. It was my choice. I could have remained in the medical department, but there, too, the final destination would also have been a combat zone, taking x-rays in a hospital or out in the field. It probably would not have been as risky as flying missions, but I preferred being up in the air rather than fighting the war on the ground.

Speaking for myself, I can honestly say that I did not fear combat. Perhaps I was being naïve, but the fact remains that it would have been very difficult to get aboard the plane, time and time again, in a fearful frame of mind. The dangers we would be facing were real, not imagined, but each of us were of the same mindset: *we were leading a charmed life and nothing would every happen to us*. It was the only way we could do what we had been trained to do.

When we had a few minutes of free time, the conversation usually gravitated to the question of which theater of operation we would be sent. Would it be Europe, the Pacific, Africa, India or elsewhere? We were spread all over the world. Which foe was the toughest, the Germans or the Japanese? How would we fare against one or the other? Which one posed the greatest threat to our survival? All we could do was speculate as to what the future held in store as we finished up at March Field. We would have our answer soon enough.

The news reports in late August of 1944, made it quite clear that the Germans were hitting our B17 and B24 bombers very hard and many ten-man crews were being lost. Very fortunate were those who survived long enough to complete a tour of duty. We concluded that probably the Germans were to be feared more than the Japanese and the possibility of being killed was greater if we were sent to Europe. However, in the final analysis, we would learn first hand that different wars were being fought in different ways, depending upon which theater of operations you had been assigned. Either way, we would soon learn how it would feel to be exposed to enemy action.

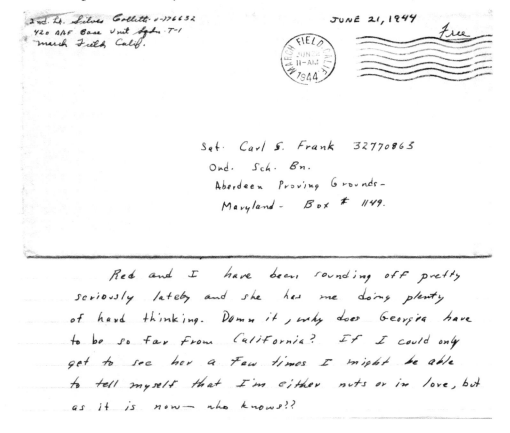

14

ISLAND HOPPING AND JUNGLE SURVIVAL TRAINING

In my letter to Carl dated August 27, 1944, I wrote:

"Leaving March Field, we flew up the coast to Hamilton Field, which was in the San Francisco area. While there, everyone on the crew had to stencil the last four digits of their serial number on everything they owned; shirts, pants, ties, etc., and be ready to leave on short notice. We were also ordered to destroy personal items such as diaries and letters which supposedly would be of value to the enemy, a conclusion which I could never understand. I had many letters from Red which I wanted to keep, and for a moment I considered sending them home, but decided against it. I read each one for the last time and then tore them up."

One last detail remained: we were to fly a five-hour flight to nowhere in order to check the fuel consumption of the engines and after a three-day wait, finally got the go ahead to takeoff. Engines were started at 10:00 AM and we were airborne at 10:26. Our destination was Fairfield Suisan Air Base, which was only about forty or fifty miles away. We enjoyed the five hours of flying which took us over the Grand Canyon, Yosemite National Park and Hoover Dam (or was it Boulder Dam back then?) finally touching down at 1527 at Fairfield. A flight line taxi picked us up for the trip to the operations office where we checked in, were relieved of our 45 pistols and field glasses, filled out a few forms and were free of any duty. I had dinner at the officer's club, wrote a few letters and finally turned in at 11:00 PM. The next day, the crew reported to the hospital for a final medical exam and lecture.

Flight crews reporting to Fairfield were supposed to be there for only two or three days, at the most, and then depart for an overseas destination. It was apparent that a sort of *this is the last good meal you are going to have for a long time* mentality prevailed, because they served steak and french fries every night. The permanent cadre went out of their way to give us a good send off and made those last few days as nice as possible. Playing cards and table tennis occupied most of our time while we waited for the order to depart. Of course, something went wrong. The two or three day stay stretched out to ten days, because it had been determined that fuel consumption was too high, and adjustments had to be made. Time began to drag, and we had long since had our fill of table tennis and card playing. As usual, there was always someone who came up with the right quip at the right time. Perhaps it was Wade who said, as we moved with the chow line, "What, steak again?" We had actually had enough of that too!

Soon afterward the word came down that the fuel consumption problem had been corrected. On September 11, 1944, we lifted off the runway at 0645 hours, and began, as Wade so ably described as *our great adventure*. Our destination was Oahu in the Hawaiian Islands.

It is difficult to describe what I thought and felt as California slowly faded from view in the distance. There was no doubt that none of us had ever had an experience such as this. Sitting in the plane, hour after hour with the engines droning, gave me an opportunity to study the members of my crew. Frank McCullough, the first pilot, was from Wichita, Kansas. He was about twenty-four years old, tall, with dark hair and handsome. He wasn't the *bubbly* type. To the contrary, he struck me as being a little bit of a loner. Wade Schroeder, the co-pilot, was from Washington State, twenty years old and an easygoing person. After getting his wings, became an instructor in Basic Flying School, flying the BT13. Cliff Risley, the navigator, was 19 years old and I believe came from Illinois. We got to know each other quite well when we shared the same room at March Field. George Hynes, the flight engineer, was from New York City. Albert Eltz, the radio operator, hailed from Reading, Pennsylvania. Rex Reno was the lower ball turret gunner, Robert Scott's position was the nose turret, Charles Stratten had the tail spot and Cliff Schraeder was a waist gunner. I seriously doubt that any of these men were over twenty years old. To sum up, eight out of ten were hardly more than kids, and the other two were in their early twenties. To them, the government had entrusted a brand new airplane, worth thousands of dollars, and in effect said, *we know you can do the job*. Now all we had to do was to prove that their trust had not been misplaced. In all probability we were no different than all the other crews flying missions all over the world. What was difficult to understand was the fact that none of us thought we were doing anything exceptional. We were happy to be doing what we liked to do: fly.

I would be lying if I said that there was *no sweat* as we flew on. We were going on a very long, over water flight in a land-based bomber that had a very poor crew survival reputation if forced to *ditch* in the ocean. Radio silence had to be maintained, and this was before radar had come into general use. In essence, we were on our own, and Cliff Risley, the navigator, was responsible for getting us there. I lent some moral support by navigating with him, and at the same time, it gave me something to do. As it turned out, Cliff did a great job. After flying for thirteen hours and fifty minutes, we landed at Oahu at 2035 hours, California time.

September 12, 1944:

Wade and I spent the day seeing the sights in Honolulu and then, pretending we were tourists, went swimming at Waikiki Beach. It was a much-welcomed change from the stress of the flight.

September 13, 1944:

Today is my twenty-fifth birthday. I *celebrated* by getting up early and going to the flight line for takeoff at 0625. Our destination is Canton Island. It was a shorter trip, however, than the one to Hawaii. After checking in at the operations desk, we found our assigned sleeping area and waited for evening mess. When it became dark, we went to the movies and saw Charles Laughton in *Canterville Ghost*.

September 14, 1944:

Departed Canton Island at 0720, Canton time for Hawkins Field on Tarawa Island, touching down at 1:00 PM. In the afternoon, we all went for an ocean swim, and that evening, sat in on a movie titled *Thank Your Lucky Stars*. We lost a day when we flew across the date line, so now it is Friday, September 15th.

September 16, 1944:

Departed Tarawa at 0710, Tarawa time, and our destination is Guadalcanal, in the Solomon Islands. We landed at Carney Field at 1:15 PM. I was awed to find myself in these historic places, where some of the heaviest fighting of the war had taken place. Many men had lost their lives in order to make it possible for the Air Corps to have airfields from which to operate.

Chapter 14

S E C R E T

HEADQUARTERS, 1504TH AAF BASE UNIT
PACIFIC DIVISION. AIR TRANSPORT COMMAND
FAIRFIELD-SUISUN ARMY AIR BASE, FAIRFIELD, CALIFORNIA

	SECRET
	By Authority of
	The Commanding General
	Pacific Division, ATC
(OPERATIONS ORDER)	28 Aug 44 ....EW........
NUMBER 27) E X T R A C T	Date Initials

2. FAC Ltr, WD Hq AAF, Wash D.C. File 370.5, Sub:"Movement Orders, Shipment FQ---AB" dated 25 July 44 and Ltr, ATC, WC Sector, PD, Hamilton Fld, Calif, File 300.4 Sub:"Authority to Issue Travel Orders and Instructions Governing" dated 4 Dec 43 and Ltr, File #370.5/758, 370.5/759 and 370.5/757, Air Base Hq, Hamilton Fld, Calif, dated 23 Aug 44, the below listed Officers and EM will proceed in designated mil acft in connection with Project 96718-R, Shipment FQ---AB from Fairfield-Suisun AAB, Fairfield, Calif to Townsville, Australia delivering acft to RESPONSIBLE REPRESENTATIVE, FAR EAST AIR FORCES COMBAT REPLACEMENT AND TRAINING CENTER (P), Townsville, Australia and then WP by other means of transportation to Port Moresby, New Guinea, reporting upon arrival thereat to COMMANDING OFFICER, FAR EAST AIR FORCES COMBAT REPLACEMENT AND TRAINING CENTER (P), Port Moresby, New Guinea for asgmt to the Far East Air Forces. This is a PCS.

B-24L #44-41418   Crew #FQ---AB-4
APO #16409-AB-4   194th SQDN

2D Lt.	MERRITT, JAMES H.	0713965	P
2D Lt.	FOSS, NEIL E.	0770229	CP
2D Lt.	SADOWSKY, ARTHUR	02058017	N
2D Lt.	COBB, EVERETT E. JR.	0776629	B
Sgt.	Jacobs, Seymour	32651416	E
Cpl.	Fisher, Thomas T.	17133528	RO
Cpl.	Wolfe, Theodore B.	19163433	AAG
Cpl.	Patton, Laurence	31440118	AG
Cpl.	Van Campen, Warren M.	33465645	AG
Cpl.	Thomas, Quinton L.	14148343	AG

B-24J #44-41354   Crew #FQ---AB-5
APO #16409-AB-5   408th SQDN

2D Lt.	MIRES, JOHN K.	0715275	P
2D Lt.	STERNFELD, NORMAN	0774800	CP
2D Lt.	SIEGEL, SOLOMON	02058027	N
2D Lt.	HYATT, BLAND B. JR.	0776664	B
Cpl.	Johnson, David L.	16080251	E
Cpl.	Fly, Benton G.	18075954	RO
Cpl.	Sanders, John L.	39335894	AAG
Cpl.	Platte, Vincent J.	13171180	AG
Cpl.	Winter, William W.	37680441	AG
Cpl.	Lofgren, John D.	31408540	AG

B-24J #44-41356   Crew #FQ---AB-3
APO #16409-AB-3   408th SQDN

2D Lt.	MC CULLOUGH, FRANK H.	0711735	P
2D Lt.	SCHROEDER, WADE W.	0772519	CP
2D Lt.	RISLEY, CLIFFORD JR.	02056473	N
2D Lt.	COLLETTI, SILVEO G.	0776632	B
Cpl.	Hynes, George V.	32530066	E
Cpl.	Eltz, Albert J.	33828738	RO
Cpl.	Reno, Rex R.	17055554	AAG
Cpl.	Schraeder, Clifford B.	33706529	AG
Cpl.	Scott, Robert D.	35629803	AG
Cpl.	Stratton, Charles E. Jr.	37487208	AG

Except as man be necessary in the transaction of official business, indivs are prohibited from discussing their oversea destination even by shipment number. They will not file safe arrival telegrams with commercial agencies while enroute and at domestic or oversea destinations.

In lieu of subs a per diem of $7.00 is atzd for Officers for travel and temp dy accordance with existing law and regulations, except when govt qrs are used or furnished. $4.00 per day will be deducted by disbursing Offr. In lieu of subs a

September 16, 1944:
Departed Guadalcanal at 7:30 AM and arrived at Garbutt Field, Townsville Australia at 1:30 PM. As we staggered off the plane, I remember thinking that the Pacific is a damn big ocean. A second, very depressing thought, was that we were now about nine thousand miles from home.

In accordance with Operations Order #56, of 9 September 1944, the aircraft was delivered to the *Responsible Representative, Far East Air Forces*.

* * * * *

Garbutt Field was a typical transient facility for combat crews who would remain there for about a week and then be assigned to a group and squadron. Our *week* stretched out to a two-week disaster. The *accommodation* at the *Garbutt Hilton* was nothing more than a cot with mosquito netting and a shelf. The army of ants which shared the barracks with us soon thought that we would enjoy their company in bed. One sleepless night was enough to motivate me to seek a solution. I went to the mess hall, located the garbage area and poked around until I found eight empty cans. I brought them back to the barracks, half filled them with water, and placed them under the legs of my cot. That took care of the ants in bed problem. I believe I gave the other four cans to Wade.

Garbutt Hilton

The food was horrible. After a few days of self-imposed forced feeding we discovered a Red Cross Canteen on the flight line. The menu there was limited to coffee and doughnuts which was what we lived on when on the base. Relief came when we were finally permitted to go into Townesville. Four of us found this little restaurant that showed promise, so we gave it a try. The menu was the popular Aussie steak and eggs, but they pronounced it, *stike and eye-g's*. Finally, we had gotten something to eat that was satisfactory. As we were leaving, we thought the waitress was going to swoon because we left her a tip that was larger than the entire cost of the meal. At the going rate of exchange, the American dollar had a lot of purchasing power.

Chapter 14

Some time ago, Verna had told me that her brother, Courtney Atkinson, had been killed here at Garbutt Field. He was a pilot in the 71st Squadron of the 38th Bombardment Group, *The Sun Setters*. His B25 had just been repaired, and he was killed when he crashed immediately after takeoff. The official report to the family raised more questions than it answered, being so lacking in detail. I had hoped to check it out, but there wasn't enough time, and I had no idea where to start.

After two weeks of bad food and boredom, we left Townesville for Nadzab which was on the northern coast of New Guinea. This time, our new home was a tent, and the unit was a combat replacement and training facility.

Without question, the most memorable part of our stay at Nadzab was the three days of jungle survival training which all the crews had to complete. There are places in New Guinea, even today, that have never been explored. The jungle was very dense and the canopy of treetops joined together permitting little sunlight to penetrate. Aircraft that had crashed could seldom be seen from the air because the trees sealed off the crash site. This too, would be a new experience.

Before starting our trek into the jungle, our Australian guides briefed us regarding the schedule for the next three days. A short question and answer session followed and then as an afterthought, the guide said,

"Oh yes, I almost forgot. There are still cannibals in the area."

We were led into the jungle, and within a few minutes found it impossible to make headway without first using a machete to clear the path. It was very hot and humid and the air felt *heavy*. The canopy of treetops above our head seemed to cut off the slightest breeze. We were dressed in long sleeve khaki uniforms, and the temptation was great to roll them up in an attempt to cool off. The guides strongly advised not to do so, the better to protect us from insect bites. For the same reason, we pulled up our socks and tucked our pants cuff into them. As we hacked our way, they would select certain vines for us to cut. They pointed out those that were juicy, safe to drink and others that were edible. In addition we were warned about those that were poisonous. Someone remarked that "if the birds ate it, we could eat it too,"

123

but that theory was quickly shot down. Various types of berries were growing around us and many of them were to be avoided.

Sanitation, or the lack of it, was another topic to be addressed. While the guide was explaining the important points, I found myself smiling and laughing inwardly. What came to mind was the day, way back in October of 1941, when I was in the medical department at Camp Lee, Virginia. That was the day when we had to learn the finer points of digging slit trenches, and how bored we were with the entire subject. All that *useless information* became important now. You just never know!

Cliff Risley (back right) and Colletti (far right) with locals, October 1944.

In mid afternoon, the marching and the hacking came to a halt while they demonstrated the proper way to construct a place to sleep. It was necessary to build it above ground in order to reduce the exposure to insects and snakes. Very large leaves were everywhere, and we were taught how to construct a sleeping pad and also use them to provide cover in the event of rain. It was hard work and we had to be clever and resourceful to get the job done, the machete being our only tool. Vines were found that could be used to lash poles together as we labored to construct a framework for the bed. After eating a meal of berries and leaves, it was time to turn in. Wildlife was everywhere and the jungle was a very noisy place. I believe I can speak for all when I say that we were a little bit apprehensive when we closed our eyes.

As revolting as the experience was, we fully realized that what we had learned could be the difference between dying or surviving in the event of a bail out or successful crash landing. All our missions would be flown over terrain similar to New Guinea, so being able to live off the land was all-important. We all hoped that the day would never come when we had to put the knowledge to use.

When we returned to our camp area at the end our three-day *camping trip*, the sight of our tents looked like first class accommodations. It was a great experience, a little scary at times, but we all were aware of its importance.

Chapter 14

A day or so later, we got the good news that we were no longer orphans. We had been assigned to the 408th Squadron of the 22nd Bomb Group, of the 5th Air Force. Reading that notice triggered a memory. It was this very unit, the 22nd Bomb Group, which had occupied the barracks into which we moved at Langley Field, Virginia in December of 1941. Closing my eyes, I could see, once again, the mess they had left behind when they were forced to leave on very short notice.

The jungle survival experience signified an end to training and the beginning of flight operations against the Japanese. The date was October 14, 1944 and the target for our first combat mission was Wewak, on the northern coast of New Guinea which was about three hundred miles west of our base at Nadzab. In the Navy, they probably would have referred to it as a *shakedown cruise*, but I could not find a comparable Air Corps label.

General MacArthur was given credit for developing the so-called *leapfrog* strategy, whereby we would not attempt to eliminate all Japanese strongholds, but rather bypass them. The 22nd Bomb Group had already moved about 650 miles west of Wewak and was now based on a very small island called Owi. Although the

Using large palm leaves to make the roof of our grass hut.

Japanese force left behind was formidable, they could not be re-supplied, so in essence, they were no longer a threat.

After all the training, this would be our first mission as a crew. I would imagine we were having much the same thoughts, wondering what it would be like and what to expect. For me, there was a much more personal element, for now it would be my turn to perform. I had studied the pictures of the target area, committing to memory everything that was important. I finally put my mind at ease when I decided to stop worrying about hitting the target, but instead, concentrate on not screwing it up through faulty procedure. (Such as forgetting to open the bomb bay doors or forgetting to engage the trigger up on the sight!) Fortunately, it went well, but I have completely forgotten if I hit anything. We were a lot more relaxed, however, on the return trip home than we were when we had left. The flight time for the mission was four hours and thirty-five minutes. That evening, I started a logbook in which I recorded all the pertinent information of the missions that followed.

On October 18, 1944, we were transferred from the replacement center at Nadzab to a base on Owi Island. At long last; no more transient camps, replacement centers, or places where we didn't belong. During our stay at Nadzab, the base officer's club was off limits to the crews who were just passing through, so to speak. I guess you can't blame the regulars, because there were so many of us. We were there only two weeks, but it seemed much longer.

McCullough, Schroeder, Colletti (far right)

Left to right: Risley, McCullough, Schroeder

Chapter 14

FLAGS

These flags were issued to combat crews who were flying missions over China, India or Burma; countries that were allied with us against the Japanese with a friendly native population.

The flags were printed on silk and the writing explained that the airman was a friend who needed help in an effort to be returned to his unit, and that they would be rewarded for their assistance. They were stamped with a personal, identifying serial number and the crews were instructed to carry them when on a mission over these countries. Many of the men sewed them on the back of their flight jackets.

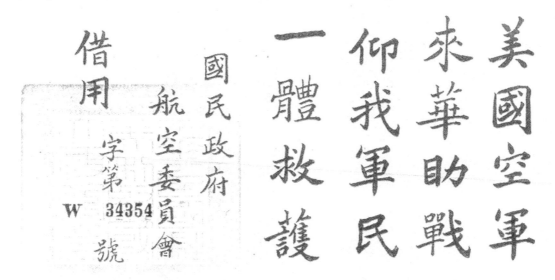

THE FLAG HAS MY PERSONAL IDENTIFICATION NUMBER

For the Duration *plus* Six Months

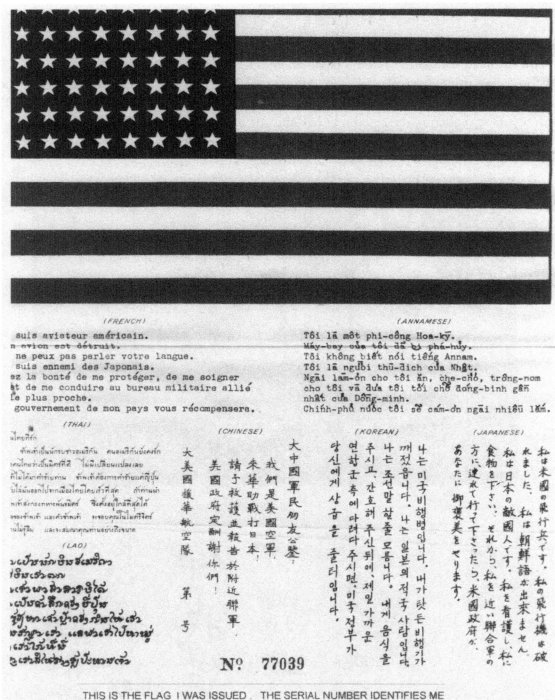

128

Chapter 14

"October 4, 1944

Dear Carl,

P38, Verna, Red Rebel! I got five of her letters today and I'm still reading them over and over. From where I sit Zom, it looks like she's got me and I love it! Boy, I'd give a months pay (and that's $260.00) just for a few days with her! There is little that we haven't discussed and decided upon in regard to our future. All I hope is that I get the chance, some day, to put the finishing touches to the deal."

Verna sent this to me when I was overseas. It was on my "night table" next to my cot. Just looking at it provided all the motivation I would ever need to do my best and hopefully hasten the day when I would see her again. Some men had pinups of movie starts, but why indulge in fantasy when the genuine article was waiting for me at home? Eat your heart out, Betty Grable!

15

408th SQUADRON, OWI ISLAND, DUTCH EAST INDIES

Patch from my flight jacket.

Using a magnifying lens, you would still have difficulty finding Owi Island on the map in the Dutch East Indies. It is located just below the Equator, off the northwestern coast of New Guinea, at 1.08 degrees south latitude and 136.12 east longitude. It was a very small coral island just a few miles away from Biak Island, which was much larger. (Today, Biak is a very important destination and transfer hub for flights going to that part of the world.) The airstrip we used went from water to water, which might have contributed to the loss of one of our planes. Since we were on Dutch soil, the *Dutch Rule* applied, which meant that we had to drive on the left side of the road. That took a little getting used to since all our vehicles had the steering wheel on the left side.

I still have a very vivid image of the day we arrived at Owi and became members of the 408th Squadron. We were greeted by the operations officer, Moe Reuther, and after a few welcoming words, led us to the tent area and instructed us to select a tent. We chose one and as we entered, we could see that it was occupied by others, since all their belongings were there. Turning to Capt. Reuther, we told him it was already in use, but he said it was okay because they were all sick with either scrub typhus or malaria, were off flying status and that they would probably be away for weeks. In addition, others had been lost on a mission to Balikpapan, Borneo, but their personal effects had not yet been removed. Not a very morale boosting beginning for green crews about to get their first taste of combat.

Later that day we experienced another memorable event: We got two shots and our arms soon began to hurt.

In the evening, the squadron bombardier invited the new *1035's* (which is the military occupation specialty number for a bombardier) to his tent. He introduced himself and then opened a bottle of wine and welcomed us to the 408th. It was a very nice gesture and a much-needed change from the *orphan designation* we felt during our stay at Nadzab.

It wasn't till a few days later that I realized how easy it was for the veterans to identify the new, green replacement crews. They simply had to look at our faces to see if we were growing a moustache, which was something most of us never had the guts to do back in the States. Here, far away from civilization, we got to thinking that no one could see us or cared so it was a good time to experiment. I gave up after two weeks when I realized that the lip adornment did little to make me look like Clark Gable or Tyrone Power.

The following is from the book, "The 22nd Bombardment Group in World War II, Volume III, Photo Supplement 1941-1945." Text and photographs produced by Lawrence J. Hickey, Edited by Col. Don L. Evans, USAF Ret. There are many mission reports, but I have narrowed the selection to correspond to the approximate time period of my tenure with the 408th Squadron. I quote:

October 10, 1944 - 19[18]

"The 22nd Bomb Group was the second of three 5th Air Force Groups over the target during a major raid against the strategic Japanese oil installations at Balikpapan, Borneo. The 19th Squadron, with four aircraft, was leading the 18-plane Group formation as it reached the target area. At this time the first of about 35 Zero and *Raiden* fighters from the Japanese Navy's *331st* and *381st Kokutais* began to attack the formation aggressively, making both firing passes and hurling phosphorus bombs into the massed B-24s. At 1055 hours, a pair of A6M5 Zeros approached the left side of the diamond formation from high and directly ahead. The nose turret gunner on the 33rd Squadron's, *LIBERTY BELLE* fired at the plane on the left as it came directly at him. It caught fire and blew up in front of the Squadron. The second Zero peeled off and headed for the 19th Squadron, which was flying ahead and to the right. The top turret gunner of *LIBERTY BELLE*, and probably other gunners, opened fire. It appeared that the plane caught fire then dove straight into the right wing of the B-24J-180 #44-40774, which was at 11,000 feet directly to the left of the mission leader. Both the Zero and the Liberator disintegrated in a ball of fire. The left wing of the B-24 broke off and the plane fell from the formation in a shower of debris. There was no chance of survivors."

October 10, 1944 - 408[19]

"B-24J-125 #110005 was one of the four planes of the 408th Squadron which reached the target area on the unit's first mission to Balikpapan, Borneo. During the approach, the #3 engine on this plane was apparently damaged by a Japanese phosphorus bomb, which exploded nearby. Following the bomb run at about 1055 hours, the damaged Liberator began to lose altitude and lag behind the formation. The cripple then came under repeated attacks by several Japanese fighters, operating in pairs. About 20 minutes into the return flight, six crewmen were seen to bail out of the badly shot-up aircraft. Several seconds later, the aircraft exploded, tearing off the tail section and blowing two more crewmen clear. Their chutes opened and they fell into the sea in the same area where the other six had come down, about sixty miles east of the target. One observer reported that the Japanese fighters strafed the men in the chutes on the way down. A submarine standing by on lifeguard duty was notified of the downed men's position, but search efforts were unsuccessful, and all aboard were eventually declared dead."

* * * * *

Malaria, spread by mosquito bites, and scrub typhus, the result of tick bites, were causing more casualties than the Japanese, so what we had learned in jungle training was quickly put to use: keep arms covered and pants cuffs tucked into the tops of our socks. The ticks were in the grass and would dig into our bare legs if they were exposed. As for the climate, it was very hot with very high humidity. No matter how much you *toweled off* one never felt dry and our skin was always clammy. Cuts or scratches never seemed to heal and everything would mildew in a very short time. There was a problem with athlete's foot (ringworm) which was probably aggravated by the continual presence of moisture on our skin. The remedy for alleviating the itching was an application of potassium permanganate, a dark purple liquid. Since the athlete's foot found its way to other parts of our bodies, we soon resembled people who had been painted up for Halloween. It was comical to see men with purple armpits, feet, hands and a *matching purple crotch* when we undressed!

Finally our mail caught up to us. I received twelve letters in one day, and much to my delight, five were from Miss P38. As usual, I saved them for last and waited until I could steal away from everyone for a very private reading. The day was made.

<u>October 14, 1944 - 408</u>[20]
"During a major coordinated raid by the 5th and 13th Air Forces on Japanese oil installations at Balikpapan, Borneo, B-24J-125 #42-109992, *LOST ANGEL*, was one of five aircraft from this squadron which were approaching the target at 11,500 feet. Interception by Zero fighters from the *331st* and *381st Kokutais* was intense, and several of them lobbed phosphorous bombs at the B-24 formations, in addition to conducting more conventional attacks. The formation turned right to avoid the onslaught and flew directly into a barrage of flak. *LOST ANGEL* was hit forward of the cockpit and turned left towards the water, passing under another B-24. Flames were visible through the windows in the bombardier's compartment. At that point a Japanese fighter attacked the plane from the rear, and the Liberator was subsequently seen descending rapidly with one engine on fire and smoke streaming from another. Moments later between five and seven crewmen bailed out. The plane fell away in a vertical dive and crashed near the target at 1044 hours."

* * * * *

Two milestones were reached on October 20, 1944: I had now been in the service for three years and would fly my first mission from this base. The target was Davao Headquarters on the large island of Mindanao in the Philippines. Flying northward, we crossed the equator as we departed, and re-crossed it again on the way back; a fact that always awed me. Unfortunately, I have no written reports of that mission and I don't remember how successful it was. The logged flying time was eleven hours and twenty minutes. Total combat flying time, for two missions, was now fifteen hours and fifty-five minutes. Only about 375 more hours to log before my tour of duty would be complete. A very distressing thought.

Chapter 15

October 25, 1944 - 408[21]

"Six B-24s from the 408th began taking off from Owi Island, NEI, at 0245 hours on a Group search mission for a Japanese task force reported to be crossing the Mindanao Sea in the Philippine Islands. Immediately after lifting off, B-24J-175 #44-70726 crashed into the water about a mile beyond the end of the airstrip. Of the eleven crewmen aboard, six were rescued and five were killed. One of the men who was saved apparently died later, although his identity is uncertain, and another required the amputation of a leg. The cause of the crash was attributed to mechanical failure."

A typical mission in the 408th would begin by checking flight operations to see if you were scheduled to fly the next day. After evening chow, the selected crews would attend a briefing where all-important elements of the next mission would be presented. In turn, the operations, intelligence, weather, bombing, navigation and armament officers would address the group and cover material in their own field of expertise. Takeoff time, course, altitude, squadron position in the formation and mission leader would be disclosed. Bomb load, target information, availability and location of air-sea rescue ships, submarines or PBY Catalina aircraft was also made known. After the general briefing, the pilots, navigators, bombardiers and gunners might gather separately and conduct their own briefing. The bombardiers would huddle with the squadron bombardier and study pictures of the target, looking for important landmarks that would make it easier to identify. What might appear to be conspicuous, in a black and white 8 x 10 photograph, very often was a lot harder to identify from the air. Obviously, if the bombardier couldn't pick up the target, the mission would be a failure.

An amusing sidelight to the mission was the trip down to the flight line. Whereas the majority of men would be transported in trucks, many would pile into the few jeeps that were making the trip, and occupy every inch of available space. It was not unusual for six or eight men, complete with Mae West's, parachutes and other gear sitting on the hood, or in the back or hanging half in or half out of the jeep. The driver had no forward vision whatsoever so he would look at the edge of the road (driving on the left side) and make corrections as the road turned. Of course, with so many on board, a few loud shouts of "danger ahead" were a big help to the blind driver. The thought that crossed my mind was that the trip to the flight line might be more dangerous than the mission itself.

A common problem on most of these islands was the lack of fresh water, and Owi was no exception. Showering was limited to a few hours in the afternoon from 4:00 to 6:00 PM. Water cans were filled and brought back to the tents, but that was usually saved for drinking. I remember how ridiculous I thought it was for one of the crewmembers to have brought an electric razor. As it turned out, he was smarter than all of us. He had no problem shaving, since we had an electric generator for the camp. Those who tried to lather up with salt seawater soon learned that it was quite an experience.

Much to my delight, softball games were a daily occurrence and there were great rivalries, such as the pilots against the bombardiers or co-pilots against the navigators. Crazy lunatics that we were, we would begin to play in mid-afternoon, out there under the blazing sun. That we were only fifty miles or so from the Equator didn't faze us. When the game was over, we would head for the ocean, a few hundred feet away, and swim out to a rubber life raft that had been anchored in deep water. It was very important to avoid touching bottom with your feet because of the danger of being cut by the sharp coral. The water was beautiful in color, clean, warm and refreshing after playing a nine-inning game in the sweltering heat. We would swim until the showers were turned on, and after showering and dressing, head for the mess tent for chow. More than once I thought what a wonderful place this would be if there was a luxury hotel on the site with air-conditioning to get rid of the heat and humidity.

According to my "Record of Combat Experience" form, the identifying number for the mission of 26 October 1944 was entered as "300-A 1." For me and my crew it was Mission No. 3. At the briefing the night before, we were told that our target would be Japanese naval forces. Takeoff was before dawn and we would be loaded with the maximum permissible bomb load and fuel. The takeoff was a nail biter, because it seemed that we would never get lift off, needing the entire runway before we finally staggered into the air. Little did we know that we would be participating in the Battle of Leyte Gulf.

Newspapers and books have described it as the greatest naval engagement in history, without equal in the number of ships involved or the size of the *battleground* which covered an area of 100,000 square miles. It was also described as the largest air battle between carrier and land-based aircraft.

There were four separate, geographical areas of engagement, and we were involved in what was known as the "Battle of Surigao Straits" which was a narrow strait between the islands of Leyte and Mindanao. If I remember correctly, the Japanese force, though superior to the American, was caught in the straits and were engaged by our surface ships, Navy and Army Air Forces.

Trying to hit a moving target such as a ship taking evasive action, is a very difficult task for the bombardier. You cannot expect a flight of B24's, flying in formation, to safely perform erratic course changes. In addition, it cannot be done quickly, so the best you can hope for is to try to *bracket* the target and hope that someone scores a hit.

The lead bombardier had his hands full, trying to track the fast moving ships. I do not think we scored any direct hits, but the fact that the Japanese had to take evasive action made it easier for other units to inflict damage. After dropping our bombs we peeled off the bomb run and made a turn to the south for the trip back to base. It was then that a check of our fuel supply indicated that we had a problem: we didn't have enough fuel to reach Owi. Luck was with us, however, for only a short time ago our forces had been able to push the Japanese off Morotai, which is in the Halmahera Island Group, roughly midway between the Philippines and New Guinea. It was within range despite our limited gas supply. Much to our relief, the primitive airstrip was usable and we were able to land, refuel and continue on to Owi. I remember thinking that we

Sink 13 Leyte Ships; 4,000 Japs Perish

By WILLIAM C. WILSON

Allied HQ., Leyte, P.I., Thursday, Nov. 30 (U.P.).— American bombers and fighters destroyed 13 Jap ships, including three destroyers, and killed an estimated 4,000 more enemy troops in turning back the sixth attempt to land reinforcements on Leyte, it was announced today.

Fighter planes, aided by a small number of medium bombers, of Lieut. Gen. George C. Kenney's 5th Air Force participated in the two-day attack in which seven troop transports, three cargo transports and three destroyers were sunk.

The battle began Tuesday afternoon when the Jap ships were observed in the Camotes Sea, and most of the convoy was destroyed that day. The Americans completed the destruction yesterday, bringing enemy losses in all attempts to reinforce Leyte to 46 ships sunk, including 17 destroyers, and more than 21,00 troops killed.

Believed Vet Jap Division.

Gen. MacArthur said the troops killed in the latest attempt to reach the port of Ormoc on Leyte's west coast, might have been from the veteran Jap 2d Infantry Division. Prisoners taken on the rainsoaked Leyte ground front said they had been told that division was expected to arrive to bolster their wavering defense line in the 18-mile long Ormoc corridor.

Front dispatches reported that the convoy, two ships of which were destroyed after reaching Ormoc, was discovered Tuesday afternoon and was bombed and strafed unmercifully during the remaining daylight hours.

Seven troop transports, three of them of 750 tons, the destroyers and one of the three cargo transports, which were of 1,000 to 2,000 tons each, were sunk "well out at sea," MacArthur announced. Seven Jap fighter planes attempting to protect the convoy also were shot down.

66,000 Enemy Casualties.

Terming the attempts to reinforce Leyte "desperate ones," MacArthur reported that two cargo vessels, which also possibly carried some troops, managed to reach Ormoc and succeeded in partially unloading before they were sunk in the wreck-strewn harbor.

Destruction of the new convoy brought the enemy's losses at sea to 26 transports totaling 92,750 tons and 17 destroyers.

The bulletin also reported that American torpedo bombers and fighters had bombed and strafed the airdrome and troop bivouac areas at Legaspi, on the southern tip of Luzon, and that other planes in widespread missions over the Philippines and Netherlands Indies had sunk 12 Jap ships or barges and damaged nine.

Dispatches from the front said that despite the bad weather American patrols were steadily penetrating deeper toward the Ormoc corridor from dominating ridges on the east and that minor clashes were occurring as the Japs occasionally threw in local counter-attacks.

NEWS AROUND THE CLOCK

from the Daily News is broadcast over WNEW at 1130 on the dial. Regular edition 24 times a day on the half hour. Wakeup editions weekdays from 6:45 to 8:15 on the hour and quarter hour. Extra editions on the hour, whenever news is urgent. Bulletins at once.

DAILY NEWS, THURSDAY, NOVEMBER 30, 1944

NY Daily News, November 30, 1944[22]

had left in darkness and we were returning in darkness. It probably was without doubt the longest, and one of the most tiring missions we would fly. Officially, it was entered into the combat reports as fifteen hours and fifty minutes. The crews that were on that mission were given an award in recognition of their participation in the Battle of Leyte Gulf. Now, we were authorized to wear another ribbon on our uniform, below our wings.

Comparing notes later after mess, we all came to the same conclusion: it was only our third mission, but at this rate, we would become veterans very quickly. Flying for almost sixteen hours in a noisy, vibrating, uncomfortable land-based bomber, over hundreds of miles of water, was a radical new experience. When I closed my eyes and tried to sleep that night, all I could see was the ocean and Japanese ships making sweeping, evasive turns while I frantically and unsuccessfully tried to keep the crosshairs of the bombsight on the target. Much to our relief, a check of the board showed that we were not scheduled to fly the next day. We needed a break to recuperate from the last mission.

"*October 18, 1944*

My little rebel just sent me three more snapshots of herself that keep me smoldering every time I look at them ~ what a girl and do I go for her! I'd like very much for you to meet her ~ she has heard me talk about you so very much that she feels like you've been friends for years. But talking to her is as close as I'll let you get, Zom!

Your Pal,
Sil"

Life on Owi soon settled down to a daily routine. If not scheduled to fly, I would usually write letters during the day and take advantage of natural light. The power generator we had would permit only one fifty or sixty-watt bulb per tent and, little as it was, we were happy to have it. Trying to write or read under that dim light, however, left a lot to be desired. There was the usual softball game in the afternoon, if we felt up to playing after a long mission, followed by the ocean swim. There were other duties, such as officer of the guard or mail censor, which we had to pull. After dark, we would sit under the stars to watch a movie (which I believe was 16-mm) and wonder why it was so dim, but this was the norm. One movie I remember seeing was *The Mask of Dimitrios* starring Zachary Scott, who played the part of an unscrupulous louse. There was malaria and scrub typhus to worry about, so we would keep covered up at all times while at the *cinema*. An *Atabrine officer* was stationed at the exit door of the mess hall and it was his job to see that every man swallowed the pill. The result of this was that in a few weeks, everyone's eyes took on a yellowish color. In addition, we had to take a salt tablet every day to replace the salt lost from the constant sweating.

Although pilot Frank McCullough was not an outgoing type personality, he, Wade, Risley and I shared the tent at Owi, and we got along very well. One night, Frank and I started a game of 500 Rummy, but after playing for a few hours, decided to keep a perpetual score rather than terminating the game at 500. The game went on for our entire stay at Owi. Taking a cue from Zachary Scott, we played a *cutthroat, utterly without scruples* game, unwilling to discard a card that the other could use. We checked the score, before leaving Owi for the move to our next base, and were amazed to learn that only two hundred points separated the winner from the loser. The final score was in the thirteen thousand plus range, but I can't remember who had won.

When my first pay arrived, I was pleasantly surprised to see that it was $260.00. This, of course, included extra *hazard* pay. For all the good it did us, it could have been $2.00, since there was nothing you could buy with the money. With that much unspendable money floating around, card and crap games became popular and some sharks did quite well. I decided to send it all home except for $25.00, and that was more than I needed. When I stepped up to collect my first pay, my thoughts reverted to the day of my induction into the Army on October 20, 1941, when as a private, I was getting the grand sum of $21.00 a month! Well, I was getting paid but very little in 1941, but then again, I wasn't being shot at either!

When we had left Nadzab for Owi, I had put my uke in the nose compartment, near the nose wheel. Somehow, it got shifted around and when the wheel was retracted, it caught the uke and split the end off where the tuning pegs are located. It was a long crack that could be repaired with some model airplane glue and string. Problem was that I didn't have the glue. It was then that I remembered that it was possible to make glue by dissolving celluloid in acetone. I managed to find the celluloid and the acetone down on the flight line, got some thread out of my sewing kit and then took the strings off the uke. That done, I mixed the glue, applied it, and bound the break with the thread, being certain to wind it very close and very tight. When it had dried, I smeared more glue over the thread. It worked!

My next mission, No. 4, was on November 5, 1944 and once again, it was a memorable one. The target was an airfield in Cebu, in the Philippines. It was a typical mission, airborne before dawn and long hours of flying over open ocean. The bombing was good and by all means, it was a success. A moment after bombs away, the bomb bay doors were immediately closed and Frank put the plane in a shallow, diving turn to reduce the chances of being hit by ground fire. Once we had cleared the target area, he followed the customary procedure whereby every man on the plane would call in to report any damage or malfunction. One by one the reports came in, "no damage," "no problem here." Hynes, the engineer, seemed to be slow in making his report, so McCullough repeated the call. It was then that Hynes said that there seemed to be something wrong with the gas gauge. It was reading very low so he checked it a second and third time with the same result: According to the gauge, we didn't have enough fuel to fly 700 miles back to Owi. Now, the unanswerable question was, *did we take a hit in the tank, or is the gas gauge wrong?* After much thought, the only logical decision was to assume that the gauge was ok and that our fuel supply was low. In short order, McCullough contacted the flight leader and explained the problem. In an effort to achieve the greatest fuel efficiency, he throttled back, leaned out the fuel mixture and slowed the plane down to a point just above stalling speed. One of the other planes in the flight came alongside and flew escort for a while, but soon, he pulled out and we were left alone. At this point, it all came down to the navigator, Cliff Risley, who was busy plotting the best course to follow and an estimated time of arrival (ETA). Having done that, there was little to do except sit there and hope the engines would keep running. What made us sweat, however, was the fact that Owi was a very small island, about three miles in diameter. Secondly, as typical in the South Pacific, cloud cover would greatly increase in the afternoon heat making it difficult to see a small island. Cliff had given us an ETA, but the question was what do you do if the ETA runs out and you don't see Owi? Did we pass over it, because of a strong tail wind, and not see it because of the clouds? Perhaps we had a strong head wind which reduced our ground speed, so we haven't gotten there yet, therefore we need to keep going. Another possibility was that a cross wind had blown us off course and that we missed it either to the left or right. Radio silence had to be maintained regardless of our situation, and radar, as we know it today, had not yet come into common use. No one spoke of it, but certainly the possibility of having to ditch was something that we had hoped to avoid. The B24 had a very poor crew survival reputation due to its design. The wing was set high on the fuselage, and did not contribute to the *surfboard effect*, when compared to the B17, which could skim across the water while slowing down. It was *white-knuckle time* for the ten men aboard, but once again luck was with us. A few minutes before the ETA ran out, McCullough dropped down under the clouds and there straight ahead was the most wonderful sight: Owi Island. Following standard procedure, we were de-briefed by the intelligence officer, Capt. Frank Meyer II, and then went to the medical tent for a chat with Dr. Rest. A shot of liquor was available there for those who wanted it, but I declined mine. Someone, I'm sure, managed to get two. Officially, the mission flight time was fifteen hours and thirty-five minutes. This *green crew* was changing its color pretty damn fast. Four missions, total flight time, forty-seven hours twenty minutes.

* * * * *

It is my contention that the average man or woman today has no conception as to what it was like to fly in a combat aircraft. Flying from Newark to Florida for two hours and fifteen minutes in a 727 or 737, in a soundproof, air-conditioned cabin, in a comfortable seat, with on-board toilets, is hardly the basis for understanding what combat crews had to endure. There was no soundproofing. The roar of the four engines and constant vibration seemed to be amplified by the metal skin of the fuselage, much the same way sound is amplified by the body of a guitar. All that separated the crew from the outside was the very thin metal of the fuselage. The interior was cluttered with wiring, plumbing, cables, oxygen tanks, 50-caliber machine guns, ammunition belts and other items too numerous to mention. Radio equipment was mounted on shelves, supported by L-shaped, sharp, metal brackets that were sure to jab you somewhere or snag your parachute or Mae West strap as you attempted to go from one end of the plane to the other. The lower ball turret, located between the waist area and the beginning of the bomb bay, occupied a good part of the available floor space, making it necessary to circle around it when moving through the fuselage. A U-shaped beam, about ten or twelve inches wide, spanned the bomb bay and it was the *connecting road* as we moved from one end of the plane to the other. Walking its length wasn't difficult to do with the bomb bay doors closed, but it was frightening to *take the walk* with them open. The upper Martin turret was mounted behind the pilots which further reduced the available space. As I had mentioned earlier, the bombardier, navigator and nose gunner had to get down on hands and knees, duck under the flight deck and crawl past the nose wheel in order to reach their work stations. Moving about the plane required agility, and certainly, a clumsy person would have more than a few problems. If it should be necessary to relieve oneself, the bomb bay doors were the designated area, but it had to be done cautiously. There was always a movement of air through the bomb bay, and a careless person would be sure to suffer the inevitable spray that would be blown onto his face. Out of necessity we all made it our business to *do our business* before we boarded the plane for takeoff. Today, we have a very descriptive, terse phrase which says it all, but which was not in use in 1944; it was not *user friendly*. Perhaps one can now better understand how we felt after completing two fifteen hour missions. To put it succinctly, *now Zombie*.

Regardless of the mission length, lunchtime had to wait until we had dropped our bombs and felt assured that we had cleared the danger zone. Since I, the bombardier, now had nothing to do, and since the others were still at their assigned places, it fell to me to break out the lunch and start serving. The *menu of the day* usually was whatever was available in a can, and perhaps two loaves of bread. Using a dull knife, I would slice the bread and then open the can, being thankful for the can opener that the cook thoughtfully provided. On this memorable day, we had a large can of vienna sausage. When I finally got the lid off I could see that what was once liquid, had now turned into a semi-frozen, grayish looking, lard-like mass. Just the sight of it was enough to make you forget you were hungry, but stupid me, I went ahead, closed my eyes and took the first bite. I almost got sick. To this very day, I cannot eat anything with white gravy because the image of half-frozen lard just won't fade away.

* * * * *

Mission No. 5, 319D-1, November 14, was a return visit to Licanan Airfield on Cebu Island to complete the job we had started on November 5th. On our way to the target I began to wonder what new adventures awaited us considering the events of the last two outings. Happily, it was routine with no worries about running out of fuel. Things were getting better, since the official flying time was *only* eleven hours and fifty-five minutes. In addition, I wisely anticipated another stomach turning, lard lunch but this time I avoided the problem by bringing a can of tomato juice. After takeoff I placed it on the nose wheel doors located behind me, and it was cold when I drank my *liquid lunch*. Fortunately, juices were available and that was all I would have for lunch on future missions.

While on the subject of repulsive food, number one on my list was the so-called chipped beef on toast which was regularly served. Much before my time, some brilliant Einstein type succeeded in giving it the name it deserved and which was used by everyone to describe it: "Shit on a Shingle (S.O.S.)." It too had white gravy that had the unique ability to destroy appetite on sight. Some of the guys really liked it, which was beyond my comprehension. Perhaps they were from another planet where edible food was scarce. As for me, I never had the guts to taste it, the visual experience being sufficient to avoid it.

Mission No. 6, 320-1, November 15, 1944, target: Lapaz Airdrome, Mindanao

Mission No. 7, 326D-1, November 21, 1944: target: Matina Airfield, Mindanao, 11:45

Mission No. 8, 329D-3, November 24, 1944: target: Matina Airfield, Mindanao, 12:00

There was an interesting sidelight to one of these missions. In 1944, Linden, New Jersey had a population of about twenty-two or twenty-three thousand. I have no idea of how many men from Linden were in the Air Corps or how many of them would be in the 5th Air Force, 22nd Bomb Group, 408th Squadron at the same time. Certainly the percentages against such a happening were very unbelievably high. Even more amazing was that there were three of us, from Linden, flying the very same mission! Sergeant

John Mihlik, Sgt. Jacobi and I were on that mission. John Mihlik lives about four miles from me, but I could never learn anything more about Jacobi. It was an incredible coincidence.

Unlike Hollywood movies, we did not have our own plane. The mission board would show the crew makeup and the number of the plane they would use. Another departure from convention was that some of us were being assigned to fly with different crews. Why this was so has always been a mystery to me. Perhaps they were trying to mix inexperienced personnel with veterans, but I would have preferred to remain with my own crew.

Invariably, we were overloaded on takeoff. The distances to the targets were very great requiring maximum fuel to be carried. In order to make it successful, adequate bomb loads also had to be carried, the net result being that we usually exceeded the supposedly maximum takeoff weight. This contributed to the crash of one of our planes which staggered into the air on takeoff, and retracted the landing gear immediately in an effort to gain airspeed quickly. They never made it. I believe the plane mushed down into the sea. I do not remember if any of the crew survived. At the end of November 1944, we said goodbye to Owi and moved northward to a new base on Anguar, in the Palau Island Group.

Airlifting ourselves to new base in Anguar, Palau Island, November 28, 1944

#984 Shoo Shoo Baby

16

ANGUAR, PALAU ISLAND GROUP

Owi slowly faded from view as we headed northward toward our next base, Anguar in the Palau Island Group, about five hundred fifty miles away. Upon landing, it was clearly evident that it would be a completely different environment. It was a barren, coral island. Very little was left standing after the heavy fighting needed to push the Japanese back into the hills, just a month before our arrival. There they remained an ever present danger, holed up in caves, and capable of infiltrating into our camp area. Guards were needed, especially at night, and those who had been assigned to guard duty did so with the intention of shooting first and asking questions afterwards. The move was in keeping with the so-called *leapfrog strategy* which seemed to be very successful. The object of all this, of course, was to liberate the Philippines and then go on to Japan for the final showdown.

After landing, we were taken to our camp area which looked liked *tent shanty town*. The floor of our tent can best be described as a layer of coral rocks, quite capable of inflicting wounds to bare feet. At first opportunity, I went looking for some of the steel mats that were put down on runways, lugged them back to the tent and placed them alongside my cot. Now I had something to stand on while putting on my socks and shoes. The paths to the mess hall, latrines and operations shack were covered with rather large coral fragments that could easily result in a twisted ankle. Owi, by comparison, was a resort.

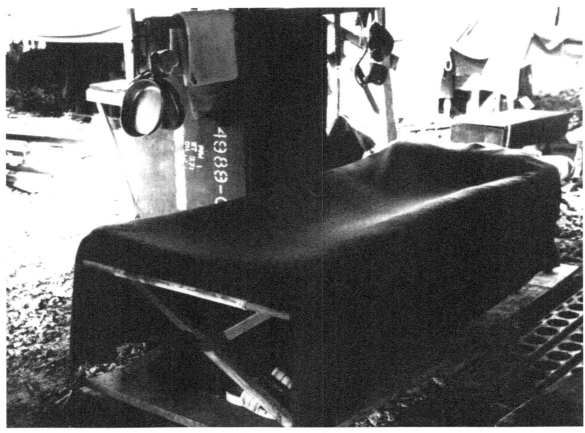

My bed at the Anguar Ambassador Hotel, Palau Islands. We had it all, including "coral lawn."

Mission No. 9, 335A-6, November 30, 1944 was our first one from Anguar. The target was Legaspi Airfield on the island of Luzon in the Philippines. Time: 10 hours, 45 minutes.

Mission No. 10, 341-A, December 6, 1944: Target: Lahug Airfield, Cebu. Time: 9 hours, 45 minutes.

Mission No. 11, 352-A16, December 17, 1944: Target: Bacolod Airfield, Negros Island. Time: 11 hours.

We had always known that eventually we would begin flying missions to the most important target in the Philippines which was Clark Field on the island of Luzon. We also were of the opinion that it would be there that the Japanese would put up a tough fight in order to keep this very important facility.

Clark Field was on a plateau, about sixty miles north of Manila and had a long history. I believe it had its origins during World War I and had figured prominently in the development of aviation in that part of the world. Immediately after Pearl Harbor, the Japanese scored a major victory when they captured it; and in the process, reduced many of our aircraft to junk. It was vital to them, and our strategists felt that it had to be retaken before we could continue on to Japan itself. Fighter planes had attacked it; but we, the 22nd, would be the first heavy bomber group to hit it. Now, flying from Anguar, it was within range of our B24's.

Looking westward, the flat plain of Clark Field soon gave way to low hills and they in turn, gradually rose and became mountains. For the bombardiers, what we liked when we studied pictures of the target, was the sight of Mt. Arayat; a symmetrical mountain rising from the middle of the flat plain. It stuck out like the proverbial sore thumb, and I always thought it was shaped like a chocolate Hershey kiss. This landmark, our *initial point*, was what we would be looking for. Once there, we would turn left toward the airfield and make a bombing run on our assigned targets. For once, locating the target would be easy. It was a successful mission and one from which we derived great satisfaction. It was my 12th mission, No. 357A-20, Time: Fifteen hours and the date was December 22, 1944.

* * * * *

Long ago, we learned that every time we moved to a new base, our mail would be disrupted and it would take weeks for it to catch up to us. The move to Anguar was no different. It had been a month since I had received any mail from home, but happily, there were a few from P38. There are no words to express how important it was to hear your name called at mail call. We were out of touch with the world with only bits and pieces of information filtering down to us long after it ceased to be headline news. It was not unusual to receive letters that were recently written reach us before those that were sent a month ago. It was fun trying to figure out what was being referred to, in letter #1, which had not yet been received, when reading letter #2. Music? Eskimos probably knew more than we did as to what was number one on the hit parade. I still had the patched-up uke, so the old songs got plenty of playing time.

In one of her letters, P38 told me that her brother, Edwin, was with an anti-aircraft unit on Peleliu which was the island just north of Anguar. We had never met and there was no way to get there without a boat. So near and yet so far.

December 26, 1944 - 408[23]

"Flying out of Anguar, in the Palau Islands, the 408th Squadron led a Group formation to bomb a Japanese aircraft dispersal area at Clark Field, Luzon, in the Philippine Islands, from 11,000 feet. Ten minutes after bombs away, what was probably a Japanese Army Ki-84 Frank fighter assigned to the *30th Sento Hiko Shudan* (30th Fighter Flying Divisional Group), attacked the lead element out of the sun at 1145 hours. The nose turret gunner in the plane on the right wing of the formation, B-24J-175 #44-40723, was killed and the Liberator's right engine was shot out. Although badly damaged, the plane made it safely back to base without further incident."

GRAHAM, Sgt. Thomas W; Aerial Gunner

December 26, 1944 - 408[24]

"Completing its first pass, the Frank fighter, in the incident above dove between the lead aircraft and the left wing plane, then rolled over to attack again from 10 o'clock below. During this pass under the formation, it raked the belly and tail of the lead plane, B-24J-90 #42-100310, which was piloted by the Squadron Commander, Maj. Ferdinand R. Schmidt, with machinegun fire and 20-mm. cannon shells. One projectile hit an ammunition tray which exploded, killing the right waist gunner and badly wounding the radio operator, T/Sgt. Vergil R. Skore, who was manning the left waist gun. Fire from gunners on either wing of the flight apparently hit the Japanese fighter at this point and smoke was seen trailing from the plane. Three crewmen on one of the B-24s, reported seeing the pilot bail out. The damaged plane, nicknamed *STRIKE (II)*, flew directly to Tacloban Strip on Leyte where Woodward's body was removed. The badly wounded radio operator was taken to Hollandia aboard a hospital ship, and was later returned to the States to complete his recovery."

WOODWARD, T/Sgt., Billy B; Aerial Gunner

For the Duration *plus* Six Months

Anguar, Palau Islands, December 1944. It would soon be Christmas and I was writing a letter to Santa Claus. I told him that I didn't want any toys. There was just one thing on my list; *send me home*! I guess he never got my letter because I'm still here. Maybe I should have put a stamp on it because our free postage privilege did not extend to the North Pole.

Chapter 16

Quoting from my letter of December 31st to Carl:

"I read a book Christmas Eve, played a game of cards with some friends and went to bed. The next day, Christmas Day, I played ball and came away with a beautiful black eye, the result of colliding skulls with the shortstop, Major Schmidt, the Sqdn. Commander. I went to the medical tent where they took a couple of x-rays, (that certainly brought back memories of Langley Field!) found no damage and sent me away. Some Christmas gift. We have a league here on the island, and we are in first place. I play second base, but I would much rather be out in centerfield."

Still retaining the memory of good swimming at Owi, Wade and I thought we would check out the beach at Anguar and get away from the heat. First, we had to find the beach since it was cluttered with shot up landing craft and an assortment of other rusting hulks. The surf looked kind of rough, but we stupidly gave it a try. In a few moments, we realized that we had better get the hell out of there before we would be bashed up against one of the souvenirs left over from the invasion. So much for cooling off.

Going to the *evening cinema* at Anguar could be less than enjoyable. The possibility of having our cave dwelling *neighbors* infiltrate under the cover of darkness was always a possibility. Then again, looking at the bright side, it was free.

Without doubt, the wackiest thing that happened at Anguar was that we were almost shot down on a non-combat mission. This is the way it happened. Five of the crew, McCullough, Wade, Hynes, Risley and I were sent up to *swing a compass*. What this meant was that we had to check the accuracy of the compass, by flying in various directions, and it could be done nicely by using the bombsight. Since the geographical direction of the runway was known, using the sight, I would line up with the runway and the compass would be read. Any deviation would be noted and a card would be placed with the compass to indicate the error. We were flying low, about a thousand feet, as we made a pass over the runway and continued northward over Peleliu and then over Babelthuap before turning to head back to Anguar. It was then that we noticed, to our amazement, the black puffs of anti-aircraft fire around us. What we didn't know was that there was a great concentration of Japanese still on the island. They were quite capable of sending up a barrage when a fat target presented itself, flying low and straight, right over their guns. Mac really hauled ass to get us out of there. I learned years later that another B24 had been shot down when they innocently flew over Babelthuap, such as we had done.

Mission No. 13, 3A-1, January 3, 1945: Target: Mabalacat, Luzon, Time: 14 hours, 5 minutes, was a disaster and I identified it as such in my personal mission list. I have long since forgotten the details, but I do remember that every man on every plane was required to write a written report. Some of the reports were very brief, but our crew went into great detail, even quoting intercom conversations that were exchanged. To the best of my knowledge, nothing more was heard from Group Headquarters about that mission.

I now had one hundred fifty-five hours of combat flying time and had qualified for "Rest and Recreation." The only problem was that we were too far away from Sydney, Australia, where others had gone in the past, and there was nowhere else to go. That being the case, I just kept flying missions.

It was the middle of January 1945 when we ceased operations from Anguar and prepared to move up to Guiuan on the island of Samar. Once again, we were cautioned about the health risks on Samar; the familiar scrub typhus and malaria. There had been some deaths from these diseases, and we were reminded to keep covered up and protect our legs.

For the Duration *plus* Six Months

Still just a big flirt, but Sid ole Boy, it's you I really love.

17

WELCOME TO SAMAR, THE KITCHEN IS OPEN

The flight from Anguar to Samar was routine. After crawling off the plane, we boarded trucks for the trip from the flight line, traversing roads where the mud was almost half way up the truck wheels. Finally, the trucks stopped and we were told to get off, since this was our new campsite. As we stepped into the muddy road, all I could see of the so-called *campsite* was a hill about twenty-five feet above the road. The top of the hill was barely large enough to pitch a tent, and worst of all, it was covered in very tall grass; the very situation we were warned to avoid. When we got to the top, we noticed that there were very large, coral-type boulders everywhere, further reducing the available level ground we needed to set up housekeeping. Disgusted as we were, there was no time to waste if we were to have shelter before dark, so setting up the tent was our next task. Taking stock of the area, we finally found a suitable site, situated between two very large boulders, and proceeded to put up the tent. When finished, we gazed at our new home: a tent with a 20-inch high, luxurious growth of grass inside it to keep us company. The next task was to open up a cot and set up the mosquito netting above it, hoping that there were no mosquitoes trapped inside. It was now chow time, and we eventually found the mess tent and were served something that looked vaguely like food, but some doubt existed in the minds of those who had guts enough to eat it. Memories of Townesville came to mind, where we had survived on coffee and doughnuts at the Red Cross Canteen on the flight line. Unfortunately, I did not see one when we landed. Considering the bright side, we didn't have to worry about gaining weight.

Needless to say, we did not have any light in our new quarters, having to use our flashlights once it got dark. It had been a long day, it was getting dark and we didn't have a thing except a cot, mosquito netting and a flashlight, so the only sensible thing to do was just go to bed. Under civilized conditions, we would wash up and brush teeth, but that was out of the question since the only water we had was what was left in our canteens. It was at that very moment that a new problem arose to challenge us. I was standing alongside the cot, hands, shoes and clothes full of mud, trying to figure out how I could undress without exposing myself to mosquitoes or ticks. Every possible solution seemed to have a down side and was soon discarded. Completely frustrated, I said "the hell with it" and decided to sleep with my clothes on. I pulled up the mosquito netting just enough to slide under it, sat on the edge of the cot, took off my shoes, pulled my feet in. and quickly tucked the netting back in place. At last! Now my only concern was the possibility that there might be mosquitoes, spending the night with me, inside the net. Muddy as they were, my clothes would provide some protection.

Strange sounds awakened us during the night, something which we could not immediately identify. Finally, we realized that it was the sound of rats jumping from the nearby rocks and scurrying around on the roof of the tent. This was something that was not covered in *Samar 101*. In addition to Wade and myself, there were two squadron mates sharing the tent. Though no word had been spoken, I would bet money that we all had considered one possible solution to the rat problem: Get our 45 pistols and shoot them. Welcome to Samar.

The first order of business the next day, was to get rid of the grass in the tent. While working, I wondered where our *roof friends* had gone and if they would return to entertain us again. We knew the solution to making life more livable: we needed to get some plywood to construct a floor. We also knew where to get it; go to the Navy. The Navy had everything; good food, showers, building material and what ever else we might need. Armed with two hundred dollars American money, we trudged down to their camp site and told them that we wanted to buy some plywood and would be willing to give them two hundred dollars for it. The ensuing laughter could be heard back on Owi. Money was worthless, so we left empty handed. Back in our hilltop paradise, some good soul produced a bottle of scotch, so we visited the Navy again and this time offered them the liquor for the plywood. That did it! I believe they even delivered it since we did not have the means to haul eight pieces of 4 x 8 plywood. Our construction project, however, had to be put on hold because the Air Corp was of the opinion that it was more important to fly a mission than have a floor in our tent. How inconsiderate of them, we thought.

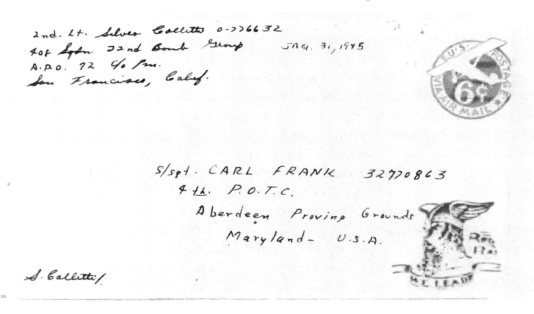

"Dear Zom,

Mail call overseas is anywhere between the hours of 0001 and 2359.99. Last night a whole batch of mail came in and I almost suffered a breakdown, nervous, one each, when I found a November 2nd letter from Earl, two on October 20th from P38, and October 20th letter from you in addition to one of January 11th. Perhaps you can now see why I say the mail situation was a little screwed up!

You're not kidding when you say "I have a case." I do and I know it. If it isn't the real thing, Zom, then I'm going to make an awful fool of myself because I've told my folks how I feel about her. She took advantage of an opportunity I gave her, to write to my folks when I asked her to forward some pics to them. She told them the whole works, started with "I love him" and ended up the same way! Now if only I could whittle down the 11,000 miles that separate us!"

Chapter 17

Mission No. 14, 17A-1, January 17, 1945 took us to Luzon to bomb an airstrip at Legaspi. Time: 6 hours, 15 minutes.

Mission No. 15, 20A-1, January 20, 1945. The target was the Bambam disposal area. It was one of our best missions. It was also my last mission in the month of January, and we took advantage of the down time to try to improve our living conditions.

On January 31, I went over to the operations tent to check the mission schedule. My name was up on the board and I had to read it more than once before I convinced myself that I had read it correctly: "Mission No. 32A-l, February 1, 1945: Target Corregidor Island. Lead bombardier: Colletti."

If I recall correctly, the target was a building known as the *Blockhouse* and was difficult to hit because it was protected by natural barriers. Results were average. What I do remember, however, was the realization that I was flying over an area that had great historical significance. Regardless of my accomplishments, whether much or little, it gave us a great deal of satisfaction in knowing that we were doing our part in driving out the enemy.

Mission No. 17, 36A-1, February 5, 1945: Target Corregidor. I was the lead bombardier and this time we did very well.

Mission No. 18, 41A-1, February 10, 1945 was the third mission to Corregidor, but I was not the lead bombardier. I now had a total of one hundred eighty-six combat hours.

* * * * *

The standard operating procedure in making a move from one base to another was to send half the outfit to the new location and keep the other half behind. Then after the forward base had been established, the rear echelon would move up. Therefore, the net result of all this was that our so-called *mess hall* and *kitchen* was in reality, nothing more than a tent. The stoves occupied what space there was, so a good deal of the pot scrubbing, washing and food preparation had to be done outdoors. The instrument of choice for delivering water to perform these tasks was a garden hose, and quickly, the area around the kitchen became a muddy mess and remained so thanks to the daily rain. Needless to say, the ambiance contributed greatly to our dining pleasure under the stars.

Reveille, for those scheduled to fly, was about 3:00 AM, well before dawn. Considering our intelligence level, it was difficult to understand why any of us believed that it was worthwhile to have breakfast. Perhaps I enjoyed the feeling of pain, for I was one of the hardy souls who got his butt out of bed to feast upon the offerings of the day. With open mess kit in hand, in total darkness, I joined all other fools in a single file line about two hundred feet long. The line was not straight, however, since we had to snake around the large boulders that graced the area. In the distance, we could see the solitary light on the roof of the kitchen, piercing the darkness. Half asleep, we proceeded slowly, eventually reaching the food server, standing under the light, who plopped the *food* into the mess kit. Now, all that remained was to find some place to sit down and eat. Since the choice was limited, we would select one of the coral boulders and hope that the rats didn't mind the intrusion. Breakfast, the very first day on Samar, was identified by someone as being a pancake. We had pancakes on the second and third day. On the fourth day, nothing had changed, except the fact that the line was a little shorter because some of the men had come to the conclusion that it wasn't worth the effort. Surely, I thought, this would soon change for the better, so I continued to show up.

This went on for twenty-seven days! Being a stubborn ass, I was determined to see it through. On the twenty-eighth day, the menu was changed to french toast. On the twenty-ninth day, we were back to the pancakes. Finally, I too came to the conclusion that *I should have stayed in bed.*

"Kitchen" January 22, 1945

There was one interesting sidelight to one of those mornings. While trudging in line, half-asleep with my open mess kit in hand, it began to rain. When the fool ahead of me moved up, I would move up, until we finally reached the promised land; the kitchen. My *reward* was dropped into my mess kit and I turned to find a place to sit. What I hadn't realized, and couldn't see because of the darkness, was that I had about a quarter inch of water in the pan and my pancake was sloshing around in it. Lesson learned: water is not a good substitute for pancake syrup (which was not available.)

At long last, the food situation on lovely Samar seemed to improve, now that the pancake debacle was behind us, but there are always exceptions. On the way to the mess hall one day, I had no way of knowing that the menu called for my *favorite*, chipped beef on toast, which was always referred to as S.O.S. In my book, S.O.S rated on par with half-frozen vienna sausage as a *substance to be avoided* unless you had become desperate enough to eat tree roots. When it was my turn, the server informed me that they were all out of toast leaving just the chipped beef. It was then that I turned to Wade and said,

"Today the kitchen ran out of shingles, so they just served the shit. I wonder what they will be serving tomorrow?" Whatever it was, I didn't plan to be there to find out.

One of the first things I learned on that long trip from the United States to Australia was the importance of toilet paper, an item which we never think about until you find yourself in a situation where you don't have any. Then, you think about it, but that does little to solve the problem. The smart thing to do was to hoard a roll and always take it with you to the latrine. Once there, you looked around to see if there was any available. If there was, you saved your hoarded roll and used the *in-house roll*.

The one bright spot on the otherwise poor food situation was what we called the *Fat Cat*. This referred to a C47 transport plane, which made a trip back to Australia once a month. Everyone would chip in five dollars and the money was used to buy anything that would survive the trip back to the base.

I believe it started in Owi, and I don't know if it was authorized, but it certainly was a lifesaver for it kept me supplied with the juices I drank while on a mission. I believe they waited until the very last moment, before making the return trip, to load up with fresh eggs and milk. Since we did not have any refrigeration, the perishables had to be used quickly. We went from the ridiculous to the sublime, eating eggs and drinking milk three times a day. When it was gone, we went back to S.O.S.

View from camp area to road. Morty Boyle on far left.

Rear view of tent on slope of the hill. Front is on the ground.

    Happy were we when we finally finished working on our hill top house. There never really was enough space on the top of the hill, so we decided to make an engineering change. We were indeed fortunate in having Morty Boyle, the squadron engineering officer, as one of our tent mates. He helped us get a few empty 55-gallon steel drums in addition to nails, tools and building material. Using our collective wisdom, we decided to move the tent back onto the slope of the hill, with one end on the ground and the other end supported by the steel drums. Next, we put down a half-ass-frame and then laid the plywood on top of it. Ergo, no mud in the tent. While I had the tools, I constructed a simple washstand that was large enough to hold two steel helmets. One helmet was used to lather up, and the other was filled with rinse water, but the nuisance of lugging five gallons of fresh water still remained. I have no idea where he found them, but Wade came back to the tent one day with four horseshoes, none of which matched. Boyle got us two metal rods for stakes, which we promptly drove into the ground in front of the tent. The fact that one stake was on higher ground than the other, didn't faze us. So what if we had to pitch uphill and then downhill? It just made the game more interesting. After a day or two of itching, however, it became obvious that we were doing a lot of sweating and needed a bath. Since we didn't have a tub, we cleverly thought to take advantage of the daily afternoon rain. We would begin pitching horseshoes, working up a sweat while keeping an eye on the developing cloud formations. Using our superior intellect, we tried to determine when the first raindrop would fall, and when the time seemed right, began to lather up. We congratulated each other on being so clever, but what we hadn't considered was how *cold* the rain would be as we stood out there, bare-ass-naked, shivering while the rain rinsed off the soap. Of course, when the rain stopped the heat returned. Despite the shivering, we thought it was a good idea because we didn't have to wait for the showers to be turned on. With each passing day, we were learning how to cope with Samar.

Wade (left) and Silveo pitching horseshoes, February 1945

Mission No. 19, 44A-1, February 13, 1945, Target: Japanese Naval Force, Time: 13 hours, 20 minutes. Once again, I was the lead bombardier for my flight, but we could not locate the naval force which was almost completely hidden by cloud cover.

The mission, though disappointing, was a milestone for me since I would be the lead bombardier for all the missions that followed.

Rain, mud, disease, poor living conditions and bad food were not the only conditions which we faced in our daily existence. The so-called *business* we were in was hazardous even when not engaging the Japanese. Had any of us applied for life insurance, I am certain we would have been dismissed as jokers and turned away as being poor risks. Week after week of flying long missions in overloaded planes was not the safest way to earn a living. The event of January 22, 1945 sadly proved just how risky it could be.

Colonel Robinson, age twenty-six, was the commander of the 22nd Bomb Group. The "Red Raiders" logo which identified us was inspired by his red hair. He had flown more than seventy missions and had received a great many decorations.

On this particular day, Colonel Robinson was aboard the B24 that would be leading the first daylight mission to Formosa. They were carrying four, two-thousand pound bombs and maximum fuel load. As they accelerated for takeoff, their left wingtip struck a parked Navy Corsair, chopping of more than six feet of the wing. The B24 then staggered slightly into the air finally striking a large Sea Bee bulldozer type machine that was working on the far end of the strip. There were multiple explosions followed by a big fire as the onboard fuel ignited. The eleven men on board the B24 and the Sea Bee equipment operator were all victims of the fire. All operations were cancelled for the remainder of the day. Obviously, the business we're in is not conducive to longevity.

Red Raiders logo[25]

I clearly remember the thoughts I had, way back when I had flown the first few missions, about the *enemy* we could do nothing about: the weather. We had the means to retaliate when attacked by the Japanese, but there was nothing we could do about the weather. Returning from a mission, I would stare in awe at the multiple thunderhead clouds, lined up like pickets on a fence, spread across the horizon. Somewhere, on the other side of the clouds was Owi or Anguar. To get there, we only needed to fly over hundreds of miles of ocean and somehow find a way to get past the clouds. We knew we could not go over them, since they rose to an altitude of thirty to forty thousand feet, much higher than the ceiling of the B24. We could not circle around them, because our fuel supply was insufficient. Going through them would be suicide, due to the violent, vertical winds within the cloud. The only option was to go down on the deck and fly under the cloud where our only worry was very heavy rain and very little visibility. Mother Nature had the ability to make us feel insignificant. I would rather take on the Japanese.

A check of my record revealed that I had logged two hundred combat hours. Three hundred hours was needed to complete a duty tour, so I needed but one hundred more. Of course, this criteria was not etched in stone, and in February, it was raised to four hundred hours. That was in effect for just a short time when it was changed again to a new, formula system where points were awarded based upon the difficulty of the mission. In addition, one point was awarded for every five hours of combat time with a total of one hundred points needed to complete a duty tour. Nothing like having the rules changed in the middle of the ball game. Then again, look at all the fun we were having at government expense!

I was pleased to be flying as lead bombardier, regardless of the increased responsibility. At the briefing the night before, I tried to learn all I could about the mission, including the level of expertise of the other bombardiers. It is said that self-evaluation is fool's work but I always felt that I was professional in doing my job and had thoroughly prepared for the task ahead.

A typical mission required the lead ship to find and identify a previously selected, prominent landmark or terrain feature which would then be referred to as the *initial point*. Once there, we would turn onto a heading which would lead to the target. The distance from the initial point to the target could be short or long, but somewhere along that route, the bombardier would have to begin his bomb run.

The lead bombardier was responsible for *killing the course* and not be concerned with getting hits with his bombs. Certainly, it would be better if he could score, but it was more important to lead the other planes in the formation to the target. The other bombardiers, relieved of the course task, could concentrate on *killing the rate*, meaning not to hit over or short of the target.

On the bomb run, it was essential for the pilot to maintain constant altitude and airspeed and quickly react to the course corrections that I was making with each turn of the course knob on the bombsight. After I had made my final corrections and had synchronized on the target, the bomb run would continue until bombs away. It was during that time, while flying at constant airspeed, constant altitude and constant course, with the bomb bay doors open, that we became sitting ducks for anti-aircraft guns and intercepting enemy planes. Obviously, reducing the length of the bomb run would reduce the risk. Depending upon the distance from the initial point to the target, evasive action would be taken until I reached the point where I had to level off and begin the bomb run. After nineteen missions, I had enough confidence in myself to shorten the bomb run to thirty or forty seconds, and was happy with the result after trying it. It gave me great satisfaction to report on the intercom: "Bombs away, let's get the hell out of here," which were the words all the men on the mission were anxious to hear. I was conscientious about doing my job, but I also believed in survival.

Back on the ground, we all got a laugh from an incident which took place about a week after setting up our tents on Samar. Lt. Jim Cooty was the squadron armaments officer and was responsible for guns, bombs and turrets, etc. He was not a flying officer and there was something about him that was a little odd. His tent was next to ours and at the end of one day we noticed that he had returned with half of a 50-caliber machine gun. The next day, he brought the other half. Considering his job, we paid scant attention. Soon, parts of a Martin gun turret and ammunition belt found their way to his *Hilltop Hilton*, and then another machine gun. Finally unable to contain his curiosity, Morty Boyle cornered him and asked, "Cooty, what the hell are you doing with all this stuff you've brought back?"

He replied, "As soon as I get everything set up, I'm going to shoot those damn rats off the roof of the tent." We didn't know if we should laugh or be concerned! Fighting to keep a straight face, Boyle noticed a paper back book in Cooty's back pocket and asked,

"What's the title of the book?"

Reply: "Strange Fruit." As it turned out, he *was* smarter than everyone. He went home on a Section 8: Mentally Incompetent. We all should have been that nutty!

Of all the missions I had flown to date, I derived the greatest satisfaction from the three to Corregidor Island, because I could identify with that target in a rather peculiar way. In order to understand the reason for this, it is necessary to go back to December of 1941, when I was in the medical department having been transferred to Langley Field, Virginia soon after the attack on Pearl Harbor.

One of the outstanding radio newsman of that era was Gabriel Heatter who might be thought of as the Walter Cronkite of his day. If memory serves correctly, he came on at 9:00 at night and we would listen to his broadcast, lying in bed in total darkness, since the lights were turned off at that hour. He would begin his broadcasts with his trademark first few words, "Ah, there's good news tonight," but in reality there was little good news coming from the Philippines because the Japanese were able to do as they pleased with little or no resistance. One of the most important topics of his broadcasts was the Bataan Death March and what was happening on the island of Corregidor. He spoke of the atrocities being committed there upon our troops who had surrendered, and to Filipino civilians. It did not make for easy listening and coming on the heels of Pearl Harbor, one could not help but feel outraged. Whether we admitted it or not, I for one could not help but feel *the need to get even*. Someday, somehow, the tables would turn and I hoped that, in some small way, I could contribute to it. That day did arrive on February 5, 1945 when I was the lead bombardier on a mission to Corregidor. It was *pay back time* for me, since we plastered the target.

For some of us, there was a religious conflict that had to be addressed as our bombs exploded on the ground. The Bible said "Thou shalt not kill," but how could we live with that commandment when we were in uniform and had taken an oath of office? As for myself, I wasn't a very good Catholic. However, I did attend mass while overseas and received, as was the case with many of the others, special dispensation to perform my duties. I had no way of knowing if that sufficed for the devout, since we seldom discussed it. Each man kept his own counsel and coped with the conflict as best he could. I lost no sleep over it and took comfort from the fact that we were bombing military targets, such as airfields, ports, ammunition dumps and supply centers that were in countries that had been overtaken by the Japanese. I had no guilty feelings about doing my job when I thought of the unprovoked bombing of Pearl Harbor. It was very satisfying to know that the tables had been turned and they, the Japanese, were now on the receiving end of our bombing. Perhaps another way of saying  what I felt was to recall one of the more popular songs of the day: "Praise the Lord and Pass the Ammunition."[26] This is part of the lyric: "Praise the Lord, we're on a mighty mission. All aboard, we're not a-going fishing. Praise the Lord, and pass the ammunition, and we'll all stay free." What was our state of mind? If we didn't fight and win, we all might have ended up speaking English with a Japanese accent and worshipping Buddha. I believe that I can accurately state that we all hated the Japanese, at that time, and felt no guilt in doing what we had to do.

One thing I could never understand about some of my squadron mates was their indifference in regard to survival, for it seemed that they had quickly forgotten what we had learned back in the jungles of New Guinea. The missions from Owi and Anguar had been flown over hundreds of miles of open ocean, where this knowledge was useless, but now that had changed. Operating from Samar, our targets were primarily over landmasses; the Philippines and Formosa, where this knowledge could be used.

Our parachute back packs contained such items as a machete, fishing line and hooks, a signaling mirror, specially designed to reflect the sun toward a rescue craft, a compass, some simple medications and morphine which was to be used to kill pain (The morphine eventually had to be removed because some of the idiots were getting high on it.) There were probably other items which I have forgotten. It was my belief that in the event of a bail out or successful crash landing, we would have a fair chance of surviving if we had some protection. The pilots, navigator and I were always aware of our approximate geographical position, so we had some idea of the best direction to walk in an attempt to seek help. In addition, the Filipinos were not the enemy. Keeping this in mind, I always wore my best, comfortable shoes, underwear, best pair of socks and a hat for protection from the sun. Our flying suits had long sleeves, which was a must. What I saw, instead, was outright stupidity; I can't think of any other word to use. I distinctly recall one bombardier going on a mission dressed in a flying suit, *moccasins*, no socks, no underwear, small overseas cap and a big smile. His feet would have been chopped liver in a matter of days.

Taking inventory of the parachute backpacks would have revealed that the machete had been left under the cot in the tent, where it had been used to open coconuts or chop tent stakes to a point. The mirror was probably hung up somewhere to be used for shaving. The fishing line and compass were everywhere except where they might be most needed. So much for the backpack! Parachutes were seldom checked to see if the ripcord was bent, in which case the chute might not open. They were thrown around, used for pillows and never given proper care. Unbelievable.

* * * * *

Much to my surprise, days went by without my name up on the board. My last mission was on February 13th, more than ten days ago. I wasn't unhappy about the chance to rest, but my curiosity led me to check with the operations officer. The answer was simple: I had two hundred combat hours; more than many of the other bombardiers, so I sat while they flew. Toward the end of February 1945, we got the good news which we had been eagerly awaiting; at the end of the month, we would soon be leaving Samar for Clark Field, Luzon and we would be airlifting ourselves. There wasn't a dry eye in the place when we got the word.

Many times, I have searched my limited vocabulary in an attempt to describe how we felt about *this* island, but unfortunately, words failed me. Many years later, I read these few lines, written by someone who probably had a *Samar experience* of his own. I cannot take credit for the statement, for all I did was substitute one geographical location for another. I quote: "If the powers that be, in their infinite wisdom, decided that it was necessary to give the world an enema, THIS is where the nozzle would have been inserted." Even Winston Churchill on his best day could not have said it better.

ADDRESS INFORMATION

Another of Lt. Colletti's pin-up girls—!

"Colquitt, GA
February 20, 1945

Dearest Colletti,
Just finished reading your last letter again and am glad you like my "art work." First time I saw these sketches in the newspaper they reminded me of the native girls in the picture my brother Courtney sent from the Philippines.

Latest news flash. Thirteen of the air bases in this section of the country are going to close within a month's time. Got it from the inside, but personally I don't understand it. Something big is definitely up.

Napier Field is on the list and Roy plans to get a three-day pass so that he can visit us before he is shipped out. We'll also celebrate our birthdays. Can't believe I'll be nineteen.

Carl wrote and said that he might be transferred, so I sent him the picture I had promised to send to you ~ so you will have to get it from him.

Say, our mailman is a lulu! The Post Mistress didn't want to send that package containing the film to you, but he did some fast-talking and they're on their way to you. He told her he just couldn't let me down since we write so many "sugar reports" to each other!

You asked me about the German POWs and I will try to answer some of your questions. I believe the reason *that they are allowed to work on the farms is because the farmer's don't have enough help to gather the crops now that so many of the farm boys are away in the armed forces. They are not forced to work, it is on a voluntary basis and the farmers pay the P.O.W's at an hourly rate for the work they do.*

It is really funny to see how they come out to the farms - the prisoners are riding in a truck and there are guards in a jeep in front and behind the truck. No one can understand why there are so many guards because it is unlikely the prisoners would try to escape! Where would they go? AND, where would they have it so good!?! They have a camp at the air base in Bainbridge complete with their own kitchen and their own cooking staff. They make a list of the supplies they need and the base supply officer gets it for them. I know one thing, their favorite meat is pork.

No one is afraid of the prisoners. Actually, if they were dressed in American uniforms and mixed in with a group of our servicemen, you could not tell the German from the American. I had always thought of Germans as being blond with blue eyes, but not so. Just goes to show you how little I know.

Mama thinks every young man is one of her "help" and treats them as such, making sure that there is plenty of ice water for them when they are working out in the fields. When they come up to the house at lunchtime, she has iced tea, cold milk, cake and cookies for them. She asked the guard if LuLu (our cook) could fry some chicken or something for them but the guard told her they had good lunches prepared by their own people. That was when he told us about their arrangements for cooking back at the base.

One of the POWs heard me playing the piano one day and he asked the guard if it might be possible for him to play the piano. You should have heard him! He had been a concert pianist in Germany and he made our upright Baldwin sound like a grand piano. After he played for a while, he started playing boogie woogie - the other workers were stamping their feet and shaking everything else trying to keep time with him.

I certainly didn't have the talent this cat had on the piano, but I sure as heck could outshoot him. As silly as it might seem, the prisoners and guards often spent their break time in a competition to see who could shoot the best. When doing their "target" practice the prisoners and the guards would brag about their shooting ability, but I just had to be a smart ass and say that I could do that good myself. I had to prove it to them before they would believe me. Heck, nobody could hit a bull's eye better than daddy could and he taught me how to shoot when I was knee high to a grasshopper. You must think it odd that I would be doing target practice with POW's and I suppose it is odd. When they arrive, the guards do whatever they want and the POW's are on their own. For the most part, guards' guns are just lying in the jeeps and nobody worries about them. I don't know how they decided to start with the target practice. Now you can understand why none of the POW's would want to go home. Here they have a roof over their heads, receive medical attention, enjoy the nice weather, get paid for any work they do, get all the food they want plus they don't have to worry about bombs blowing them up. Wish that our boys would be treated half as well.

Good heavens, Mama just reminded me I was supposed to visit grandmamma and check on how she is doing. Calvin saddled my horse an hour ago – so as the lone ranger would say "high ho and away!"

Promise to write you tomorrow and remind you of how much I miss you.

All my love,
P38"

18

CLARK FIELD, LUZON, PHILLIPINE ISLANDS

On March 1, 1945, we loaded our precious belongings into our flying boxcar, said goodbye to Samar, and hoped that all the unpleasant memories would soon be forgotten. Next stop: Clark Field, Luzon. It was on December 22, 1944 when Clark Field was first hit by heavy bombers and we had the satisfaction of being on that fifteen-hour mission. Now, we would be taking over as the new occupants.

As we approached the outskirts of the base, I twisted my head so that I could once again see Mt. Arayat rising on the plain below. What a difference a few months makes! To leave Samar and come to Clark Field was to return to civilization.

Our new camp area was smooth, level, dry and the tents were laid out in a neat, large, rectangle about 300 feet long. The latrine was located well beyond the last tent, and it was a long walk if the call of nature could not be suppressed (more about that later.) It was a standard GI six-seater (or eight?), but best of all, it was *screened in*. Buildings constructed from bamboo became the mess hall, kitchen and operations office. The commanding officer had the first *accommodation* (which was a rectangular hut) and Wade, Boyle, Eisele and I shared the tent next to the hut. There were open air showers and you could actually feel dry after toweling off. Native women appeared on the scene and were hired to do our laundry. The cost was next to nothing, but they always insisted that we give them a new cake of soap with every wash. Obviously, the soap was more precious to them than the money. We hired two of them. I named one "Tondelayo" and the other "Scherezade."

Tondelayo and Scherezade

After unloading the boxcars, we erected our tent, retrieved our precious plywood, put it down, extended the tent flaps to a horizontal position and tied them

there. Now there would be ventilation through the tent. Surely, all this luxury would spoil us! However, one vexation to the spirit remained: we still had to lug the heavy, five gallon GI can to the mess hall and back in order to have water for drinking and personal needs. Surely, I thought, there must be a better way.

* * * * *

I had not flown a mission since February 13th, and had begun to wonder if they had forgotten I was there. Maybe, they were giving me my R&R, but whatever the reason, the *vacation* gave me time to set up housekeeping which meant opening up a cot and pushing my B4 bag under it.

Bamboo was plentiful, readily available, came in all sizes and was what the Filipino natives used to construct our buildings. Watching them work gave me an idea.

I cornered Morty Boyle and gave him a list of the tools and material I needed for a project I had in mind. Noticing that he was not too enthusiastic about my request, I suggested that perhaps he would like a bottle of beer. It was shameful, to see how I used the leverage I had, but everything is fair in love and war and we certainly were at war. Of course, he granted my request and I marveled at the persuasive power a bottle of beer possessed.

In this part of the world, you could win money betting that it would rain sometime in the afternoon, and it was this observation that led me to think about constructing a water collection system.

Boyle didn't disappoint me; he got all the stuff I had requested. I had not told anyone of my project, so he just looked at me and wondered what I was up to. Early the next morning, I went to work hoping to beat the heat, but within a few minutes, I was drenched with sweat. A few of my friends walked by, shaking their heads and making snide remarks about a "damn fool killing himself under the broiling sun." Boyle had brought me a new, unused, clean 55-gallon steel drum. I laid it on the ground, and then marked an 8 x 4 rectangle on the side, a few inches from the end of the drum. Then the fun began. Using a chisel and a hammer, I kept banging away until I had cut out the rectangle, making enough noise in the process to make people think there was a Chinese New Year celebration on the base. That attracted more detractors, but I ignored them and their insults, and continued working. I used the 2 x 4 lumber (courtesy of Boyle), to make two X shaped frames, which I joined together with a few 2 x 4's about two feet long. That done, I moved the X-frame to the edge of the tent flap and then placed the drum on the frame, with the hole I had cut out facing upward. Now, I had drawn a few more kibitzers, but who, strangely enough, seemed to be developing some interest in the proceedings. It wasn't until I began the next task that *the look of enlightenment* could be seen in the eyes of my skeptics. I had located a bamboo pole, about ten feet

long and five inches in diameter, split it in half and then knocked out the little partitions on the inside. Net result: a ten-foot long rain gutter. I placed the gutter, open end up, under the edge of the tent flap and secured it in place with the far end higher than the end that terminated over the hole in the steel drum. It was at that moment that I heard some mumbling to the effect that *the idea seemed to have possibilities.* By this time the yokels who had been razzing me the most began to study the sky, hoping that it would soon rain. The last thing I had to do was to remove the plug, which was screwed in at the lowest point on the end of the drum, and screw in the spigot that was a standard GI item and engineered to fit the drum. Had I charged admission, I could have made a good buck because I had attracted a rather large crowd. The rain arrived on schedule and soon began to run down the roof into the gutter. I covered the hole in the drum, not wanting to capture the initial dirty water, and then removed the cover and let the water flow into the drum when it looked clean. Within a few minutes, I had 55 gallons of *soft* usable water! To complete my brainstorm, I set up the two helmet wash stand, that I had brought from Samar, and positioned it a few feet away from my cot and adjacent to the spigot on the drum. I didn't use the water for drinking or brushing teeth, but it was so nice to just reach over and rinse off my sandy, dirty feet before going to bed. Soon, I noticed something strange was taking place. Those who had laughed the loudest were those who had to make the longest walk from their tent to the water tank, lugging the heavy can. Naturally, it was they who were first to ask if it was okay to get some water. With dramatic gestures and talking like a *big shot* I answered, "Take all you want, I've got plenty." It was a true statement because the drum would fill up every day!

Perhaps I derived the most satisfaction from my endeavors, when Major Rierson (the adjutant who shared the hut with the commanding officer) asked if he could fill up his 5-gallon can. Talk about being in favor with those who mattered. I had it made!

It was March 15th when I checked the board in the flight operations hut and saw that my assistance was needed to help win the war, so the home improvements I had in mind would have to wait. Walking back to the tent, it occurred to me that I had not flown a mission in a month, due to the fact that I had piled up many combat hours.

Mission No. 20, 77A-1, March 16, 1945, was a ground support strike against a target in northern Luzon, "up the road a piece" as the saying goes. Looking through the sight, all I could see were trees and more trees. I never did know if it was a success or a bust, due to the nature of the target. It was very short, only two hours ten minutes of flying time.

One of the first things we noticed when we arrived at Clark Field was the great number of aircraft that the Japanese had left behind when our forces pushed them out. I put a new roll of film in my camera and Wade and I began a walking tour. Parked far under the trees were various types of fighter planes. Many were in good condition, needing minor repairs to make them airworthy while others were no more than junk. At first, we were a little wary, thinking that the planes might have been booby-trapped, but from all indications, they just didn't have enough time to do their dirty work. In another area, we located an airplane junkyard piled high with old airplane parts; a sight I had never seen before. It occurred to me that the ground support mission I had flown in the past, might have been to head off and slow down the fleeing Japanese, thereby making it possible for our ground forces to catch up to them. There were many other damaged Japanese planes scattered around in open fields. Looking at them made me wonder if I had had a hand in reducing them to junk when I participated in that first heavy bomber mission to Clark Field.

HEADQUARTERS
ALLIED AIR FORCES
SOUTHWEST PACIFIC AREA
OFFICE OF THE COMMANDER

March 2, 1945.

Dear Mr. Colletti:

    Recently your son, Lieutenant Silveo G. Colletti, was decorated with the Air Medal. It was an award made in recognition of courageous service to his combat organization, his fellow American airmen, his country, his home and to you.

    He was cited for meritorious achievement while participating in aerial flights in the Southwest Pacific Area from October 20, 1944 to November 30, 1944.

    Your son took part in sustained operational flight missions during which hostile contact was probable and expected. These flights included bombing missions against enemy installations, shipping and supply bases, and aided considerably in the recent successes in this theatre.

    Almost every hour of every day your son, and the sons of other American fathers, are doing just such things as that here in the Southwest Pacific.

    Theirs is a very real and very tangible contribution to victory and to peace.

    I would like to tell you how genuinely proud I am to have men such as your son in my command, and how gratified I am to know that young Americans with such courage and resourcefulness are fighting our country's battle against the aggressor nations.

    You, Mr. Colletti, have every reason to share that pride and gratification.

    Sincerely,

GEORGE C. KENNEY,
Lieutenant General, U. S. A.,
Commander.

Mr. James S. Colletti,
45 West Twelfth Street,
Linden, New Jersey.

Chapter 18

Danny Giordano was my first cousin. His mom and my dad were brother and sister. We were about the same height and weight, but he was two years younger than I. To my surprise, in a letter from home, I learned that he was stationed here and was an enlisted man with an anti-aircraft unit. I was anxious to see him, but he was based on the other side of the field, well beyond walking distance, which meant that I needed transportation. My tent mate, Morty Boyle, had his own jeep. Obviously, he had the solution to my problem; but first, I had to figure out a way to make him think that it was I who was doing him a big favor to let me borrow it. After much deliberation, I came up with a plan which I thought might work.

About every two weeks, we received a cigarette and beer ration. When I got mine I put in under my cot, making sure that it was easily seen. I did not smoke or drink, but Boyle did. I waited a few days to determine if he was out of cigarettes or beer and when convinced that he was, I made my request. Of course, the answer was no. Very innocently, I sprung the trap and remarked that he might like to have some of the stuff I had. He then asked, "How long do you need it and how far are you going?" I had him! The next day I went to see Danny.

Danny Giordano

I had no trouble locating his unit, which was on the other side of the field, and it was great to meet up with him, here, six thousand miles away from home. I had brought my camera and we had a few pictures taken together. I had promised Boyle that I would have the jeep back on time, but before I left, Danny took me into his tent and opened up a *spare* footlocker. My God! He had just about every kind of food that had ever been canned! (The explanation for this *gold mine* was quite simple. Danny's family had lived in Little Italy, in downtown New York City, since they arrived in this country around the turn of the century. Uncle Joe knew every shopkeeper or grocer in the neighborhood, so he was able to get first crack at whatever canned goods were available. Not an easy thing to do with a war going on.) I left with an assortment of tuna fish, sardines, peaches, pears or whatever else I desired. I gave him a few rolls of film, which he had never been able to find, so it worked out quite well. The upshot of all this was that we all benefited when I borrowed the jeep. To explain: One of the things that Wade, Boyle, Eisele and I enjoyed doing was playing hearts. Whenever possible, we would begin the game at about seven and play for a few hours.

165

There was no allegiance to anyone. We would gang up on the low man, with the familiar, "Get Wade" or "Get Colletti" if it seemed that he was about to win. Pity the poor loser, for it was he who would have to go to the mess tent and try to convince the cook that we were in dire need of a loaf of bread. To come back empty handed meant that they couldn't get into my stash of canned food, a fate worse than death. In the days that followed, I had no trouble borrowing Boyle's jeep when I wanted to visit Danny, even though I had no beer or cigarettes with which to bribe him. They sure enjoyed that nine o'clock snack!

There were two more projects to complete, while I still had some down time. I managed to convert an old, wooden box into a so-called night table, which I placed at the head of my cot. Now I had a convenient place for my pen, pencils, papers and toilet kit. The top of the table, however, was reserved for the most important thing: a picture of P38. Someday, with a little luck, I hoped I would no longer have to settle for a picture.

Project number two involved making what was basically a folding beach chair with a piece of canvas attached at the top and the bottom with arm rests about 12 inches longer than normal. When seated in the chair, I would place a board across the extended arms, which in effect, became my desktop.

I had to thank the Georgia Rebel for her contribution which led me further into the lap of luxury. She had sent me six, hand rolled linen handkerchiefs. They were beautiful, but I had a better use for them. She was aghast when I wrote saying: "I had received them; thank you and that I had sewn them together making them into a pillowcase for my dirty pillow." I was one of the few who had a pillow, dirty as it was, given to me by one of the men who had gone home. In every sense of the word, this was a major improvement.

Things were really looking up. I had a pillow with a pillow case, a desk to write on, a chair to sit in, food in cans, a night table with my girl's picture on it, a wash stand with two helmets, personal water supply and a jeep to go visit Danny. Man, I had it made!

Soon afterward, I returned to the *real world* when I saw that I was scheduled to fly the next mission. The vacation was over.

Mission No. 21, 93A-1, April 3, 1945. Target: Shipping in Hong Kong Harbor. This was a mission I would never forget.

The weather was fine when we took off and set course for Hong Kong, but it began to change a few

Assume the position of a soldier!

hours later. A thick layer of clouds had moved in, greatly reducing visibility. We were leading the mission and McCullough felt that it was safer to get above the overcast where visibility was much better. The ocean below, however, was completely hidden from view. The navigator had computed an estimated time of arrival over the target area, but he could not determine the strength of the wind or its direction because of the extensive cloud cover. When the ETA was about to run out, Mac nosed the plane down through the clouds, slowly losing altitude. Finally breaking out of the overcast, we all were amazed to see that we were over land: China! Apparently, we had been pushed by strong tail winds which could not be determined without reference to the ground. The only way I can describe the terrain below was to compare it to a can of worms, since there wasn't a straight line to be seen. I did not see two roads or paths that crossed each other at right angles. Mac made a 180-degree turn and in a very few minutes Hong Kong came into view. There was a lot of activity in the harbor, and I selected what I felt was a major ship, and began to line up for my bomb run. The ship began evasive action, and I tried to stay with it, but their maneuvers made it very difficult to keep the target in the crosshairs of the bombsight. It was not easy, or safe, to get a flight of B24's to make radical course changes. Once again, the best we could do was to bracket the target and settle for a number of near misses.

The following is an account of the mission from the book, "The 22nd Bombardment Group in World War II, Volume II, by Walt Gaylor, 1986, page 608," pertaining to mission No. 93A-1. I quote:

3 April 1945: From the 408th's Combat Narrative[27]

"Shipping in Hong Kong Harbor was drawn into our sights today. 6 planes were assigned, taking off at 0750. Target was reached a few minutes after 1200. Soon afterwards 1 Zero-type Zeke made a level pass from 2 o'clock over the target on the plane in A-3 position. At 800 yards, A-3 fired 3 short bursts. Zeke pulled up and reversed direction towards the NE. No damage was inflicted. Despite heavy ack-ack, the harbor received 47x1000-lb bombs. There were 5 near-misses on a possible heavy cruiser. 42 bombs were released in the harbor. One bomb that hung up was manually released safe. Much shipping was observed in the harbor. 15 rounds of cal-50 ammo were expended."

I was the bombardier with the *hung-up bomb*.

A device called a shackle is attached to hooks on the bomb, and then the shackle and the bomb are placed in an electrical device which is attached to the bomb rack in the bomb bay. When the bombsight completes the electrical circuit, the bomb will be released. Obviously, the releasing device had malfunctioned and the only solution was to force it open manually. I would use a *very sophisticated tool* to release the bomb: a long screwdriver. When we were safely away from the target, I contacted the flight deck and told them what I was going to do. After opening the bomb bay doors, I walked out on the 12-inch wide catwalk, screwdriver in hand, to the mid point of the bomb bay and grabbed the V-shaped strut which supported the catwalk. I was wearing my oxygen walk around bottle and a chest pack parachute. I encircled the V-strut with my left arm and leaned out as far as I could, in an attempt to reach the faulty shackle. I came up short because the chest pack parachute was in the way. I contacted the deck and told them that I was removing my parachute and would try again. The second attempt also failed because now the walk-around oxygen bottle was in the way. Obviously, I had a problem. Our altitude was about 12,500 feet above the ocean which I could see much too clearly (judging from the butterflies in my stomach) through the open bomb bay. I figured I could hold my breath for a while, but if forced to breathe, I would be running the risk of losing consciousness for lack of oxygen. (It was at that moment that I wished that I had remained at Langley Field taking x-rays.) I called the flight deck again, informed them of the problem and that I would try once more after removing the oxygen bottle. I took a few deep drags of oxygen, unhooked the bottle and slid my arm up to the highest part of the V, thereby extending myself further out over the open bomb bay and closer to the shackle. Working by feel, I finally got the screwdriver into position, used it as a lever and forced the shackle to open. The bomb was released, the plane gave a slight jump, with the loss of a thousand pounds, and I hauled ass off the skinny beam just as I started to feel light headed.

Perhaps my little waltz with the thousand-pounder over an open bomb bay at 12,500 feet had been written up, but I doubt that it had ever been acknowledged. It would have been nice if someone had taken note of the fact that something unusual had happened, but it was not reported. Sometime later, I learned that the 7th Air Force had a different perspective in regard to unusual events. They cited one of their bombardiers for doing the very same thing I had done. Bully for him. He deserved it.

Maybe this would be an appropriate time to mention something which irritated everyone who was in the Pacific Theater of Operations. We were well aware that the war in Europe had been given priority. We were also well aware that what was happening there made for better headlines. Very often the newspaper story would identify the unit, such as the 8th or 15th Air Force, and go on to report what they had accomplished. For us, second-rate cousins that we were, a typical communiqué might read: "MacArthur's Liberators or MacArthur's ships hit important targets today." Seldom if ever, were the units identified; everything carried the MacArthur label. We weren't looking for medals, but it certainly would have boosted morale if we had felt that the people back home knew we existed and weren't spending our days and nights chasing native cannibal women, clad in grass skirts and carrying a spear. Even now, seventy years later, the irritation still exists.

Mission No. 22, 97A-12, April 7, 1945, Target: Facilities at Tainan, Formosa (now Taiwan) Time: 8 hours, 20 minutes. There were fires burning when we left the target.

Mission No. 23, 102A-2, April 12, 1945. Ground support mission. Target: Japanese ammunition dump. Time: 3 hours, 30 minutes. This was one of the most successful missions I had flown. I quote from my letter to Carl dated April 13, 1945:

> *"I flew a mission yesterday and led 'B' flight again. This mission gave me a great deal of satisfaction because it was the best I have done as a lead bombardier. I had a plane on my left and right wing and all three strings of bombs trained right through the target. It looked that way from the air and the mission photos proved our observations to be correct. Check off one Jap ammo dump. It just isn't there anymore."*

Quoting again from the 22nd Bomb Group Book:

April 15, 1945 - 33[28]

"In conjunction with two other heavy bomb groups, the 22nd was participating in a coordinated strike against Shinchiku Airdrome on the northwest coast of Formosa, when it encountered accurate, heavy caliber flak over the target. At 1401 hours, only five seconds before bombs away, the plane in the #3 position of the 33rd Squadron's first flight was apparently hit in the fuel tanks by a large AA round. An instant later, this B-24J-190, #44-41031, loaded with 6000 pounds of frag bombs, exploded in a blinding flash. *PATIENT KITTEN* immediately disintegrated and the debris showered to the ground 10,000 feet below. No chutes were observed and there was no chance of survivors. Three other planes in the six-plane 33rd formation were damaged by shrapnel and fragments of the exploding aircraft."

Chapter 18

* * * *

Clark Field was spoiling me. The food was a big improvement from what we had at Samar, the living area was comfortable and the weather, although hot, was not as humid. I was playing softball on the squadron team and we beat two officer's teams of other squadrons. The terrain here was flat and we were able to lay out a good playing field. To top it off, I received a letter, dated December 12, 1944. I wondered where it had been for the past four months.

"Lest you should forget that I love you, Red"

169

With the help of the natives, a stage had been set up in the movie area. The enlisted men put on a show, depicting themselves as the Andrews Sisters, and lip-synched to the girl's recording of "Rum and Coca Cola." They did a great job! The unanswered question was, where did they get the women's clothes? When there were no stage shows, we reverted to the standard practice of bringing a chair to the movie area in the afternoon. When it got dark, we would get our raincoats and helmets and walk over to our reserved seats. If it should begin to rain, raincoats and helmets were put on and we would sit there and watch the movie in the rain. We never had it so good.

As previously mentioned, our camp area was a large rectangle. The latrine was located well beyond the last tent making it a touch and go situation for anyone who couldn't maintain control during the long walk to the streamlined, screened-in beauty. For a number of nights, we were awakened by the sound of a single Japanese plane flying overhead. Someone with an Einstein type brain came up with the perfect name for this intruder: *Piss Call Charlie*. The purpose of their mission was nothing more than to deny us a good night's sleep, but one could never be sure, so an alert was always sounded and we had to find shelter. There were four officers in the tent directly opposite ours and one of them decided that he had enough of this crap of getting out of bed and seeking shelter, so he decided to do something about it. The very next day he

Officer's camp area, Clark Field.

was out there in the hot sun, digging a foxhole that reached to the very edge of his cot. Now fully prepared, all he had to do if *Charlie* showed up was to roll off the cot into the foxhole. Mission accomplished -- for a few days. Being the lazy creatures which we were, it dawned upon some of the *about to lose control urinators* that the foxhole was made to order for emergency evacuation of the bladder. Wow! This is great! Soon, it became a favorite pit stop for all those who weren't camels and couldn't hold it until they reached the latrine. All went well until the hot sun began to bake the soil and it was at that moment that our squadron commander happened to be returning to his nearby dwelling. The wind, unfortunately, was blowing in his direction and carried with it an odor that certainly wasn't roses in the moonlight. Following his nose, he found the offending foxhole and told the four occupants to "Fill up that damn piss hole right NOW." All this aggravation because of *Piss Call Charlie*. Sometimes, life just isn't fair.

* * * * *

From the standpoint of preparation, most missions were similar. The briefings were generally the same, touching upon all the important aspects such as target, bomb load, crews, etc., but the mission itself never became routine. There was always the possibility of a new adventure every time we lifted off and headed for the target. Such was the case with this particular mission to a target in Formosa, which possibly took place the latter part of April.

We were the lead plane that day, and as usual, I checked the bombsight on the ground about half an hour before takeoff. Everything checked out fine. Following the procedure I had established months ago, I checked the sight once again while we were about forty-five minutes from the target. This time, I could see that it was malfunctioning. I called McCullough and told him of the problem. His reply was the standard reply in such a situation,

"Okay, we will let plane number two take over the lead."

"No good Mac, Lt. Cu------ missed the briefing, last night, and knows almost nothing about the target. He will probably drop his bombs when he sees ours go out."

"Then I guess the only thing to do is let number three take over."

"Not a good choice. The bombardier is green. I'm not too impressed with him."

"Well, what do you want to do?"

"I think I can fix the sight."

"What do you need to do to fix it?"

"I have to take the sight apart and get to the inside."

"*You what?*"

"I need to remove the screws on the end of the sight, take the end cover off and then make an adjustment."

"Are you kidding?"

"No."

"Okay, but it sounds crazy." I did it and it worked. We went on and had a successful mission. The explanation for this radical solution to the problem had its roots back in Victorville; for it was there that I became intrigued with the Norden bombsight. As we studied it, I began to develop a deep appreciation for how cleverly it had been designed and for the precision that was built into it. The desire to learn more than what was required to pass the final exam, gave me the knowledge I needed to make the repair in the air. Strange as it might seem, as I began to remove the screws, I remembered the comments of a few of my classmates as we left the classroom after taking the final exam. "Why the hell are they making us learn all this crap? We'll never have any use for the knowledge, so why waste time on it?" I had the answer for them, but there was no way I could convey the message.

It was in late April or early May, when I got the word that I had been appointed assistant squadron bombardier. Now it became my job to prepare the report for yesterday's mission, take it to the office to have it typed up, and then deliver it to the group bombardier. In addition, it was my job to go down to the flight line, meet the returning planes, and inquire about any malfunctions they might have had with the bomb racks, the sight, etc. A *negative* benefit was that I could be the receiving end of a good chewing out if someone decided it was *my fault* that the target didn't slide over and re-position itself under the falling bombs so that the bombardier could claim a direct hit. Some job.

May 1945 was a very busy month. On May 1st, I flew Mission No. 27. This was followed by missions on May 5th, 11th, 13th, 18th, 26th and 30th. They were all against targets in Formosa except for the May 5th mission which was to Amoy Airdrome in China. Some of them were easy but there were days when we encountered heavy resistance. There were injuries from anti-aircraft fire and planes were limping home on two or three engines, at times landing at auxiliary fields due to leaking gas tanks. The Japanese were beating a path back to Japan, and they were using Formosa as a staging area. It was the intent of the Air Corps to deny them the use of the facilities there and make it difficult or impossible for them to use the ports that were vital to their retreat.

Regardless of how many missions we had flown, takeoff was always a tension-filled event. More often than not, we were overloaded for the simple reason that you needed the extra fuel to complete the mission and a big enough bomb load to make the trip worthwhile. On more than one occasion, I wished that I had never had pilot training because the training gave me first hand knowledge of the struggle Mac and Wade were having just to get the plane off the ground. During those white-knuckle moments, ignorance surely would have been bliss. There were times when it seemed that we would be running out of runway before achieving takeoff, and once airborne, hoping that we wouldn't mush down, as the B24 was known to do, loaded with bombs and gasoline. Fortunately, there was a lighter side to life.

Wade, June 1945

Chapter 18

July 1945

When we first arrived at Clark Field, one of the first projects on the agenda was to build our so-called officer's club. Bamboo was plentiful and the Filipinos were very adept in using it. Quickly, they had constructed a large framework and stretched a tent over the top for the roof. Somewhere, somehow, they found enough cement for the floor and the finish was smooth enough for dancing. A bar was set up at one end, and there were a few tables available for letter writing or just sitting around.

There were many nurses stationed in the nearby hospital, a fact which I am sure was not lost on the wolves of the 408th. At last the *club* was finished and soon it was not unusual to have female officers as guests. As one might suspect, there is a story that goes with this.

"Sunday, June 3, 1945

Dear Carl,

Before I get to writing about other things, I must tell you about something that happened last night that had everyone laughing for hours. Two of the officers had invited nurses as their guests and it was very strange indeed to see women walking around the camp area. It was about 7:00 PM when a large, black cloud loomed on the horizon and appeared to be moving toward us. It so happened that the two nurses were in need of 'some toilet' so they walked out to our beautiful, screened in, GI six-seater to heed nature's call. One of the guys, who by act of Congress was described as an 'officer and a gentlemen', strategically positioned himself to ward off any males from intruding upon their privacy. Without warning, the black cloud opened up and it began to pour, accompanied by very strong winds. In fact, the wind blew so hard that it picked up the latrine roof and walls and dumped them about twenty feet away. Before they could say, 'I've been caught with my pants down' the startled girls found themselves sitting on the pot exposed to the elements and prying eyes. They both grabbed their underpants, pulled them up, pulled down their skirts and ran like hell for shelter! The entire camp had a good laugh at their expense. As for the nurses, they were good sports. After the shock had worn off, they too couldn't help but laugh about their most embarrassing moment."

Another major event in May was the receipt of orders promoting a number of 2nd lieutenants to 1st lieutenant. It made Wade Schroeder very happy, for his name was on the list. In fact, he was so happy that he got skunk drunk, removed all his clothes and proceeded to run around the camp area stark naked. Knowing Wade, *the Human Sponge* (Ha!) it occurred to me that he would not remember a damn thing about his escapade once he became sober, so irrefutable proof would be needed. I picked up my camera and went out to find him. Then I had a second thought: I needed my hard-to-get film for more important things than making a pictorial record of his posterior for posterity, so I put the camera away. This decision had a down side, however. My sneaky, devious mind easily understood how valuable a picture of his butt could be. It would have provided me with great leverage; if for instance, I should want to blackmail him for a candy bar or some other very important, hard to get item. All I would have to do would be to threaten to send his wife, Fran, the x-rated picture and he would cave in. After further thought, however, I realized that I had made the right decision, since he was my best friend, and I was such a nice guy.

The final touch to that very memorable month was when the clerk in the orderly room presented me with order #151. It was dated May 31, 1945 and went on to say: "As of this date the following named second lieutenants are hereby promoted to the rank of first lieutenant." My name was on the list. Now it was my turn to get drunk and run around naked, but I didn't drink so I couldn't emulate Wade. Insofar as having a picture taken of the *non-event*, I was the only one who had a camera and I surely didn't want to waste the film!

Finally, the officer's club was finished and we all were eagerly awaiting the biggest social event of the season: our first dance. We *booked* a sixteen piece orchestra (I think they were all men from our own group) and they were quite good. I had forgotten how great it was to listen to a live band. The Romeos of the 408th lost no time in seeking partners from among the local Filipino girls, nurses and Red Cross workers. It was going to be a blast. The blast, however, turned into a bust because only two women made the scene. What a waste, good music and no partners. I had made no attempt to get a date, for the

Colletti at the officer's club, June 1945

simple reason I didn't know anyone to ask. My social life had ended that night in Fresno, when I was on a blind date and sang a solo of "They're Either Too Young or Too Old." Regardless, the band sounded good. Soon afterward, we scheduled another dance which was quite a success.

Our preoccupation with social activities had given us a much-welcomed break, but there was a war going on and we were still very much involved. Mission No. 34, June 5th, took me to a place called Taichu, in Formosa. On the 16th and 18th, Missions No. 35 and No. 36 were targets in the northernmost part of Formosa. The target was the seaport of Kiirun which was extremely important to the Japanese who were using it as a staging area in their retreat to Japan. The group systematically reduced the piers, warehouses and surrounding areas to junk, making it virtually useless to them.

The next day, I entered the last two missions in my personal log and noticed that I had about 330 combat hours. Projecting ahead, I would need to log about 400 hours before I would reach the 100 point total, which was required to complete a duty tour. Difficult missions earned more points, but it also meant that the risk was greater. Either way, I was close, but as the saying goes, "no cigar."

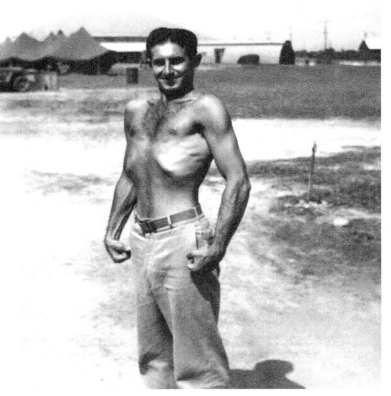
"Tarzan" Colletti

Rudy Riccio*

Rudy Riccio was the aircraft commander of another crew. He joined the squadron about the same time we did but was not part of our island hopping bunch that made the trip from San Francisco to Australia. He was tall, slim (weren't we all!) about my age and his home address was Elmhurst, Long Island. Perhaps we had flown together previously, but I was not sure.

The letters I received from Mom and Dad were written in Italian, and they were careful to keep them simple. I had never really learned how to read Italian, but I could usually decipher what they had written even though I could not interpret every word. When I got stuck, I went to my interpreter; Rudy Riccio. I will never forget the very first time I gave him a letter to read, because the first words he spoke were,

"Ah Ne." (A meaningless phrase, which I can only spell phonetically.) That, however, was not what they had written, and which I easily understood to be, *Dear Son*. (I compared his "Ah Ne" to an opening remark, such as *well* that someone might say before beginning to speak. At least, that was the way it struck me.) We both began to laugh the moment the words left his lips! From that moment on, we never greeted each other with a *hello*. From that moment on, hello was out and "Ah Ne" was in!*

* * * * *

Balikpapan, on the eastern coast of Borneo, was the biggest oil producing area in that part of the world. The Japanese, so badly in need of oil, took control of it soon after Pearl Harbor and had captured a major prize. Now, years later, the British were going to attempt to retake it, and air support was essential to their effort. Japanese airfields in the Celebes and Borneo had to be neutralized and the 22nd Bomb Group, among others, had been selected to do their part.

Three crews were to leave Clark Field and go south to Morotai, in the Halmahera Islands. From there, the target for the first mission was Mondai Airdrome and the second Limpoeng, both in the Celebes. The third target was an airstrip in Oelin, southeast Borneo. I groaned when I saw the names of the lucky crewmembers: Lead pilot: Riccio. Lead bombardier: Colletti. Borneo! New Guinea was bad enough.

---

*Rudy lives in Colorado and we have kept in touch over the years via the phone or e-mail. When we call, we do not identify ourselves by saying, "This is Rudy" or "This is Colletti." When he picks up the phone, I utter, "Ah, Ne" and immediately the laughter begins! The incident remains fresh in our minds despite the passing of seventy years.

We were briefed thoroughly before leaving Clark Field, and it was a typical briefing with two exceptions: Much to our dismay, we were told that there was no air-sea rescue in the area, no submarines or surface ships. Nothing. We were on our own if we went down.

The second morale-deflating bit of information had to do with the fact that in the event of a survivable crash landing in Borneo, we would be exposed to an animal which might attack humans without first being provoked: the orangutan. Not very reassuring.

Some of the thirty men selected for the mission were, like me, close to completing their tour of duty, needing only three or four more missions to reach the cherished 100-point mark. With the goal in sight, we became a little *edgy*. I had never been apprehensive or jittery about flying a mission; but now, for the first time, there was a nagging gut feeling inside me that this might be the day my luck might run out. I hated to think that it would happen in some Godforsaken place such as Borneo.

The distance from Clark Field to Morotai was about seven or eight hundred miles, which put us closer to our old base on Owi than to Clark. When we

Dutch East Indies, Morotai, June 24, 1945

checked in, it was like reliving a bad dream. We had a tent, mosquito netting, Mother Earth for a floor and the few things we had packed. It was a transient camp, dedicated to the proposition that we would be there for only a few days, so why bother to make any improvements? The food, unfortunately, was what we expected: Lousy.

Proof of my anxiety was evident when I went down to the flight line to check out a parachute and for the first time, also checked out a flak vest, an item which I had never previously used. I took a step to leave, but quickly went back and checked out another vest and steel helmet. Later, when we neared the target area, I put the helmet on and put the second vest *under me*. I had been in the jewelry business for only three short years, but I had learned how important it was to protect the *family jewels*. I hadn't had the opportunity to start a family, but I had high hopes!

Mission No. 37 (for me) was No. 176A-1 in the official record. Date: June 25, 1945 and the target was the airstrip at Mandai, in the Southwest Celebes. Time: 10 hours, 30 minutes.

Mission No. 38, 177A-1, June 27, 1945: Limpoeng Airfield, Southwest Celebes. Time: 11 hours.

Mission No. 39, 181A-1, June 29, 1945: Olin Airstrip, Borneo. Time: 13 hours 50 minutes. It was a very successful mission, leaving many bomb craters for the Japanese to fill. We had been intercepted by Japanese fighter aircraft; but fortunately, they inflicted little damage. The interception, however, entitled us to a few more points, bringing us closer to the cherished 100.

As Borneo slowly faded in the distance, I knew that we all breathed a sigh of relief. One more landing at Morotai, one more de-briefing and we could then say goodbye and head back to Clark Field and civilization. As we droned on, it amused me to think that the Japanese were probably pissed off because their airstrips were full of holes. What they had no way of knowing, was that the lead pilot, Rudy Riccio, was from Elmhurst, New York; and the lead bombardier, Silveo Colletti, was born in Manhattan, and both were of Italian descent. How the fates had conspired to bring these two together, ten or eleven thousand miles from New York, was beyond my comprehension.

The return trip to Morotai was not without its nail biting moments. Once again, it was the old balancing act of carrying enough bombs and/or fuel to get us there and back. The fuel reserve had been figured a little too close, and strong head winds over the Makassar Straits drained the gas tanks faster than anticipated. When we finally reached the vicinity of the airfield, we were sweating out the possibility of running out of fuel in the traffic pattern, but Rudy got us down in a hurry, much to our relief. Quoting from the 22nd Bomb Group Book:

June 25, 1945 - 2^{29}

"On June 24th, the 2nd and 408th Squadrons sent contingents to the Molaccas [sic] in the Netherlands East Indies to stage out of the 13th Air Force base at Morotai in support of the Allied landings on Borneo. At 0555 hours the next morning, six planes from the 2nd Squadron took off from Pitoe Strip, leading the 408th on a strike against the airdromes at Mandai on Celebes Island. The 2nd Squadron began its bomb run at 1113 hours, encountering heavy flak. The formation was also attacked by Oscar fighters, one of which was reported shot down. Although the planes were briefed to break to the right over the sea after their bomb runs, B-24M-30 #44-42431 was apparently experiencing mechanical difficulties during the target approach because it turned left on a heading which would have taken it directly over the town of Makassar. No one on the mission actually saw the plane crash, but several crewmen of the trailing 408th Squadron formation saw a large column of smoke rising from a fire at the probable crash site at the edge of the foothills about 10 miles east-northeast of Mandai Airdrome. An aerial search of the area the next day located a grass fire near this site and possible mirror flashes nearby. It was speculated at the time that survivors of the crash set the fire to attract the attention of search aircraft. After the war, further investigation on the ground revealed that the B-24 had crashed near the village of Maros. Natives had buried Lt. Shellington, identified from the name in his hat, at the Christian cemetery at Maros. Six other crewmen had been buried by natives at the crash site in the countryside about eight or nine miles east-northeast of Maros. Four crewmen were captured by the Japanese two days after the crash and were taken by truck to Makassar, where they were executed at the local headquarters for the Japanese Navy *Kempei-Tai*. The remains of the crew were returned to the United States for burial in 1952."

The death of anyone, regardless of which squadron he was in, was not easy to accept, but strange to say, we did very little to formally acknowledge the loss. It wasn't that we didn't care, but rather it had to do with the fact that we knew of the inherent risks we faced every time we climbed aboard the plane. We didn't dwell upon it or perform rituals such as you might have seen in a Hollywood movie. We didn't smash the dead man's cup or stand at attention and salute with tears in our eyes. Perhaps the chaplain would say a few choice words, but I do not recall anyone making a public statement. This might have been interpreted as indifference, but that was not so. We cared, but we downplayed it and learned to live with it. I have no doubt that each of us asked this silent question of himself, "Who would be the next to die?"

Chapter 18

In most instances, we were far removed from the tragic event, as compared to the men on the ground who would be physically close to the actual loss of a friend or comrade. A good example of this is the loss of *Ascent Charlie* which disappeared on the June 22nd mission or the men lost on the June 25th mission. There were no remains. No bodies in coffins to drape a flag over or recite pretty speeches. There was very little we could do.

I learned a very valuable lesson way back in 1942, a few months after entering the Army. *It was best not to make close friends.* The reason for this was very simple. It had to do with the fact that today you would be together, but tomorrow you might be notified that you would be shipped out with hardly enough time to pack or bid farewell to anyone. Casual relationships made it a lot easier to say, so long, good luck and drop me a line if you get the chance. In a way, it might be said I had erected a protective device, a *mental barrier* that would shield me from the sadness that comes with saying goodbye. With the exception of Wade Schroeder I was able to adhere to my adopted philosophy.

Perhaps there was a rule or regulation somewhere, which spelled out the procedure for gathering the personal effects of the deceased, but I believe it was usually done by those who were closest to him, usually his tent mates. Fortunately, I was greatly relieved for never being called upon to perform this sad task.

To repeat a statement I made earlier in this book: "I never did like that part of the lyric of the Air Force Song which said: 'We live in fame or go down in flames.'"[30] What fame?

I had been so completely preoccupied with the Morotai, Borneo experience that I had forgotten that Wade was gone. He had flown his last mission on June 12, and soon afterward received his orders sending him home. I could only imagine what his thoughts were as we said goodbye, but I am sure that he had to be thinking about seeing his son for the first time. All he ever had were the pictures his wife Fran, had sent him of herself and the baby. It was so strange to see the corner of the tent which he had occupied, now devoid of pictures, clothing or shoes. Just a bare cot. It was then that I realized, more than ever, that the war had created many crazy situations and relationships.

The standard army tent measured sixteen by sixteen feet, and for a year, Wade and I had shared that small space with two others. One thing was certain: under those conditions you got to know a person very well and it would have been a very difficult existence if you were incompatible. We were lucky, for we quickly became friends and discovered a sure fire way to *compliment* each other and that was by never missing an opportunity to be insulting!

It might have started one evening as we left the briefing for the next day's mission when Wade turned to me and said,

"Do you think you can do us all a favor tomorrow and make just *one* bomb run? It's bad enough we have to go over the target once; but if you screw it up, we'll have to do it twice and I might never get the chance to see my son." (I don't remember his exact words, but that is close enough.) Another day, he got on my case again with some remark to the effect that, "How come all the other crews come back with great results, and all you do is drop bombs in the ocean and kill a lot of fish?" This all started after I was flying as the lead bombardier, and of course he was just trying to get my goat. Another day, he was quite pleased with himself when he took me aside and in a hushed voice told me, "Don't forget to open the bomb bay doors, *this time*, before you drop the bombs." The fact that none of this ever happened was conveniently forgotten. Of course, it was all a game. There was never any malice in the insults. What we had accomplished was to perfect the technique of giving left handed compliments!

It was not all one sided however. We were sitting around just breezing when a discussion began as to which member of the crew was most important. Naturally, the pilots were of the opinion that it was they, since they were the aircraft commanders and were responsible for the plane and crew. (I knew that sooner or later this question would come up, and I had prepared for it weeks before.) I let Wade rant and rave for a while and then I sprang my trap. I asked him to please answer a few questions, and he said okay. I proceeded step by step:

"How many men are there on the crew including yourself?

"Ten."

"Why are we here?"

"To fly a mission."

"Why do we need to fly a mission?"

"To hit the target."

"What happens when we get to the target?"

"We drop our bombs?"

"Who drops the bombs?"

"The bombardier."

"Okay," I said. "Let me see if I understand what you have said: We are here to fly a mission, to a target and then the bombardier will drop bombs on the target, right?"

"Yes."

"Now answer the next question, true or false: By your own admission, isn't it true that the *only reason* you and the others are here is to put the *bombardier over the target so that he can do his job*?"

"Well......." Then I shut him up completely when I added:

"In essence you pilots are nothing more than taxi drivers!" Maybe I didn't win the argument, but I could live with a draw.

Left to right: Mires, McCullough, Schroeder, Colletti - Dutch East Indies

Chapter 18

A few days after returning from Morotai, I was told to report to the operations tent. When I got there the clerk handed me a sheet of paper bearing the title, "Record of Combat Experience," signed by Lt. John Mires, the squadron operations officer. It was a list of the missions I had flown, dates, targets, total combat flying time, etc. My eyes worked down to the bottom of the page where I read, and re-read the final entry: "total points, 101." As of June 29, 1945, my tour of duty was complete, and I was relieved from any further combat flying. It was over. I was eligible to be rotated back to the United States. I was going home.

RECORD OF COMBAT EXPERIENCE

COLLETTI, Silvee G. 1st Lt. O-776632 — NAME, RANK AND SERIAL NUMBER
BOMBARDIER — CLASSIFICATION
408TH BOMB — SQUADRON
22ND BOMB (H) — GROUP

No.	Mission Number	Date	B-24's Target	Total Combat Flying Hours	Accurate Anti-Aircraft Fire	Interception With Fighters Without Hits To	Aircraft Lost On Mission	Aircraft Accident	Grand Total of Points
1.	294A-1	10/10/44	Davao, Mindanao	11:20					
2.	288A-8	10/14/44	Balikpapan, Borneo	4:35				4	
3.	300A-1	10/26/44	Jap Naval Force	15:20	1				
4.	310A-1	11/5/44	Open Airstrip	15:35		3			
5.	319D-1	11/14/44	Licanan Airdrome	11:55	1				
6.	320D-1	11/15/44	Licanan Airdrome	11:55					
7.	326D-1	11/21/44	Matina, Mindanao	11:45					
8.	329D-3	11/24/44	Matina, Mindanao	12:00					
9.	335A-6	11/30/44	Legaspi, Luzon	10:45					
10.	341-A	12/6/44	Lahug, Cebu	9:45					
11.	352A-16	12/17/44	Bacolod, Negros Is.	11:00					
12.	357A-20	12/22/44	Clark Field, Luzon	15:00	1	1			
13.	3A-1	1/3/45	Clark Field, Luzon	14:05	1				
14.	17A-1	1/17/45	Legaspi, Luzon	6:15					
15.	20A-1	1/20/45	Bamban, Luzon	6:30	1				
16.	32A-1	2/1/45	Corregidor Island	7:10					
17.	36A-1	2/5/45	Corregidor Island	5:15					
18.	41A-1	2/10/45	Corregidor Island	6:10					
19.	44A-1	2/13/45	Jap Naval Force	13:20					
20.	77A-1	3/18/45	Ground Support	2:10					
21.	93A-1	4/3/45	Hong Kong, China	8:35		1			
22.	97A-12	4/7/45	Tainan, Formosa	8:30					
23.	102A-2	4/12/45	Ground Support	2:30					
24.	107A-2	4/17/45	Shinchiku, Formosa	9:15					
25.	113A-4	4/23/45	Matsuyama, Formosa	9:55	1				
26.	119A-6	4/29/45	Armed Night Recco	10:05					
27.	121A-4	5/1/45	Tainan, Formosa	8:00					
28.	125A-2	5/5/45	Amoy Island, China	9:30	1				
29.	131A-3	5/11/45	Toshien, Formosa	7:40					
30.	133A-5	5/13/45	Tuguegarao, Luzon	4:00					
31.	139A-1	5/18/45	Tainan, Formosa	8:15	1				
32.	146A-6	5/26/45	North Echague A/D	3:45					
33.	150A-1	5/30/45	Takao, Formosa	7:35	1				
34.	156A-1	6/5/45	Incomplete Mission	8:00					
35.	167A-1	6/16/45	Kiirun, Formosa	9:20	1				
36.	169A-1	6/18/45	Kiirun, Formosa	9:20	1				
37.	177A-1	6/27/45	Limboeng, Celebes	11:00		3			
38.	176A-1	6/25/45	Limboeng, Celebes	10:30		3			
39.	181A-1	6/29/45	Celin Airstrip, Borneo	13:30		3			
			TOTAL HOURS:	363:05					
			POINTS:	72	18	14	4		101

CERTIFIED CORRECT:

John K. Mires

JOHN K. MIRES,
1st Lt. Air Corps,
Operations Officer.

Last mission June 29, 1945. 101 points, duty tour complete. No more missions to fly.

Much to my dismay, however, being eligible and actually saying goodbye were two different things. The recently adopted policy required that a replacement arrive before I could leave. In the meantime, there was nothing to do but wait. How I despised that word.

Most of the month of July 1945 was spent writing letters, waiting, pulling officer of the guard duty, waiting, mail censor, waiting and whatever else they could find for me to do. Time dragged on. Every time new personnel arrived, I would look to see if any of them were wearing bombardier's wings. If so, perhaps he was my replacement, and I would soon be on my way home. No such luck.

Left to right: Colletti, Jones, Lapsley, Siegel, Sullivan, Meyer, Stemfield

A short time after Wade's departure, Boyle and I were sitting around making small talk, when he began to laugh. Since I didn't see Bob Hope in the tent, it was only natural to ask what was so funny. He replied that he was thinking about the caper he pulled off a few weeks ago that involved Wade.

Captain Mortimer Boyle, the squadron engineering officer, was about five feet, eight inches tall, perhaps thirty years old and had worked for the New York Telephone Company before entering the service. He had his own jeep with the words, "408th Sqdn Eng," written on the base of the windshield, and he had a problem: He needed shelter for his supplies and equipment, but his requisitions apparently fell on deaf ears.

The solution to the problem could be found locked away in a huge supply depot in Manila -- but unfortunately, there seemed to be a war going on and getting what you needed, through regular channels, was almost impossible. When confronted with situations such as this, one must be resourceful, rise to the occasion and employ a tactic known as *midnight requisitioning*. Actually, this can be more accurately defined as *stealing*. Of course this method could also be used in broad, open daylight if the perpetrator knew how to pull it off, and *Mr. New York City, Morty Boyle* (as Wade called him) sure knew how to do it.

Chapter 18

Lt. Innocence, twenty-year-old Wade Schroeder, became involved when Morty asked if he would like to accompany him on a trip to the supply depot in Manila; an invitation Wade accepted. They left the squadron area in the 408th jeep, followed by a 6 x 6 truck driven by an enlisted man. There was no problem getting into the guarded depot, and Boyle soon found what he wanted: completely disassembled buildings, packed in a crate and which could easily be erected on a building site. There were two problems, however. One, he didn't have authorization for the buildings and two, he didn't have the means to get them loaded on the 6 x 6 truck. Problem #2 was neatly solved (or so Wade believed) when Boyle bribed a crane operator with a bottle of bourbon. The enlisted man, seeing the Captain's bars and "408th Engineering" on the jeep, asked no questions and quickly loaded the items onto the truck. Now it was time to solve problem #1: no authorization for the items. In a speech, Winston Churchill said it eloquently when he used the phrase, "This was their shining hour" to describe an act of heroism, and this was Boyle's shining hour. He told Wade to get in the truck and sit up front with the driver. They were instructed to wait until Boyle (driving his jeep), had reached the gate. There Boyle would park off to one side; and at that moment, they should slowly begin to drive toward the guarded gate and continue on through. Once in the clear, they were to haul ass out of there and disappear. As the 6 x 6 slowly approached, the guard could clearly see a commissioned officer in the front seat, so he suspected nothing and let them pass. It was then that the guard asked Boyle for the required papers for the items on the truck. Boyle replied, "What papers?" He didn't know anything about the truck that went by, he was there on some other business -- he didn't know the men in the truck!

It wasn't until some time later that Wade realized he had been duped by Captain Boyle, and was cringing at the thought of being arrested and spending half a lifetime in a Philippine jail and would never get to see his newborn son. Then he asked himself, "Did he invite me to go along because I was just too dumb and naïve?" Of course not, they were tent mates!

Wade and Silveo

During one of our bull sessions, a few of us spent an evening discussing how different our duty tour might have been if we had gone to the European Theater of Operations. All we could do was to speculate and imagine, but we did arrive at a few conclusions. We agreed that the Germans would have been a tougher foe than the Japanese, but we also felt that we in the Pacific faced some hazards which the men in Europe were spared.

Our war was quite different than the one fought over Germany. Flying long ten to fifteen hour missions over water could be boring, but never worry free. Many were *sweat missions* filled with anxiety and concern over the possibility of mechanical failure or of running out of fuel hundreds of miles from land. In such an event, we had the option of bailing out or going down with the plane, praying that we would be found by whatever air-sea or surface rescue vessels had been deployed. The chances of surviving an ocean ditching in a B24 were not good, when compared to the B17, whose low wing design created a surfboard effect that helped it skim over the water while it slowed down. The B24, because of its shoulder high wing position, usually *stubbed its toe* when the nose touched the water, bringing it to an abrupt halt. Over land, and depending upon our geographical location, we probably would be helped by friendly natives. But on our own, knowing how to survive in the jungle was not exactly the field of expertise of city-bred boys. In addition, we strongly felt that being captured by the occupying Japanese was a death sentence, needing only to recall the inhumane treatment of prisoners on the Bataan Death March. From what we were led to believe, the underground in Europe, composed of forces loyal to the Allies, hid, fed and helped return many downed airmen back to our own lines.

Regardless of what part of the world you were flying, the weather was always a factor; but in my opinion, we in the Pacific were subject to its dangers more so than the crews in Europe. The warmer climate created large storm clouds which were awesome to see, but deadly to aircraft. The sight of them frightened me more than the enemy. We had more health problems, such as malaria and scrub typhus, but I doubt if they were a cause for concern in Europe. As I previously mentioned, there were times when we had more men off flying status because of these diseases than from enemy action. Living conditions were radically different. If

"War Hero" with Air Medal, June 1945

not mistaken, the crews in England were housed in Quonset huts while we slept in tents. I do not know if they had bedding, but I do know that we had only the bare, standard army cot and little more. For the most part, I would assume that they were dry and reasonably comfortable, while we had to contend with high humidity while slogging around in mud. (Ah, Samar!) They probably remained in the same quarters, during their entire tour of duty, while we resembled Gypsies. We no sooner had *made ourselves at home* when it was time to pack up and move to a new base, where the process would then be repeated. I spent hours seeking ways to make life a little easier, such as catching rain water off the tent roof and making a night table out of an old wooden box I had found. At least that provided a place to put the picture of the girl I hoped to see again some day.

When off duty, they could put on their class "A" uniform and go to the nearest town where they could associate with civilized people, find entertainment, go dancing or seek female companionship. The female companionship they succeeded in finding proved to be quite a sore point to the English men in uniform who, economically speaking could not compete with the better paid, free spending American servicemen.

They, the English, were able to vent their feeling of displeasure with this great, concise, very accurate statement, when they said of the Americans: "They are overpaid, over sexed and over here."

For those of us stationed in places such as New Guinea, the choice seemed to be limited to seeking out one of the cannibal beauties living in the jungle. We had a standing joke, concerning them. "The longer you remained here, the whiter the native women seemed to become." (Now, all we had to do was to figure out a way to get the bone out of their hair!) Food? I do not know what was on their plate, but it had to be better than what we had. I distinctly remember eating a piece of meat which had the same gray color as the caribou that was being walked through the camp area at that very moment by one of the natives. The only difference was that one was on my tray and the other was on the hoof. Milk and eggs? Only a memory. The bottom line: they had a tougher foe, but our standard of living was much lower. We had to be more resourceful as we tried to adjust to life in a strange, unfamiliar and sometimes hostile environment.

There wasn't too much news available regarding what was happening elsewhere in the world, and it would have been an understatement to say that we were poorly informed. At the outdoor, evening cinema, newsreels were shown of battles or combat situations, but the events had usually taken place weeks before. What we learned through the mail, was also out of date, since the mail lagged behind every time we moved up to a new base. As for the broadcasts from Tokyo Rose, it was clearly evident that they were nothing more than outright propaganda and could be dismissed as such.

We were well aware that the war in Europe had priority when it came to supplies, equipment or material. The show in Europe was the main feature. We in the Pacific were the *extra-added attraction* on the double bill. We understood it, accepted it, learned to live with it, but we surely didn't like it.

Lt. Picconi and Colletti, Manila, July 1945

Colletti and Lapsley, Morotai

I got hair like my pop used to have!

Sure—Sure—I know— you and your promises! I can remember when you used to tell me that we'd go out three or four times a week! Now the only time I get to go out is when I go to the Hospital—!! Silveo Colletti— if I didn't love you I'd tease ya!

Colquitt, Georgia.
May 28, 1945

Chapter 18

Street scenes. Angeles Luzon, Philippine Islands 1945

Wade Schroeder, Clark Field June 1945

Remains of Shoo Shoo Baby. I flew four missions in this plane.

Chapter 18

Clark Field, May-June 1945

B29 #714

A04 #602

B29 #714

B25 Honey

B17 #483547

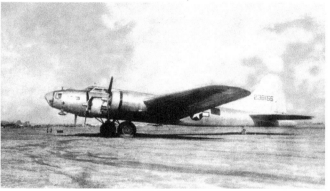
B17 #238155

Million $ Baby

Kansas City Kitty

Clark Field, May-June 1945

It Ain't So Funny

P38 #5825 Mexican Spitfire

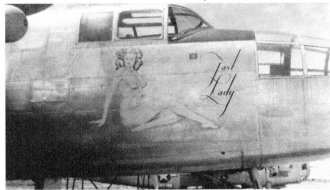
Fast Lady

Round Trip Ticket

Mad Russian

P51 #70 Me Darlin

Cocktail Hour

Slightly Dangerous

Chapter 18

Clark Field, May-June 1945

Rum and Coke

P38 Stardust

F6F #916 Boots

F6F #916 Boots

Red-Hot Riden-Hood III

Sleepy-Time Gal

th' Duchess

P47 Thunderbolt #64

19

OKINAWA, JAPAN

As the Japanese retreated northward, it became obvious that it would be necessary to leave Clark Field and move up to a more forward location. Our forces had landed on Okinawa and an airfield had been prepared. The 22nd Bomb Group was on the move again, this time to Okinawa; and I was going with them regardless of the fact that I was no longer on flying status. They didn't need me, but I was going to make the move with the unit. Unfortunately, I no longer had my "T.S. Card," so I couldn't get it punched.

It was the last week of July when we began to break camp. It would be a typical move; take everything you owned or whatever might be of use. In one respect, however, it would be different for me. Since I was no longer required to fly, there was no hurry to transport me to the new base. This time, I would be taking an ocean cruise on an LST with eight other officers. As I boarded the ship, I could see that the deck of the LST was completely covered with items of all description; jeeps, trucks, supplies, water tank cars, etc, with little or no room to spare.

Clark Field, July 1945. Frank McCullough (in photo) and I were trying to decide which of our "treasured possessions" should be left behind due to lack of space in our B24's.

When we were about to get underway, one of the ship's officers welcomed us aboard. He invited us to dine with the captain and his officers in the wardroom, which was large enough to accommodate our small group of eight. A few instructions followed: Line up in the passageway to the wardroom at the specified time, and remain there until the captain had entered and sat down. Then we could file in and choose a seat. Needless to say, there was a tablecloth on the table, dishes, utensils, cups, glasses and a mess attendant to serve. (Egad! These guys really knew how to live, but we already knew that the Navy had everything, from previous experience!) Visible proof that our mothers had raised no fools was the fact that we made very sure to line up half an hour ahead of time.

Sailing northward, we soon left the Philippines behind. I knew that we would pass close to Formosa as we sailed north to Okinawa. I wondered how close we would come to the island that I had come to know so well from the air. I had flown many missions there and I knew it would be strange to view it from aboard ship. I have no memory as to the number of days we sailed, but I did know that I would not be going home for quite some time. All I could do was to wait.

On LST to Okinawa August 1945.

On the second day, the weather began to change and the seas became a little rough as we plowed through the China Seas. When we lined up for the next meal, I noticed that two of our group had decided to pass up the meal. On the third day, the weather worsened and a few more decided to remain in their bunks. The LST certainly was not built for comfort. It rolled severely from side to side, and everyone aboard could feel it shudder to its very core when the flat prow plowed into a large wave. This was not fun anymore. After a few days of this, there were only two dedicated flyboys lined up in the passageway awaiting the arrival of the captain. I was one of them. I had never been airsick, but I would be lying if I said that I had not lost my appetite. Still, I was determined to stick it out. As we stood at the doorway leading to the wardroom, we could see the mess attendant going about his job. I believe he was a Filipino of very small stature; but whatever he was, he pretended not to recognize the green in the gills look on our faces. We watched him as he moved a small table into our line of sight, close to the very entrance of the door where we were standing. Then he got a large drinking glass, placed it on the table, and making certain that I and the other fool could see, took a *raw egg* out of his pocket, cracked the shell, dropped the egg in the glass and then swallowed it! Ugh! That did it! We both came to the same conclusion: we had lost our appetites! We did an about face and hi-tailed it out of the passageway as fast as our wobbly legs could take us. Later, we both agreed that he was a mean little bastard for he knew just how to show up the Air Corps!

It was the 4th of August when the LST was run up on the beach on Okinawa, and it was about 1:00 AM when the front ramp was lowered. It was then that I was collared by one of the ship's officers and appointed officer in charge of unloading. To this day, I don't know why I was selected to supervise this operation since I surely had no qualifications for the job. Seeing that I was stuck with it, and in view of the fact that there was no place to go, I positioned myself on the beach and assumed a *man in charge* posture. In the darkness, I might have easily been mistaken for General MacArthur, but the lack of a corncob pipe was a dead giveaway. All went well, until I noticed that what had once been a large group of workers had now dwindled to about a dozen. I probably would have joined them, had I known where to go, but they had disappeared without a trace. Regardless, I made the most of the few that remained.

In port, Okinawa, August 4, 1945

My attitude changed quickly, however, when an alarm was sounded warning us of the possibility of Kamikaze attacks. Suicide bombings were becoming more common as the desperate Japanese spared no one in an attempt to turn the tide.

Later that morning, I was rescued when trucks of the 22nd arrived and brought me to our new camp area. Except for the food, I'd had enough of the Navy and that undersized mess boy who had perpetrated that low down, mean raw egg trick.

* * * * *

Our new camp area was a long, narrow rectangle, extending over uneven terrain. Water tanks on trucks indicated that once again we would be hauling water in 5-gallon cans. I began to walk and when I reached the most distant part of the camp area, I was surprised to see that it ended at a cliff. I guessed that it was about a hundred-foot drop to the ocean. Looking to my right, I could see a rather nice beach and some swimmers in the ocean. I went back and found McCullough and another officer named Hammond and reported that I had found an ideal location to set up our tent.

At last, our building materials arrived and we started work on our new home. This time, however, we were going first class. We decided to construct a framework and then find something to use for the roof. I looked forward to the construction task, since it would keep me from thinking about the delay in going home. After we got the floor down, there was an immediate need to erect a guardrail because the floor came to within a few feet of the cliff. Without a parachute, the hundred-foot drop could be a little too thrilling.

Erecting our "home away from home" on Okinawa, August 1945. The front faces the ocean about 200 feet below. McCullough is wearing white coat and Boyle is assisting. Hutton is standing on steel drum. Colletti on ladder.

When we had finished, we surveyed our handiwork and felt quite pleased with the construction job we had done. In addition, I had located my water collection system and wasted no time in getting it set up, and not a minute too soon.

Some of the officers had hired natives to lug the heavy, water fill cans, for we were camped quite some distance from the tank truck. Unfortunately, some of the

natives were caught stealing so they were all banned from the camp area. Now, it was back to carrying heavy 5-gallon cans. It was then that Lt. Colletti, he with the personal water supply, once again discovered that he had more friends than ever. To meet the increased demand, I mounted a second drum above the first, let it fill and then opened the spigot to let the water run into the lower drum. Wade Schroeder, had he been here, would have been very proud of me.

Then everything changed on August 6th when we learned that the atomic bomb had been dropped on Hiroshima. We in uniform were probably more ignorant than the civilian population back home, insofar as knowing what was going on in the world. We questioned each other, what's an atomic bomb? How big is it? Who dropped it? Everybody had questions, but there were no answers. As more details became available, we realized nothing like this had ever happened before.

We barely had time to begin to understand what this meant, when the second bomb was dropped on Nagasaki on August 9th. The entire world was stunned, unable to grasp the full significance of these two events. Then we began to think the unthinkable, that the war might soon be over. But all we could do was wait.

Slowly, things settled down to a daily routine. I was assigned various tasks; mail censor, officer of the guard and served as a member of a court martial board. I welcomed any duty that relieved the boredom of sitting around with nothing worthwhile to do.

Although we were aware that peace talks were taking place, we were stunned when it was announced that the Japanese had agreed to our surrender terms on September 2, 1945. Since I was off flying status, I can only imagine how those who were flying reacted when they realized that they would not have to fly any more risky combat missions. At last, it was possible to think about going home.

Using the front porch of new Okinawa home.

Most of us were of the opinion that the Japanese would never surrender; that they would defend their homeland regardless of the cost or number of casualties. We were also well aware that we would also suffer heavy casualties if we went ashore on the Japanese mainland. Fortunately, that horrible confrontation had been avoided.

I had a visitor, a few days later, in the person of Joe Friedman, the squadron adjutant. Naturally, our conversation turned to the big story of the day, the use of atomic weapons; but I felt that there was more to this visit than current events.

"Colletti," he began, "I have been checking the personnel files, and I learned that you had been an enlisted man and had experience in running the orderly room. As you probably know, I need someone to replace me; and I think it would be a great opportunity for you. You could submit your own orders for promotion to captain, and then go on to see Japan as soon as the peace treaty is signed. The job is yours if you want it."

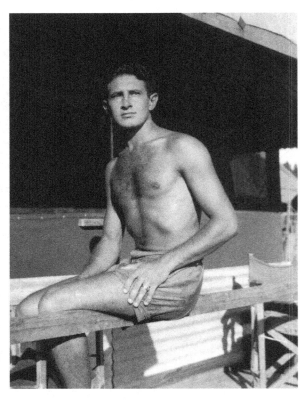

I replied "Joe, I know it is a great opportunity for someone who wants to make the service their career, but I'm a civilian at heart. Thanks for the offer, but the only place I'm going is home." He said he understood.

As he left, the last word I had spoken, *home*, made me think of Jack Cole, who had the bed next to mine at Victorville. I remembered his classic remark, "When this damn war is over, and I get back to

Chapter 19

Jackson, TN, I'm going to hang out my shingle and it will say, 'Jack Cole, at Stud.'" He wanted to *make a bomb run* on the female population of his hometown. As for me, the only woman I was interested in was P38, thousands of miles away in Georgia.

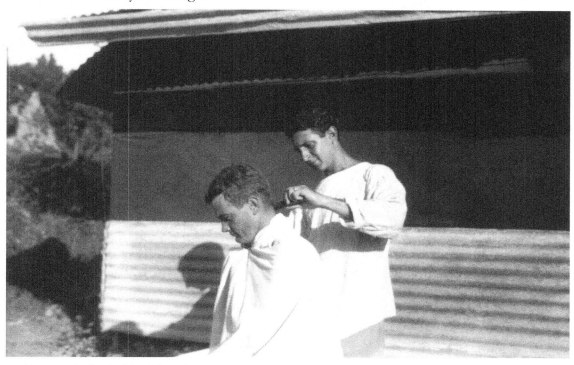

I became the "barber" by default. None was available and no one cared how they looked. Lt. Hutton is the *lamb*.

Mires, Boyle, Colletti, McCullough, Hutton - Okinawa 1945

197

Outdoor laundry – strip, and wash what you're wearing, too.

View of private beach from tent.

Chapter 19

On September 7, 1945, all the wheels in my head began to spin when I was given order #247, dated September 4, 1945. I was hereby relieved from active duty with the 408th and would board a war-weary B24 (which was going to be scrapped) for the trip back to Clark Field. From there, I was to proceed to Nielson Field, Manila to begin processing for the return to the United States.

I was part of a small group that made the flight from Okinawa, and I believe that we all were concerned with the airworthiness of the plane, hoping that it would not fall apart in the air.

Eldridge Okinawa, leaving for home (Colletti second from right.)

Seeing Clark Field again was wonderful, for it would be the first step in the seven thousand mile trip home. From Clark, we got a ride on a C47 that was going to Nielson Field. The next stop would be the processing center in Manila and then finally head for the United States.

"September 9, 1945, Manila

Dear Carl,

I am having a difficult time trying to find something solid to write upon. The best I can do is sit on my cot and hold the paper on my knees.

Perhaps you are wondering what I am doing in Manila. Well, they're finally sending me home and this is the first stop. My orders came through on the 7th.

This is a processing center, and it reminds me of my first few days in the Army. Chow lines two blocks long and inadequate washing facilities, but who cares I'm on my way! The food is good, a major improvement over Okinawa, which was awful. Right now, I am waiting to be processed, check my records, etc. That should take a few days. Once that is done, it is a matter of sweating out transportation. I am almost certain that I will be going on a long boat ride.

Till then,
Sil"

The processing center was quite large, but it was still a transient camp. I had remembered to bring my hoarded roll of toilet paper the first time I used their facilities, knowing that places like this would leave a lot to be desired. Unfortunately, I was right. I was also right about another thing: this was going to be a slow process, but then again, I had become accustomed to waiting. There was little to do except write letters and wonder how much longer it would be before I would be on my way.

Having nothing better to do, I decided to hitch a ride into Manila and take a few pictures. I was under the impression that it had been declared an open city, to be spared, but what I saw was a city that had been heavily damaged. Rubble was everywhere, visual proof of the fierce fighting that had been waged. While walking around like a tourist on vacation, I saw a Red Cross Canteen. In a moment, I remembered how I had lived on their doughnuts and coffee when in Australia. Much to my surprise, they had ice cream, something I had not tasted since leaving the United States over a year ago. There was no choice, just vanilla, but that was fine. *It only cost seven dollars.* It was worth it because it was a milestone, a connecting link to the life I had left behind.

At long last, the waiting came to an end. I would be going home on a fully loaded, army transport ship, the USS *Haskell*, and the destination was San Francisco. Departure date was September 30, 1945.

The ship had barely left port before the first crap game and poker game began. What made these games unusual was that they never ended. When a player had had enough, he would drop out and someone would take his place. Eventually, there would be a complete turnover of players. Money that could buy nothing now found a use and a lot of it changed hands. I might have been tempted to join in, but fortunately, I had sent almost my entire pay home.

The weather was good and I enjoyed the trip, but it was slow, adding to my impatience. There was nothing to see except water until we sailed past Eniwetok Island, on October 8, 1945, then it was back to the vast expanse of the Pacific Ocean. The monotony was finally broken on October 18th, when we got the message we all had been waiting to hear: We would be arriving in San Francisco tomorrow after a nineteen-day voyage. It was exciting news.

Sleep was impossible that last night aboard ship. I closed my eyes and tried to relax, but I could not tune out the thoughts and visions that came to mind: How will it feel to see the California shoreline and sail under the Golden Gate Bridge, which by tradition indicates the departure from or arrival to the USA? Is this really happening or is it just wishful thinking? Once ashore, how many days will it take to be processed? Will I be flown home or put aboard a train? I visualized the faces of my family; faces I had not seen for a year and a half and wondered if they had changed. I knew I had changed, but in what way? How can I do all the things I want to do, and see all the people I want to see? What will I do when I return to civilian life? Loaf for a while and then look for a job? What kind of a job? How long will it take to re-start my life? When will I get to see Red? Do I want to get married or put it off for a few years? How can I even think of that when I don't have the means to support us? Everything is so screwed up.

There was no doubt, however, that the vision that was uppermost in my mind was that of P38. It had been almost two years since we had kissed goodbye; two years of writing letters and waiting. What will it be like to see her again, to hear her laugh, hold her close and dance with her? Could we bridge the two-year gap? Had she met someone else? She had made a commitment to me, in her letters, but the possibility could not be dismissed. (I remembered seeing a plane, at Clark Field, with a girl's name prominently painted on the fuselage. The name had been crossed out, however, and in bold letters was the caption: "Couldn't Wait.") I shuddered when I considered the possibility that it could happen to me.

Apparently, I was not the only one who could not sleep that night because most everyone was topside early in the morning. As we drew closer, the excitement level went up a few notches when the returning servicemen, crowding the deck, began to see the dim outline of the California coast. Slowly, ever so slowly, the landmark we were straining to see came into view, and the excitement level went up a few more notches when we could read the *welcome* sign on the side of the Golden Gate Bridge. Finally, on that never to be forgotten day of October 19, 1945, after 19 days at sea, we sailed

Passing under the Golden Gate Bridge October 19, 1945

under the Golden Gate Bridge and in so doing marked our official return to the United States. A loud cheer went up as we realized that this wasn't Australia, the Palau Islands, the Philippines or New Guinea. This was the USA -- this was where we belonged -- this was another never to be forgotten *once in a lifetime moment* that I entered into my scrapbook of memories.

After we left the ship, we marched a short distance to the motor pool where transportation was available to take us to Camp Stoneham. Parked in a straight line, spaced about twelve feet apart, were a line of trucks that had already been loaded and were waiting for the signal to leave. Apparently, the officer in charge of the convoy was determined to transform a simple every day task, such as moving a group of trucks, into a choreographed event. When he gave the signal to pull out, the entire convoy of ten trucks moved as *one*. Number two did not wait for number one to move before he started to roll. They moved as though they were coupled together. We all wondered how many hours they had practiced in order to achieve that high level of precision driving. When the preliminaries had been completed, I sent a telegram to Red and then phoned home. I kept it brief, knowing that others were waiting, anxious to make their calls.

For the Duration *plus* Six Months

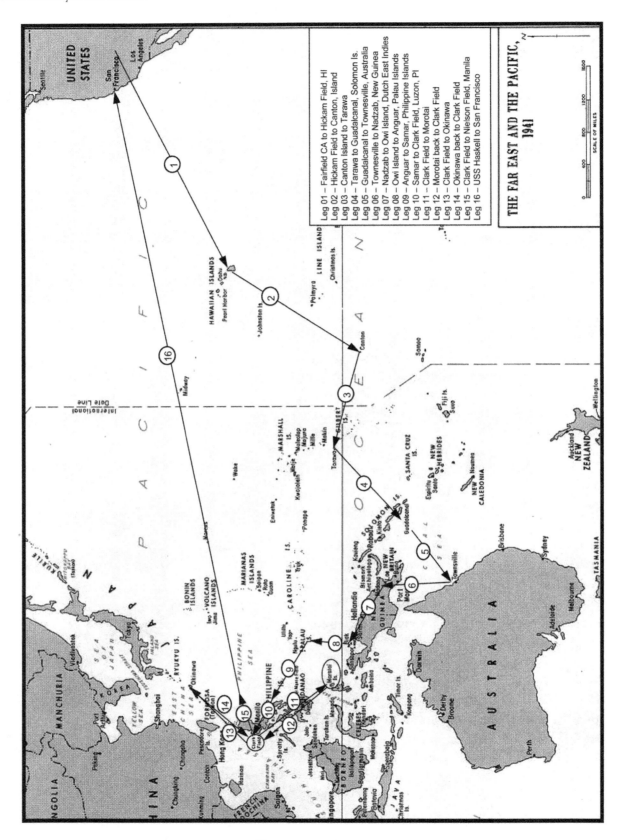

The Far East and Pacific Map[31] displaying all the legs of my trek across the Pacific.

Chapter 19

The next two days were spent going through processing and waiting for transportation. I was part of a large group that was going to the east coast. When we boarded the train, we were appalled to see what we had been given for the long trip across the country. We judged the train to be at least forty or fifty years old, with vases on the walls to attest to its antiquity. In its heyday, it might have been first class, but all we could see was an old hulk. Finally, the train pulled out and we were happy to be on our way, but not for long. There were a number of females aboard, in addition to a number of colonels and majors; and after a few hours of traveling, it became obvious that the facilities were inadequate for the women. We checked with the train crew and learned that we would soon have a layover at the next stop. When the train pulled into the station, we descended upon the wireless office and sent telegrams to our respective congressmen, senators or any government official we thought would have a sympathetic ear. It worked. At our next stop, we left the dinosaur and were put aboard a train that would meet the needs of the mixed group. We were still in coach, but it would be a lot more comfortable.

The last car of the train had a platform where passengers could stand and see the track trailing off in the distance. One of the most popular songs in October of 1945 was "Sentimental Journey,"[32] and it was sung by Doris Day with Les Brown and his Orchestra. I have a most vivid memory of a group of us standing out there on the platform and singing that part of the lyric that said, "Countin' every mile of railroad track, that takes me back." The clickity-clack was music to our ears since each clack indicated we were that much closer to home.

It was the 27th of October, 1945, when I arrived at Fort Dix, New Jersey. Physically I was there, but the mental adjustment had not yet begun. That would take time.

Three friends were with me aboard that train. Lt. Glenwood Ewald, a pilot from New York State and Lt. Sol Siegel, a navigator from New York City, were my squadron mates in the 408th. Lt. Art Sadowsky, a navigator, was also from New York City, who was with the 19th Squadron. As we stepped off the train, I turned to them and said "The wheel has come full circle, for it has been exactly four years and four days ago that I had been at this very base, when I was drafted." There is no way to describe the thoughts I was thinking or the emotional impact I felt knowing that I had returned to the very place where it all had started October 20, 1941.

October 28, 1945, Fort Dix – Sadowsky, Siegel, Colletti

The officer in charge of the detail made a short, welcome home speech and wasted little time in getting us assigned to sleeping quarters and getting us fed. If all went well, only one more day would be needed for processing. Then he told us where we could find telephones, said see you tomorrow and turned us loose.

I had called home when I had arrived in San Francisco, informing them that I would be sent to Fort Dix, and would call from there. It was still early in the day when I phoned and said that I would be on the first train that was going to Linden.

Once again, what I had learned in three years of commuting to New York was put to good use, for I knew how to decipher a Pennsylvania Railroad timetable. I was on my way. Although the travel time was only about an hour, it seemed much longer before the Linden sign came into view, and the train began to slow down, finally coming to a stop. As I stepped off, I asked myself how many times had I stood on this very platform, in years gone by, when commuting to New York? Why does everything look so familiar and yet so strange? It would be an understatement to say that what I was experiencing was so very confusing.

It was then that I decided to walk rather than wait for a bus, since it was less than a mile. I had walked but three blocks when I passed the street where Carl Frank lived. Five minutes later, on my left, the old Linden City Hall came into view. It was there that the Linden Model Aircraft held their meetings on Thursday night. Another block and another memory: Wheeler Park, scene of many football and softball games. The park was deserted, but in my mind, I could see the faces of all the friends who took part in those games. A few minutes later I reached US 1, waited for the traffic light to change and then continued walking slowly as I looked at all the familiar stores that fronted on Wood Avenue -- places that I had known most of my life. I looked up when I came to the next corner, and the street sign said Tenth Street. One more block and there on the corner of Wood Avenue and Eleventh Street was Andy's Meat Market where Mom did her shopping. I had needed three references when I had applied for aviation cadet training, and Andy had supplied one of them. It was then that I quickened my pace, anxious to reach my destination: Twelfth Street. I turned right, and as I began

Fort Dix October 28, 1945

to walk, I made mental note of the houses where my playmates had lived whom I had known since 1925. Some had moved away, but many were still living in the same house. As I walked, I recognized many of the cracks in the sidewalk, the same sidewalk that I had unsuccessfully tried to jump two squares at a time when I was ten or eleven years old. I had failed because I was too small, but it was when I finally succeeded that I realized I had begun to grow. As I neared the end of the street the vacant lot where we played softball came into view; and off to one side, I could see the area where we pitched horseshoes. In my mind, I recreated the ghostlike images of the players there on the field: Vic and Charlie Cericole, Eddie Treaschler, brothers Sal, Domenick and Joe, Morris Kamler and Tony Russo, among others. I could not help smiling when I looked at the house on the other side of the street, because I remembered that Davey Glick lived there -- the same Davey Glick that I had nicknamed *Mr. Argue-ation* because he argued every close call regardless of the game we were playing. "Was it fair or foul? Was the ball carrier in or out of bounds?" With him in the game, more time was spent arguing than playing ball -- a real pain in the ass if there ever was one. Continuing toward the end of Twelfth Street, it seemed that nothing had changed and yet everything had changed. A few more strides and I could see the front porch of the house in which I had lived since I was six years old and remembered that at the top of the steps, the number 45 was on the post adjacent to the screen door. It was then that I realized that this time I wasn't coming home on furlough or on a three-day pass for a brief return to the life I had previously known: *A visit that would come to an end much too soon; followed by tearful goodbyes and long, tiring train trips and more long months of separation. A visit that had become so confusing because I didn't know where I belonged; here or there, which made me conclude that I didn't ever want to come home on leave again because saying goodbye had become too painful. Without a doubt, it was much easier to remain on base and not be put through that emotional ringer.* But this return was different. The war was over -- the odyssey had come to an end -- I was home to stay.

I rang the doorbell, but didn't bother to wait because the door was unlocked and the emotional high that had overwhelmed me made it impossible to wait. I took two steps into the living room and a moment later Mom came rushing toward me. As I reached for her, she threw her arms around my neck and started kissing me, and I couldn't decide if she was laughing or crying, because she was doing both. Suddenly, she stopped kissing me and did the most unbelievable, unexpected thing only a mother could do. She backed off a step and then, starting at my shoulders, proceeded to run her hands *over my entire body*. At that moment, I wasn't 26 years old. At that moment I was her youngest child, her baby, and she had to prove to herself that I had not lied when I told her I had not been wounded -- that I was all there. When she was satisfied, she started kissing me again. Then it was my turn to cry.

Later that evening, the welcome home scene was repeated when Pop, brothers Dom, Sal, Joe and sister Angie arrived, soon followed by in-laws, nieces and nephews. I would wager that the very same scene was being played in thousands of homes by thousands of veterans as they opened their front doors. Only then would they feel the full impact of those two wonderful words *I'm home*.

It had been an eventful day, but I had to get back to Fort Dix to complete the last bit of paperwork. As I was about to leave, after supper, Pop gave me the keys to the family car and sent me on my way.

At last, I had the opportunity to attend to one last very important detail. I drove to the train station, which I knew would be deserted, entered the phone booth and called P38. Hearing her voice once again was all I needed to make my day complete. I didn't need a car to transport me back to Fort Dix because I was on my personal magic carpet. It had been a very emotional day, a once in a lifetime day and talking to Verna was the icing on the cake.

* * * * *

Driving time to the base was about an hour -- an hour spent entirely thinking about her and what to do. It was not a difficult decision. Talking to myself, I said, what the hell are you waiting for you damn fool? Go to her. Don't wait too long. She's waiting for you. Go!

The next morning, October 29, 1945, back at Fort Dix, was spent going over my records, making additions, corrections and checking for accuracy. Service dates, awards, decorations, insurance transfer, termination of allotments, medical records, etc. were all reviewed. I was issued a small pin of an eagle with outspread wings to be worn in the buttonhole of a jacket, which would identify the wearer as a veteran. Needless to say, it quickly got a nickname, the *Ruptured Duck*. The final item was a decision I had to make. Did I want to go into the Air Corps Reserves? If so, I was to go through the designated door and sign up. I didn't have to think twice about the decision to join the Reserves. I had worked too hard and too long to earn my commission, and I had never lost the desire to wear, or sense of pride I felt, when wearing the uniform. As a reservist, I would wear it when attending meetings. I entered the designated room and signed up. It would prove to be one of the best decisions I had ever made.

When the processing was completed, the interviewing officer shook my hand and wished me luck. As an officer, I had been *separated* from the service, not discharged. There was a difference. The leave time that I was entitled to, but which I had never received, extended my official date of separation to, ironically, December 7, 1945.

I had invited Lt. Art Sadowsky to ride with me when we left Fort Dix to go to Linden, and from there he could easily get a train to Penn Station in New York. It occurred to us that not too long ago we were flying over jungles and being shot at by the Japanese. Today, *we were both flying*, but without the need of an airplane. It was very confusing. It would take time to get our heads on straight.

It was early afternoon the next day when we left Fort Dix for the trip back to Linden after being separated from the Army Air Corps. While driving, we compared notes as to how we hoped to make the transition to our new status, *civilian*, (although technically, I was still on active duty until December 7th.) The one thing we agreed on completely was that our lives were all screwed up and that we didn't have a clue as to what to do next. I drove Art to the Linden train station and remained with him until his train arrived. Then we said goodbye for the last time, vowed to keep in touch and waved a last goodbye as the train left the station.

Linden Train Station October 19, 1945
Saying goodbye to Art Sadowsky.
We saw each other again 58 years later to the day.

When I returned home, I went upstairs to my old room and began to unpack my bag and hang up my uniform. I checked the closet and noticed a few items of civilian clothing, a pair of shoes, a few shirts, a matching set of shirt and pants and very little more…*clothes which I had last worn in October of 1941*. Obviously, I needed to go shopping. It seemed so strange to see my civilian clothes and uniform side by side in the closet, and for a moment, I concluded that the civilian clothes belonged to someone else because the uniform was mine and I had proof of that because my serial number was stamped in them. There was my bed. The bed I had not slept in since the first week in May, 1944, when I came home on leave from Victorville bursting with pride to be wearing the wings on my blouse and 2nd lieutenant bars on my shoulders. That was eighteen months ago. Looking at the pillowcase on the bed, my thoughts wandered back to the pillowcase I had made from the handkerchiefs Red had sent me when I was overseas. Talk about luxury! I was the only one with a pillow and a pillowcase. What had become of it? Boyle, McCullough and Hammond were my tent mates when I left Okinawa. Probably one of them had inherited it.

I looked out of the window in the bedroom and what I saw brought a surge of memories. The woods behind the house were still there, unchanged by time. Meandering through it was the brook that became our personal skating rink when it froze over. I was thirteen when the kids on Twelfth Street built a house in the woods, and we *appropriated* a few items from our homes to make it more comfortable. How well I remembered the most important incident that took place there. Feeling very grown up we decided that we were old enough to smoke, so this was the perfect place to do it. We had saved up enough money to buy a pack each of the brands *all the grownups* were smoking. As I recall, a pack of cigarettes cost about twenty cents, so we bought a pack of Lucky Strike (motto: Lucky Strike Means Fine Tobacco; Camels: I'd walk a mile for a Camel; Kool: Spud and Twenty Grand.) I smoked one of all the brands and what I remember so very clearly was that they all tasted like crap. Horrible! That was the end of my smoking adventure. Who needed it?

There was a special delivery letter for me, from Red, when I got home on the 27th of October. She had listed the dates when she could get away from school and when we could be together. We lucked out because she would have five days off for Thanksgiving and that was all I needed to know. I found a calendar and went about making plans.

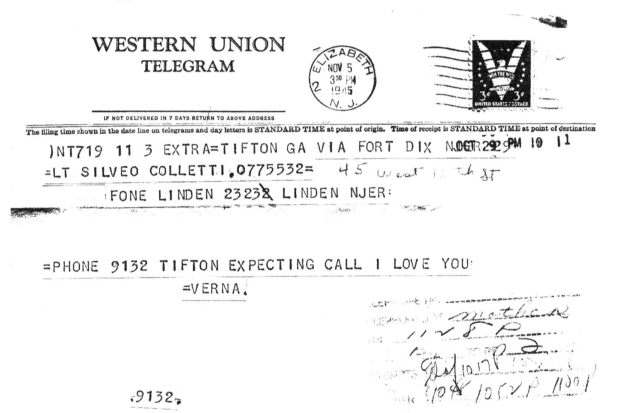

Once again, what she had written and what I wanted to read were one and the same, but something new had been added. At the end of the October 23rd letter, she signed her name *Red Colletti*. The letters of November 1st and 2nd were signed, *Verna Colletti*. There was no doubt about what she was telling me. She was *trying on the name for size* and apparently, she liked it. Now all that remained was to make it legal.

While overseas, I had written to my family and told them about Verna and how I felt about her. What I had no way of knowing was how they reacted to the news, because they made no comment; but I sensed that Mom and Pop were not too happy with my choice. They probably had visions of me marrying a local girl, preferably Italian, rather than someone so different from our lifestyle. That would have pleased them, but it was my life to live and I had already met the girl with whom I wanted to share it.

I was pleased to learn that they had exchanged a few letters, so it came as no surprise when I told them I was anxious to see her. When I mentioned it to Pop, he asked, "When are you leaving and how are you going to get there?" To the first question I answered,

"November 15th." As for question number two I answered, "I don't know." Pop had been in the United States Navy on the USS *Brooklyn*. He knew and understood how I felt.

He said, "Take the car."

As he spoke those words, I realized how stupid young people could be. When I was about seventeen or eighteen, I thought I knew everything and my parents knew nothing. Wasn't it odd how much wiser *they* had become as *I grew older*? What happened? "With age comes wisdom," as the saying goes, and I had aged a lot in four years.

* * * * *

TOP SECRETS OF WORLD WAR II

There were many top secrets during WWII, such as the development of the atomic bomb, D-Day and the Norden bombsight. To the best of my knowledge, there is still one secret that has never been revealed and that is the identity of the person who created the terse, descriptive, crisp, three word message that was read by millions of servicemen throughout the world. I believe I first saw it when we left the United States and landed in Hawaii, and from that moment on it was everywhere. Open up a book, flip a few pages and it would be there. Read the bulletin board in New Guinea, Samar, Clark Field on the flight line, and it would be there. Go to a restaurant and it would probably be on the menu. Climb aboard a B24 Liberator to fly a mission, and the message would certainly be there. Enter a bathroom or latrine anywhere in the world, and it would be prominently displayed along with many other words of wisdom. (It is my firm, unshakable belief that if the misspent brain power that was used to create all those sayings which were written on *latrine walls* had been properly used, a cure for cancer would have been found years ago.) The ingenuity of the writer fascinated me; his ability to have been everywhere was legendary. It was impossible not to smile when reading the message scribbled on the bottom of a toilet seat. There was one place where I expected to see it, but I was disappointed because it was not on the underside of the Golden Gate Bridge, as I passed under it coming home from the Philippines. Perhaps it had been there, but someone might have erased it since I am sure the writer would not have overlooked that prominent spot. To this very day, I remain intrigued by this unsolved mystery. What was the message? *Kilroy was here!*

SEPARATION QUALIFICATION RECORD
SAVE THIS FORM. IT WILL NOT BE REPLACED IF LOST

This record of job assignments and special training received in the Army is furnished to the soldier when he leaves the service. In its preparation, information is taken from available Army records and supplemented by personal interview. The information about civilian education and work experience is based on the individual's own statements. The veteran may present this document to former employers, prospective employers, representatives of schools or colleges, or use it in any other way that may prove beneficial to him.

1. LAST NAME—FIRST NAME—MIDDLE INITIAL	MILITARY OCCUPATIONAL ASSIGNMENTS		
COLLETTI SILVEO G.	10. MONTHS	11. GRADE	12. MILITARY OCCUPATIONAL SPECIALTY
	18	1"Lt.	Bombardier 1035

2. ARMY SERIAL NO.	3. GRADE	4. SOCIAL SECURITY NO.
O 776 632	1"LT.	unknown

5. PERMANENT MAILING ADDRESS (Street, City, County, State)
45 West 12th Street
Linden, Union Co., New Jersey

6. DATE OF ENTRY INTO ACTIVE SERVICE	7. DATE OF SEPARATION	8. DATE OF BIRTH
29 Apr. 1944	7 Dec. 1945	13 Sept. 1919

9. PLACE OF SEPARATION

Fort Dix, New Jersey

SUMMARY OF MILITARY OCCUPATIONS

13. TITLE—DESCRIPTION—RELATED CIVILIAN OCCUPATION

BOMBARDIER: Flew 39 combat missions in the Asiatic Pacific Theater as a B-24 Bombardier doing high altitude precision bombing of such targets as Borneo, Formosa and the Philippines. Had 21 Group and Squadron Leads.

DECORATIONS: Air Medal with 2 Oak Leaf Clusters;
Asiatic-Pacific Theater Ribbon with 8 battle stars;
Philippine Liberation Ribbon with 2 Battle Stars;
American Theater of Operations Ribbon;
American Defense Service Ribbon.

WD AGO FORM 100
1 JUL 1945

This form supersedes WD AGO Form 100, 15 July 1944, which will not be used.

Army of the United States

CERTIFICATE OF SERVICE

This is to certify that

FIRST LIEUTENANT SILVEO G. COLLETTI O 776 632 AIR CORPS
408TH BOMB SQUADRON 22ND BOMB GROUP
ASIATIC PACIFIC THEATER

honorably served in active Federal Service in the Army of the United States from

29 APRIL 1944 to 7 DECEMBER 1945

Given at SEPARATION CENTER FORT DIX NEW JERSEY

on the 7TH *day of* DECEMBER 1945

FOR THE COMMANDING OFFICER:

H C Ward
H C WARD MAJOR AC

MILITARY EDUCATION

14. NAME OR TYPE OF SCHOOL—COURSE OR CURRICULUM—DURATION—DESCRIPTION

Army Air Forces 24 weeks Bombardier and Dead Reckoning Navigation.

CIVILIAN EDUCATION

15. HIGHEST GRADE COMPLETED	16. DEGREES OR DIPLOMAS	17. YEAR LEFT SCHOOL	OTHER TRAINING OR SCHOOLING	
			20. COURSE—NAME AND ADDRESS OF SCHOOL—DATE	21. DURATION
4 Yrs. H.S.	Dip.	1937	none	none

18. NAME AND ADDRESS OF LAST SCHOOL ATTENDED
Linden High School
Linden, New Jersey

19. MAJOR COURSES OF STUDY
General

CIVILIAN OCCUPATIONS

22. TITLE—NAME AND ADDRESS OF EMPLOYER—INCLUSIVE DATES—DESCRIPTION

SALES CLERK: James S. Coletti Jewelry Merchant
   New York City   August 1938 to October 1941.
  Sold jewelry and repaired watches. Also did bookkeeping.

TYPIST: Linden Recreation Company   September 1937 to May 1938.
   Linden, New Jersey
  Typist- operated mimeograph machine and typed stencils for use by Recreation Commission.

ADDITIONAL INFORMATION

23. REMARKS

Enlisted Man T/4 X-ray technician   21 October 1941 to 10 December 1942
Good Conduct Medal.

Aviation Cadet 10 December 1942 to 29 April 1944.

24. SIGNATURE OF PERSON BEING SEPARATED	25. SIGNATURE OF SEPARATION CLASSIFICATION OFFICER	26. NAME OF OFFICER (Typed or Stamped)
Silvio G. Coletti	W. W. Von Schlichten	W. VON SCHLICHTEN MAJ. AGD.

For the Duration *plus* Six Months

ARMY AIR FORCES
Certificate of Appreciation
FOR WAR SERVICE

TO

SILVEO COLLETTI

I CANNOT meet you personally to thank you for a job well done; nor can I hope to put in written words the great hope I have for your success in future life.

Together we built the striking force that swept the Luftwaffe from the skies and broke the German power to resist. The total might of that striking force was then unleashed upon the Japanese. Although you no longer play an active military part, the contribution you made to the Air Forces was essential in making us the greatest team in the world.

The ties that bound us under stress of combat must not be broken in peacetime. Together we share the responsibility for guarding our country in the air. We who stay will never forget the part you have played while in uniform. We know you will continue to play a comparable role as a civilian. As our ways part, let me wish you God speed and the best of luck on your road in life. Our gratitude and respect go with you.

COMMANDING GENERAL
ARMY AIR FORCES

SILVEO G COLLETTI

To you who answered the call of your country and served in its Armed Forces to bring about the total defeat of the enemy, I extend the heartfelt thanks of a grateful Nation. As one of the Nation's finest, you undertook the most severe task one can be called upon to perform. Because you demonstrated the fortitude, resourcefulness and calm judgment necessary to carry out that task, we now look to you for leadership and example in further exalting our country in peace.

Harry Truman

THE WHITE HOUSE

20

GEORGIA, FLORIDA, AND A MOP OF RED HAIR

I was feeling guilty leaving so soon after getting home as I got into the car and waved goodbye, but deep inside I felt excited. I couldn't wait to get started.

For those heading south, US 1 was the way to go and there I began my trip, then switching to US 130 and onto US 13 in Delaware. Memories of Langley Field came to mind, when I boarded the ferry to Norfolk. Back on the road again, it was US 13, to US 17 and eventually Savannah, Georgia.

It was on November 2, 1943, two years and thirteen days ago, when I kissed Verna Atkinson goodbye and left the following day convinced that I would never see her again. It was not a question of being a pessimist. Rather it had to do with being realistic. There was a doubt in my mind that was rooted in the inescapable fact that we all change with the passing of time. The person she had kissed goodbye two years ago had changed, and she too probably had changed. Did the changes make any difference?

She was the most popular girl in her class, if not the entire school, doing what any seventeen-year-old girl should be doing: having fun. I was twenty-four years old and headed in the opposite direction; concerned with surviving the war, and if fortunate, how to restart my life. My class, 43J, was leaving and the incoming class would no doubt have its share of handsome, younger men than I. They would be *rushing her* while I wrote letters, which is not the best way to court a girl. Being fresh out of options, I began to write. It was the best I could do.

Leaving that train of thought, my mind wandered back to the events of the last two years when my odyssey had begun. One by one, I recalled all the stops along the way: Tyndall Field, Panama City, Florida, Victorville, March Field, Hamilton Field, Fairfield and Suisan Field, all in California. Then came the island hopping to Hawaii, Canton Island, Tarawa, Guadalcanal and finally our destination, Australia. North to Nadzab, New Guinea, Owi Island, off the northern coast of New Guinea, northward to Anguar in the Palau Islands, north to Samar and west to Clark Field in the Philippines. Missions to Hong Kong and Amoy China, back to Morotai in the Halmahera Islands, and the final missions to the Celebes and to Borneo. Back to Clark Field, to Okinawa, back to Clark Field, to Nielson Field, to Manila and then the long, 19-day sea voyage home aboard the USS *Haskell*. San Francisco, Camp Stoneman in California. Across the country to Fort Dix and finally home. Now, one more 1100-mile trip to Tifton, Georgia.

We had exchanged many letters during that time, each one adding a bit more to our growing relationship. I doubt if we realized that we had stopped writing about frivolous things while concerning ourselves more and more with matters that were important. We were pleasantly surprised to learn that we had more in common than we thought, whether it was music, aspirations, moral standards, importance of strong family ties and what we both wanted out of life. Once again, I relived all the wonderful moments of the little time we had spent together. The day I first saw her at Babcock Field eating fried chicken, and in the space of half an hour, found that I was attracted to her. Was it possible to fall in love in half an hour?

How absurd. That's crazy, but it did happen that way. Of course, I didn't know it then, but in time, I had to admit that it was so. The unexplainable mixed emotions I felt as I climbed into my plane and waved to her as I taxied out to takeoff to return to base. The feeling of sadness as I became airborne, certain that I would never see her again. I had to simply attribute that peculiar sensation to wartime loneliness and forget that it ever happened. One memory led to another; the glow that swept over me when she told me that she would be going to school in Valdosta, and that I would be able to see her again. The still vivid, embarrassing memory of the stupid, "I didn't know you with your clothes on" remark. Her astonished mother wondering what I had been doing with her seventeen-year-old daughter. Dancing with her at the college dance at Valdosta and how exciting it was to touch her for the first time and how it affected me to see another man holding her, even though they were only dancing. Telling that damn fool cadet to buzz off and stop cutting in because "she was my girl and I wanted to be with her." *My girl!* We hardly knew each other! Total up the minutes and hours we had spent together and it probably would have added up to less than two weeks. It didn't matter, it was enough. Writing letters was all I had and if she had lost interest, she could have cooled it off, written about the weather or how nice her new shoes looked with her new dress and just let it fizzle out, but she didn't. She could have sent me a "Dear John letter" saying that she had met someone else, but she didn't. Though only seventeen when we met, she had already turned down a number of marriage proposals, starting when she was in her early teens. By *Yankee standards,* southern girls married when they were very young. Following southern tradition, some of her friends had already married or were engaged. Certainly, she had the opportunity to give thought to the kind of man she wanted.

Soon after flying my first few missions, I started a letter asking her to wait for me, but after further thought, decided that it was the wrong thing to do. I knew of too many instances of married men, and those with girlfriends back home, give in to the pressure and come to the conclusion, "what the hell am I saving it for?" At the time, *my occupation* wasn't selling socks and ties in a men's store. We were being used for target practice by the Japanese, and one hit by anti-aircraft shell in the loaded bomb bay would have blown us to bits. My so-called future, for want of a better word, was much too uncertain; and I didn't want to box her in. I strongly felt that *a vow not taken was a vow that could not be broken,* so the only thing to do was to wait. In the meantime, we kept writing and I kept dreaming, but at the time, I dared not make any plans. The plans would have to wait until the future looked brighter.

There was another reason for not asking her to wait for me. I felt confident that I would not be killed, but that did not eliminate the possibility of being seriously wounded or maimed. It was a thought that I tried to suppress, but it was always there in the deepest recesses of my mind. The possibility of losing an arm, leg, eye or of suffering an injury which might reduce me to being a dysfunctional human being was very real. Maybe it had occurred to her that, physically speaking, the person who was returning might not be the same person she had kissed goodbye in November of 1943. What to do? Would she still be expected to keep the promise she had made? I concluded that it was much better not to ask her to wait and hope for the best. If my luck held out, that would be one bridge we would not have to cross.

Near Savannah, an accident up ahead made me realize that I had been driving like a robot, making turns and stops automatically, hardly paying attention to the road. An inner voice told me, you're tired. Stop. Get off the road. I saw a motel sign a short distance ahead, pulled in, got a room and settled down. At last I had an opportunity to do the most important thing, *call Verna.* Hearing her voice again made the day complete, and my anticipation level went up a few more notches. Tomorrow could not come soon enough, but at that moment, it was an exhausted, very happy flyboy who turned in and finally fell asleep.

I got an early start the next morning driving south on US 17 until I reached the junction for the turn off onto US 84 which would take me to Waycross. In my impatient, mental state, I thought that the odometer was malfunctioning because the numbers hardly changed regardless of how many miles I had driven. Making time was impossible because of the many small towns along the way, each posting typical speed reductions to twenty-five mph in city limits and school zones. At long last, Waycross came into view, a city that I knew so well from the air when I was going through pilot training at Bainbridge.

Once again, I began to daydream wondering what it would be like to see her again after being apart for two years. Two years was a long time, perhaps too long to expect a girl to wait --- a girl who was not yet eighteen when we kissed goodbye in November of 1943. Had there been a change? Was I expecting too much? Would anticipation prove to be greater than realization? Score: Questions many, Answers none.

After what seemed an eternity, I saw an *Entering Tifton* sign, followed by directions to Abraham Baldwin Agricultural College. I drove onto the campus grounds and headed for the large building, which I guessed correctly to be the main office, and parked. As I walked up the steps, the overwhelming thought that raced through my mind was the fact that *I had come to the end of an eleven thousand mile journey to be with the girl I wanted to marry.* A journey that began in Okinawa, from there to the Philippine Islands, a nineteen-day ocean voyage across the Pacific to the USA, across the USA to New Jersey and now to Tifton Georgia. A journey that I could only hope and dream that I would make some day to see the girl I wanted in my life. A journey that could have easily been aborted by circumstances over which I had no control.

* * * * *

I was wearing my *pinks and green* uniform and apparently, many of the people in the office seemed to know who I was, judging from their knowing smiles and the response I received when I asked for Verna Atkinson. I was told to go back to town where she and her classmates were waiting in a diner, which she identified by name. I thanked her, got in the car and headed back to town. It was only a short drive, but it seemed to take forever. Looking ahead, I saw the diner on the other side of the street and parked. I got out of the car, took a few steps and it was then that I saw a mop of red hair running toward me, waving in the middle of the street.

At that moment, I did not know or care if we had stopped traffic, if horns were blowing, if people were staring, if the dean of the college was watching or if we could be arrested for indecent behavior in public because we were oblivious to everyone and everything. All I knew was that in my imagination, I had lived and thought about this *day* and this *moment* for two years and now it was finally happening. *Nothing had changed --- all the doubts were gone --- there would be no Dear John letter --- she had waited for me.*

People watching these two idiots kissing in the middle of the street could easily arrive at three conclusions: they were crazy, she wasn't kissing her brother and he sure as hell was not kissing his sister. They would have been absolutely right on all three counts. Once again, no woman had ever sent a man a clearer message of how she felt.

The memories of the lonely hours spent on Owi, Samar, Anguar or other far away places -- the mud, lousy food, powdered eggs and powdered milk, *gray meat*, S.O.S., tent life, ticks, malaria, scrub typhus, ring worm, boredom, heat, humidity, not having a life -- the white-knuckle-moments we all experienced as we thundered down the runway, *overloaded* with fuel and bombs, praying that we would be airborne before running out of runway -- the pressure on me when it was my turn to do my job, as I searched the terrain below to locate the target -- putting the crosshairs on the aiming point and making coordinated course corrections with my left hand and rate corrections with my right, keeping in mind that it had to be done smoothly when leading the mission, so that the planes in formation could maintain their relative positions and not have a mid-air collision -- fine tuning my synchronization as we approached the bomb release point

-- checking and rechecking the setting I had entered into the Norden bombsight -- leaving nothing to chance -- so completely engrossed in what I was doing that I was not aware of being attacked by enemy planes or of the anti-aircraft bursts around us -- checking the bomb bay to see if I had a hung up bomb -- watching the bombs, in their downward flight, hoping that they would hit the target -- knowing that a mistake on my part, when in the lead, would make it necessary to *go around* and make another bomb run and thereby endanger every one a second time -- reliving the *sweat of flying* hundreds of miles over water, in a land-based plane for ten hours or more, wondering if we could find safe passage around the ever present storm clouds which blocked our path. Unwilling to admit to ourselves, that we might run out of fuel short of our base and have to ditch in the ocean with little chance of survival -- living from one mail call to another and how difficult it was to suppress the anxiety I felt as I waited for my name to be called -- dreading the thought that there might not

be a letter from her -- all the waiting and dreaming -- the fear that I would not live to experience this moment -- all these memories were suddenly a thing of the past as we held onto each other in the middle of the street.

Finally, we decided that it would be sensible to remove ourselves and let the waiting cars, with their staring, bewildered occupants go by. We returned to the diner, but I have no recollection of our conversation. Unfortunately, we were not alone, so there was little we could say to one another in the presence of others. But I distinctly remember how exciting it was just to be with her.

Soon, we had to leave for she was due back in school, and for the first time I knew how it felt to have her sitting close to me as I drove. She risked being grounded because the school kept a tight leash on the girls and getting into any car was a no-no; but in my euphoric state of mind, I couldn't care less about school rules. I had four years of being told what I could or could not do; but more to the point, this was a special, once in a lifetime moment for me and I wasn't going to be denied.

Looking at my watch, I saw that I had just enough time to find a place to stay, wash up and return to the college in the evening. The students were allowed to have guests on campus, but I considered myself to be more than a guest because I was going to see the girl I wanted to marry.

Chapter 20

Verna and Colletti, Valdosta, GA, November 11, 1945

I turned the car radio on as I drove back to town and heard the distinctive sound of Harry James' trumpet and a moment later, the voice of Kitty Kallen. She was singing a song which probably was being sung, whistled or hummed by thousands of returning servicemen who were experiencing what I had experienced just a short time ago. The lyric was simple, but it went to the very heart of what we were thinking and feeling as we returned to those we loved after being apart for years or months.

The emotional impact it had on me has survived to this day, has never lessened and I relive that beautiful, once in a lifetime experience every time I hear it played. That brief, sweet, incredible, never to be forgotten minute of seventy years ago that brought us together after being apart for two years, when we kissed in the middle of the street and in the process, managed to completely shut out the entire world.

"It's Been A Long, Long Time"[33]
Never thought that you would be, standing here so close to me
There's so much I feel that I should say,
But words can wait until some other day.
Kiss me once, then kiss me twice, then kiss me once again,
It's been a long, long time.
Haven't felt like this my dear, since I can't remember when,
It's been a long, long time.
You'll never know how many dreams I dreamed about you,
Or just how empty they all seemed without you.
So, kiss me once, then kiss me twice, then kiss me once again,
It's been a long, long time.

Returning to the school campus that night, it seemed that the clock had been turned back and once again, I was a teenager going out on a date for the first time. I met all her friends, we sang around the piano in the music room, and it was there that I learned the words to one of my favorite songs; "El Choclo."

We strolled around the campus grounds, hand in hand, talking, laughing (and stealing a quickie kiss when we thought no one was looking) trying to make up for lost time. How unbelievable it was to be alone with her after being apart for two long years.

We went to the movies the first afternoon she was free, but I have no recollection of what was playing because I wasn't looking at the screen. I was gazing at her thinking that it wasn't too long ago that I was watching bombs dropping over Borneo and sweating out my final mission. I had the feeling that I was seeing two scenes being played out simultaneously: One was the here and now, staring at her while holding her hand and the other of flashbacks of mud, takeoffs, landings, droning engines and fatigue. In my mind, I re-flew those long missions; wondering if I would live to see the day when we would be together again. Being realistic, I couldn't help but think that while I was writing letters, someone else might have come into her life. That one day I would get a letter where I could sense, reading between the lines, that she was gradually saying goodbye. Looking at her, in the dim light of the theater, all those nightmares were put to rest.

After the movie, we found a place to dance, and for once, there would be no one cutting in. I have a wonderful memory of the first night we went out to dinner. In her letters, she had mentioned how poor the food was at the school and how she was looking forward to having a good meal. She picked out the restaurant, and we both ordered their specialty: steak with french fries, and when we were served, I thought the servings were large enough to feed four people. I had all I could do to finish mine, feeling absolutely stuffed. A few minutes later, the waitress asked if we wanted dessert and I said "Nothing, we're too full." The words were barely out of my mouth, when I realized I had not considered her feelings, so I asked, "Would you like dessert?"

"Yes," she said, "I would like peach shortcake with ice cream" and she ate every bit of it! This redhead was hungry! Despite the passing of seventy-two years, I have never forgotten how wonderful it was to be with her, to see her sitting across the table from me, talking, smiling and saying all the little things I had dreamt about for the past two years.

Being on campus was fun but it wasn't until November 21st, the start of the Thanksgiving holiday, that we finally had the chance to be alone away from school rules and time deadlines. We drove north to Vidalia, to "carry" two schoolmates home. Then we headed south for Dunedin, Florida where we would stay with her sister Grace and husband, Sam Davis. We both were worn out when we finally arrived in Dunedin, after driving more than four hundred miles.

We spent four fun-packed days together, dancing, dining out, taking pictures and experiencing, for the first time, how it felt to be together in the same house -- still flying on *cloud nine*, excited but relaxed -- a *mini-preview* of life under the same roof as man and wife. It was then that I realized this was the perfect moment to do what I had wanted to do, soon after going overseas in September of 1944 -- *propose to Red*.

Dunedin, Florida November 1945

As strange as it might seem, and despite our open declarations of love, I had never asked her to marry me, but not because I didn't want to. I was crazy about her, and what I wanted most of all was to put a fence around her -- take her out of circulation -- making certain that she would be there when I returned. It was so tempting, but I held back thinking that it was not wise to do so while on active duty, flying combat missions, facing an uncertain future. It was obvious that we were making a commitment to each other with every letter we wrote, both knowing where we were headed. Still, there was something missing: I wanted to experience the thrill of hearing her answer "yes," when I asked her to marry me; but to describe it as a thrill does not do justice to how I was affected when she whispered that magical, three letter word. I added that moment to my list of *once in a lifetime moments*, where it belonged, at the very top. I had never been happier in my life.

On Sunday November 25th, we said goodbye to Grace and Sam and headed for Tifton, trying hard not to think that I would soon be going back to New Jersey while she remained in Georgia. But there was one major difference to this separation: the war was over and we were free to plan for a life together. I promised to send her an engagement ring, and she assured me it would be worn on the correct hand and finger.

Leaving her on Monday November 26th was one of the most painful things I've ever had to do. It hurt, but I could live with it knowing it would be just a matter of time before we would be together again. For the present, however, we would be returning to the all too familiar routine of writing letters, making phone calls and waiting; always the hated waiting.

The drive home was boring and long, but it did have one positive aspect. It afforded me an opportunity to concentrate on finding solutions to the problems facing us, for there were many. One in particular had to do with a situation I never dreamed could happen to me.

I am quite certain that my family probably wondered why we went to her sister's house rather than going to see her parents, which would have been the proper thing to do. They didn't ask and I didn't have the heart to tell them that her family, and especially her father, disapproved of me and forbid Verna from ever bringing me to his home. I was not welcomed.

Mr. Edward Atkinson, Verna's father, was born in North Carolina (probably in the mid 1870's) where his family had received a land grant from the King of England. His playmates were the Lumbee Indians and he learned their skills, culture and way of life. He told of going swimming in the wintertime, protected by a layer of bear grease, as the Indians did. They taught him how to live off the land and he became adept in various skills such as basket weaving and hunting. His skill with tools was legendary, and he was the kind of man who could do most anything with his hands. His father was a Captain in the Confederate Army which made it easy to understand why he, Edward, felt as he did about *Damn Yankees*. It came naturally to him.

For unknown reasons, he decided to forgo everything. He left North Carolina and made his way to Georgia where he met Rusell Jones. They married and had six children before they moved to Largo, Florida where Verna was born in 1926. A few years later he moved the family back to Georgia during difficult economic times (the depression), to live on a small farm that Verna's mother had received from her father.

Most of all, he was a highly principled man -- a man whose word was his bond, and it was probably this facet of his character that was responsible for his attitude toward me. Unfortunately, I soon learned that I had not three, but four strikes against me: I was a Damn Yankee, a Catholic, an Italian, and probably the most damming of all, was the fact that her family wanted her to marry someone else.

Staff Sergeant Clice Yancey saw action in Europe, serving in the infantry. He was a southerner, handsome, a year older than I, well educated and polite. He had dated Verna, when she was only sixteen, fell in love with her and asked Mr. Atkinson's permission to marry. There was no conflict with religion or nationality; he liked him as a future son-in-law and gladly gave his consent, but they overlooked one thing: she was not ready to get married. She was fond of Yancey, but did not love him and made it very clear that she did not intend to marry *anyone* until after the war was over. There were things she wanted to do -- go to college and take flying lessons. Mr. Atkinson felt betrayed, for he had given his word and in the process, I became the *undesirable other*. That was when he told Verna that she could never bring me to his home and she found herself trapped in a no-win situation, forced to make a decision no one should ever have to make.

As I drove, hour after hour, I wracked my brain trying to find a solution. For a few brief moments I concluded that we could defy everyone and get married, but in the long run, I knew it would not work. We could never be happy if she was cut off from her family, so I dismissed the thought. One fact was very clear; we were both miserably unhappy, feeling absolutely helpless, not able to think of a way to solve the problem.

For the Duration *plus* Six Months

November 28, 1945

Chapter 20

Verna Atkinson
Conquit, Georgia.
Sept. 4, 1945

RETURNING U.S

VIA AIRMAIL

Lt. Silveo Colletti O-776632
~~408 B Sqdn.~~ 22nd Bomb Group
A.P.O. ~~#~~ 337 % Postmaster
San Francisco, California.

"September 4, 1945

Colletti,

    As badly as I want to see you – I hope you don't come within the next few weeks. By that time I will either be in school or at one of my sisters – I won't be here. Then when you do come, I can see you. Since you keep asking, I'll tell you straight – Daddy said you could never come here so please don't."

21

HOME AGAIN AND EVERYTHING AFTER

In the fall of 1945, and in the coming year thousands of men across the country, such as I, were leaving the service and were confronted with the task of how to adjust to the return to civilian life. We had been gone two, three, four or more years and now it was time to pick up the scattered pieces of our lives and try to put them back together. During that time, I could not help but feel that my life had been put on hold while the *world's clock* kept ticking away. The four plus years I had served represented the time when I would have hoped to established myself, but they were gone and there was no way to make it up.

When I was drafted in 1941, adjusting to military life was easier because there were hundreds of us in the same boat; and in a way, it was sort of *group therapy*. The transition to civilian life, however, was more difficult because this was something you had to do alone.

As we began to say goodbye for the last time, a few of us would gang up on someone who had come from humble beginnings and who would soon be discharged. We would tease him by saying, "This is the first time in your life that you have had shoes on your feet, clothes to wear and good food to eat. *You have found a home in the Army.*" Why go back to living in a shack -- reenlist!

Then there were those who had achieved little in civilian life before their military service, but through rank, had reached a level of importance they had never previously known. Commissioned officers, accustomed to giving orders, would soon find themselves competing with GI Joe in the job market where they could not pull rank or go to the head of the line. Sadly, they quickly realized that they would revert to being a nobody after taking off the uniform. Without the uniform and the bars, they would be just another individual out of a job. Some, who could not make the transition, reenlisted and made the service a career. As for myself, I had no problem adjusting, despite those few, confusing days when I didn't know where I belonged. Fortunately, I had great motivation to quickly *find myself*. That motivation being how much I wanted the girl I had left in Tifton. Thinking about a life with her was all I needed to spur me on.

As I drove for endless hours, I began to take inventory of myself, adding up the plus and minus columns. Unfortunately, the minus column far outweighed the plus column. I didn't have a job, a car or the capability to support myself, much less a wife. Housing was unavailable, and lucky were the couples whose parents had a spare room into which they could move. *Doubling up* was the only immediate solution to the problem.

I had been out of high school eight years and a little over four of those years were spent in the service. The only thing in the plus column was the thirty-five hundred dollars which I had sent home when overseas. Judging by today's standards that was pitiful, but in 1945 twenty-five dollars a week was what the average worker was earning. That would be enough to fall back on in an emergency, but I still needed an income.

Chapter 21

Mom and Pop, December 9, 1945

Trying to be objective, I asked myself what I was qualified to do in civilian life. Certainly my military specialty, bombardier, was a useless skill, so what skills did I have? Not many, unfortunately. What were my options? I could look for a job, but there again, what kind of work was I qualified to do? I strongly considered the GI Bill which would have given me a free college education, but there was a problem. I had taken a general course in high school, no languages, no advanced math or other college preparatory courses. I was twenty-six years old and would then be in my thirties when looking for my first job. In addition, I didn't have any idea of what I wanted to do and it made little sense to think about college until I could make up my mind. What I realized even more was that I was tired of waiting and impatient to restart my life. It was then that it occurred to me that I was more fortunate than many others were because I could go back into the jewelry business with Dad. The more I thought about it, the more it appealed to me, and with that decision, I was able to put my mind at ease. Now I knew what I wanted to do and the sooner I started, the sooner I could think of getting married.

When I arrived home, I told Mom and Dad of my decision. They thought it was the right thing to do and the timing could not have been better. With the coming of the busy Christmas season, I could really be of use. I wasn't kidding myself, however, because I knew that for some time to come Dad would just be carrying me, since my contribution would be meager. The most important thing was that I now had a goal and the motivation to reach it. It was time to go back to work.

I was looking forward to Christmas of 1945 and the coming of the new year, 1946 for it would be my first Christmas at home since 1940. It had always been a beautiful, wonderful, family holiday and I knew this one would be very special.

Once again, the letter writing began, with phone calls to fill the gap. Verna had previously told me that she wanted to remain in school until June, and that was fine. I told her of my decision to return to the jewelry business and that I needed time to establish myself, so it was all working out. We agreed that we would try to marry in July or August. So once again, all we could do was wait. It seems that we had become quite expert in the art of waiting. Soon, we hoped, the waiting would be over. Little did I know that 1946 would turn out to be the most unhappy year of my life.

It was the second week in December when I went back to work making the daily commute to New York. Slowly, gradually, the images of military life began to fade, being replaced by familiar surroundings and people I loved. Fade they might, but they would never be forgotten.

During the Christmas holiday, I could not help but think of where I had spent the last four years. In 1941 and 1942, I was at Langley Field. I had just arrived at Victorville, on Christmas Day of 1943, to begin bombardier training. Year 1944 was spent on barren Anguar, in the Palau Islands writing letters and then going to bed early knowing I would be flying a mission the next day. I remembered the hostility shown to one of the men when he wished us "Merry Christmas." *Merry Christmas your ass*. What's so damn merry about being six thousand miles away from home? I felt sorry for him, since he meant well, but many of us were bitter and frustrated and we took it out on him. Fortunately, that was all in the past. I was now with friends and family and ever mindful of how wonderful it was to be home. New Year's Eve *celebration* was nothing. There was only one person I wanted to kiss on New Year's Eve and she was a thousand miles away. Perhaps next year would be different.

After an absence of four years, I knew that re-learning the jewelry business would be a slow process. There had been many changes in the market place, and it would take a while before I would be able to judge the value of merchandise. During my spare time, I began to tinker with junk watches that were not running, challenging myself to make them work. When I sat at the workbench for the first time, I remembered the day I took the final exam at Victorville and how helpful my previous watch repair background had been. For some strange reason, that seemed to be so very long ago.

* * * * *

During the month of January, 1946, I received letters from Red dated the 11th, 16th, 24th, 25th and the 27th stating that she was back in school at Tifton. I glowed when she wrote that she had to stop what she was doing to write me a letter, because she was listening to "Tico-Tico" on the radio and it made her think of *someone she knew in New Jersey*. There were a few other important items of note. Sister Grace and her husband Sam told her that they liked and approved of me. In addition, sister Elizabeth and husband Pat said she should marry me if she loved me; and though her mother was still not too happy with her choice (me), she didn't like her father's attitude either. Her brother Edwin had come home from the Pacific Theater and was going to return to farming where he was badly needed.

On a more personal level, she was doing very well in math, had cooked a good, complete meal at school and had been elected president of the Glee Club. She had saved the best for the last however, when she said that she wanted her engagement ring. I attended to that little detail the following month, when I sent it to her and which she received on the 26th of February. At last, we had passed a milestone. We were engaged.

Chapter 21

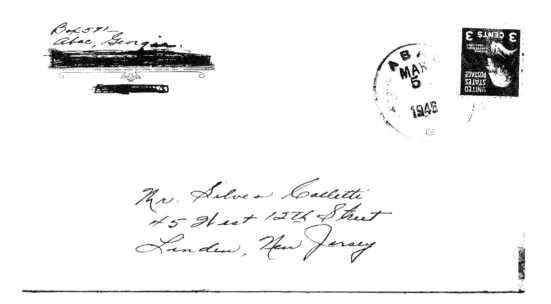

"… I didn't have a letter in the box, but I slipped my hand in anyway to see if I might have a slip saying that I had a package ~ I did, I asked for the package at the window and the minute I saw it I knew that it was a watch, so I started opening it right then and there!

After I got the top off I felt inside and was I surprised! I knew for certain what was in the little box, so I just put the box top back on and started back to my room. Fortunately there was no one in the room whenever I went in so I turned the light on and then before I opened the box I read your letter ~ then I looked at the ring. It's a beautiful ring darling ~ and it fits perfectly. I don't know exactly how to thank you, I really don't think there is even any need for me to try because you know how badly I wanted it ~ but as you so often say, 'just for the record' I'll say thank you…."

Also, in the month of February I was informed that the school had conducted a *who's who* event and she was elected as "the Girl about the Campus, most talented, most popular and wittiest." I was proud of her and now they knew what I had known all along: she was special; one of a kind. At last, I could now rightfully say that she was *my girl*, because she was wearing the ring I had given her.

There were a lot of happy reunions across the country during 1946 as servicemen began to return home. Best friend Carl Frank, returned in March, and it was great to get together again. We didn't know where to begin when we attempted to fill in the blanks when we told of our wartime experiences. There was so much catching up to do, comparing notes and laughing as we recalled the fun we had in previous years. Still, there was no escaping the fact that we had all changed, and that it would never be quite the same as it was when I left in October of 1941. We were older, and we knew that it was time to *turn the page* to thoughts of getting married and restarting our lives. He asked me about P38 and I told him that I had sent her an engagement ring and that she was going to college while I addressed the problem of becoming financially able to support her. Then, when the semester was over in June, we planned to get married in July or August. He and P38 had corresponded and exchanged pictures, at my urging, and had gotten to know each other. Soon, I hoped, we would all be together.

One Saturday evening I went to a dance at the Elks Club in Elizabeth. It had been weeks since I had last been anywhere, and I thoroughly enjoyed listening to a live orchestra. What I didn't realize was that these dances were primarily for men and women who wanted to meet after the long social drought of the war years. I enjoyed the first few numbers of the first set, and waited on the floor with my partner, for the second set to begin. It started with a rumba, "Siboney" which was the song and dance Red and I considered to be *ours*. I lied when I told my partner that I didn't know how to rumba and escorted her off the floor. For the briefest moment, I hated her because she wasn't Red. That experience put an end to going to dances since there was no pleasure in dancing with others.

March, April and May went by and we kept writing, but the waiting became more and more difficult, more so than during the war years. Then, I was not in control of my life, but now there were just two things keeping us apart: her father's disapproval and our own decision to wait until I was earning enough to support us. In her letter of May 28th, she wrote that school would be out June 11th. At last, I thought we could go ahead and plan to get married, but she admitted that she was scared to death just thinking about it.

In early June, Mama Atkinson informed her that her father was ill and had been taken to the hospital. She went to see him, and he smiled at her, although he was in great pain and was being given pain-killing drugs. About a week later, he felt well enough to go home, but she did not want to make any plans while he was recuperating, which was understandable. If all went well, she would be coming to New Jersey in August, so we went back to writing letters, telephoning and waiting.

In early July, her dad was back in the hospital having suffered a heart attack. When better, he went home only to be readmitted in late July, in serious condition. Once again, it was impossible for her to leave while he was ill. It was then she wrote, "Why don't you just forget about me? I couldn't possibly leave with Dad in serious condition. I love you so very much, but what good does it do me? You love me and stay home missing the things you could be enjoying if it were not for me." A week later, she wrote saying that she didn't know if we would ever be together and urged me to find a girl to love, that I should not wait for her any longer. I do not recall the exact words I used when I replied, but I straightened out her thinking when I told her that it would be easier for me to volunteer to return to Samar before I would ever consider forgetting her. I had a choice: I could wait or I could forget. I had long ago learned how to wait. I could teach a course on how to do that, but to forget her would be impossible. There was no way I could put an end to something we both wanted so badly. So I put that nonsense to rest and told her that I would wait for her regardless of how long it would be.

"*Colquitt, Georgia*
May 16, 1946

Dear Sil,
Please excuse my delay in answering your letter, but I was sick at the time I received it. Thanks for your Mother's Day card. It was very nice of you to think of me.
I was sorry that I didn't get to see you Thanksgiving. Verna didn't know what to do. She knew that her father had refused to see you and thought it best to call Grace.
I hope some day Mr. Atkinson will change and you can visit us. She also asked me to write to you, giving my consent. Hope I'll get to see you and talk to you in person, but always remember I want my children to be happy.

Sincerely,
Rusell J. Atkinson"

In early August, the family was advised to make funeral arrangements and her daddy died about the 19th. I would have gone to her, but considering how the family disapproved of me, thought it best to stay away. In the letter she wrote after his death she said, "Colletti, the only thing I have to hold on to is your ring -- sometimes I just sit and stare at it as if it could say something to me that would give me comfort."

In September, she wrote that she felt the need to go off by herself for a while, away from everyone and everything. Shortly thereafter, Mama Atkinson wrote to Mom Colletti that Verna had been under a great strain for the past three years, but she was free to visit me at any time. We each wrote a few more letters, and then September was gone.

It wasn't until the 10th of October that she wrote again, this time from Dunedin, Florida. She was not feeling well. She was depressed, couldn't eat and didn't know what was wrong and couldn't possibly come to New Jersey until she felt better. Weeks passed until she wrote again from Miami, on November 23rd. She had gotten a job and was working hard hoping to be tired enough at the end of the day to sleep at night. She begged me not to ask a lot of questions and to please leave her alone for a while. The letter ended with, "I love you more than ever, want to marry you, but not now." Then, about two weeks later, I learned that she was doing secretarial work for a tailor shop in one of the hotels, but what I read over and over were the last few lines. "The nicest Thanksgiving was the one we had spent together last year and that my ring is always where it belongs on my third finger, left hand."

Nothing made sense. She loved me, *but*. I was thoroughly confused, looking for logic that didn't exist; and I was determined to make her commit herself. The *macho man* in me was going to *insist* that she give me a flat yes or no answer, that I couldn't wait anymore. I had begun to write when I remembered what her mother had written, "…that she had been under a strain for three years." At that moment, I fully realized that choosing me was what had caused the problem. I put the pen down, knowing that I would surely lose her if I wrote what I had in mind. The last thing she needed was more stress, so I cooled off and went along with her request. Talking to myself again, I said, "You damn fool, ease up. Give her time and be certain to make it very clear that you love her and will be waiting until she is ready. In the meantime, be there for her if she should need you."

There was one more letter from her, postmarked December 5, 1946. Nothing had changed. I stopped writing because I knew I would make the mistake of putting more pressure on her if I did. In truth, there was nothing left to say, for we had said it all over and over. We did agree on one thing, however. We were both miserably unhappy.

I dreaded the coming of Christmas and the new year. I was happy when the holidays were over, wondering what 1947 would bring. In the month of January, it brought nothing, for she did not write at all. Finally, I received a letter dated February 3rd telling me that sister Grace and family and her brother Edwin had come to Miami and they all had a good time at the auto races. I hoped that being with some of her family might help to bring her back to me.

February 23, 1947 was her 21st birthday. I sent her a card and wrote that I loved her and that it was a year ago that I had given her the engagement ring. I asked her one question: "When are we going to start counting anniversaries?" She never answered the question.

There was a lot of time for random thoughts, on the daily commuting trips to and from New York, as I stared out the window at the passing countryside. On more than one occasion, I couldn't help but wonder if there was such a thing as *destiny* or if something was meant to be. In my mind, I went back to October of 1942, to the day when Dutch Holland came in for an x-ray, recognized me and urged me to take the aviation cadet exam. I would have missed him completely if I had been scheduled for darkroom duty that week. Coincidence? Then there was the day I met Red at Babcock Field. Simpson had five students, but on that particular day I was flying and that was the *only time* Red had ever brought food out to the field. Just once. If I had not been scheduled to fly, I would never have met her. Coincidence? I remember how angry Simpson was when I told him I had chosen twin engine advanced training. In my heart, I agreed with him that I would have made a better fighter pilot than a bomber pilot, but I had made up my mind well *before* the day we met at Babcock Field. Then I thought about the day we met in Bainbridge, when I told her that I didn't recognize her with her clothes on. I had been one of the first off the bus and she and her mother were just a few steps away when we saw each other. Had I been one of the last to get off, they would have been beyond the bus and across the street and I never would have known that she would be going to school in Valdosta. Coincidence? *Whatever will be will be*, so goes the saying, and if that is so, there was nothing I could do to change the outcome.

* * * * *

Some years before, Verna's sister LaVerne and husband Smith Humphries had moved to Greenbelt Maryland, just outside of Washington DC.

In Miami, Verna had met a pilot who was going to deliver a refurbished, personal aircraft to an Air Corps general. In casual conversation, they invited her to go along, just for the ride. She asked, "Where are you going? I have a sister living there, and I sure would like to go with you." she answered. Just one more *coincidence*?

It was late February when I received her letter telling me that she was in Greenbelt, Maryland, and asked if I could go to see her. Fifteen months had gone by since we had been together, and I had begun to think that we would probably go our separate ways. Now, she was just 200 miles away.

I carefully read and reread every word she had written for she left no doubt of how she felt. She was ready, eager and if anything, more in love than ever. I counted the hours waiting for the weekend to come in anticipation of seeing her.

I skipped work on Saturday and early in the morning, I went to Penn Station in Newark to get the train for Washington. Once aboard, I had almost five hours to think about what was happening.

More than ever, I became convinced that *someone* must have been watching over us, because being apart for long periods of time only made us more certain that we belonged together. I could not dispel the feeling that we were being tested; being brought together and then kept apart, making us prove over and over how much we cared. Maybe at last all the testing and waiting would come to an end.

As I sat there, looking out the window, I made a vow to myself. In November of 1943, I watched her walk away from me after I had kissed her goodbye, thinking that I would probably never see her again. In November of 1945, I felt sick when I watched her walk away from me for the second time. Twice was enough, there would be no third time. I would never let her walk away from me again.

A few minutes before arriving at Union Station, I left my seat, went to the end of the car and stood on the platform where I had a better view of the people waiting for the arriving train. I strained to see their faces, hoping to get a glimpse of her, but what I saw first (and which brought back the vivid, once in a lifetime memory of Tifton in November 1945) was the mop of red hair which I recognized immediately.

Finally, the train slowed to a stop, but this time it was I who did the running while calling her name and grabbing her when we came together. There was one difference, however, because we were on the station platform, not in the middle of the street, when I kissed her. Seeing her again, in that brief moment, was all I needed to rid myself of the misery and unhappiness of the past fifteen months.

She and her sister LaVerne had driven to the station and as we walked to the car, I kept staring at her as I tried to convince myself that I wasn't imagining our being together -- that this was actually happening -- afraid that what I was seeing would soon begin to fade and I would revert to reality.

LaVerne had prepared a great supper, but food was not what was on my mind. I was too excited to eat, but I did try. It was so difficult to sit there, making small talk, when there was so much I wanted to ask her -- so much I wanted to tell her, but in private. Finally, everyone said goodnight and went to bed.

At long last, we were alone.

It took but a few hours to decide when and where we wanted to get married. In two short weekend days our lives had been turned upside down, but wonderfully so.

The following weekend she came to Linden and admitted that she was scared to death at the thought of meeting the Colletti family. Whatever misgivings she might have had soon disappeared a few minutes after walking into the house, because she fit in so naturally. It was at that moment that I realized that for the first time everyone I loved was finally together under the same roof, talking and laughing as they welcomed her into the family.

I went to Greenbelt the next Saturday and together we planned our wedding. We agreed that she would retain her religion, and that we would marry in a Catholic church, in Washington DC. Many details had to be settled; getting a marriage license and a blood test if needed. The church required a copy of my baptismal papers and LaVerne had to attest that Verna had never been previously married. I also had to be interviewed by the priest who would be performing the ceremony. Hotel reservations were needed for me, Mom and Pop, and a time and a date had to be agreed upon. Things were getting a little hectic, but all I could think of was that the long anticipated day would soon arrive.

Of course something completely unforeseen and unexpected arose. At the very time when we needed to communicate quickly, on a daily basis, the country had its first *nationwide* telephone strike. Only outright emergency calls were permitted. In addition, we had switched to daylight savings time, the morning before our wedding date, and neither of us knew if Washington observed the change or remained on standard time. I was in a quandary. Desperate, I picked up the phone and was told that there was a strike and no calls were permitted. I told them of my plight, that it was an emergency and that they could listen to our conversation to satisfy themselves that I was not lying. Much to my amazement, they let the call go through. More than ever, it seemed that nothing would ever come easy for us.

We were married in the afternoon of April 27, 1947, by Father Spence, in the rectory of St. Matthew's Cathedral, Washington DC. Mr. and Mrs. James Colletti, parents of the groom and the bride's sister, Mrs. Smith Humphries, her husband and family, were in attendance.

I can still see the wonderful look in her eyes and the happiness I felt, when I put the wedding ring on her finger and how it affected me to hear her say "I do." At long last, the tormenting, miserable, endless waiting had come to an end. She was mine. Without a doubt, it was the happiest day of my life.

We have been married sixty-eight years, ever thankful for being granted the *rare privilege of growing old with the person you love*. We have been blessed with five children, three daughters and two sons, and we, in every sense of the word, are a family. (It was quite possible that there were those who wondered if we were trying to have our own football team, but we knew how to answer that question. Her parents had seven children and mine had five, so we were simply following family tradition.) End of wondering.

Every birthday is celebrated, not casually but with the opening of wrapped gifts, complete with bows and cards. This would always be followed by an event that has become a rarity in today's society; a sit down, formal dinner served on china, not paper plates. Last but not least comes the birthday cake that *Super Wife Verna* bakes, (store bought cake is outlawed here) studded with candles.

At Christmas time, it is not unusual to have two hundred fifty wrapped gifts under the tree. (The record was four hundred.) In addition, everyone has a bulging Christmas stocking hanging on the fireplace mantle, but the items therein are not included in the gift count.

It was about sixty-two years ago, when we established the rules regarding the opening of gifts. It was decided that only *one* person would open *one* gift and announce to everyone the name of the giver. When finished, the next person would do the same. All this has been recorded for posterity because cameras are flashing constantly. There is little need to rush and it is not unusual to spend about six or seven hours to do it all, but this is what they have known since they were kids and no one wants any changes. So, the ritual is repeated year after year.

Many times, during the past sixty-eight years, I have wondered how two people, who had spent so little time together, had the ability to see past the obstacles in their path and intuitively know that they were meant for each other. Years ago, I stopped trying to understand or explain the events that shaped our lives, since obviously, it was an exercise in futility.

There is one thing, however, of which I am certain: What Red and Colletti have put together has endured more than …

April 27, 1947

Chapter 21

Easter 1947

Mama Atkinson's Visit to Linden December 1947

We were living with Mom and Pop (using my old bedroom) when Courtney was born December 17, 1947. Mama Atkinson had arrived a few days before, to be with Verna, and stayed until a few days after the new baby and mother came home. (In 1947 childbirth called for a seven day confinement.) Perhaps it was the fact that she was there from the first day of his birth that endeared him to her. I have no hesitation is saying that he was one of her favorite grandchildren.

It was heart warming to see how well our parents got along, especially when it came to food. Mom and Pop loved seafood and Pop would eat most anything that was caught. Mama, living close to the land, also liked simple food so they were quite compatible. One night, he prepared one of his *specialties*, but it wasn't seafood, it was *brains*. He offered some to her, feeling quite certain that she would not care for it, but she fooled him and ate more than he was willing to share! There was one little problem during her stay with us, and that had to do with communication. She could understand very little (or nothing) of his *version of English* and would turn to me and ask, "What did he say?" and I would have to interpret!

There was another highlight to her visit: It began to snow about the 24th of December and it didn't stop until it reached a record twenty-six inches! She would go out with a cup and spoon, find some clean, untouched snow, scoop it up and put vanilla and sugar on it. I have pictures of her standing beside a huge mound of snow. It was fun to see how she reacted to it.

Many years later, we made a trip to Georgia, in July of 1964, and Courtney was old enough to get a driving permit. He became her personal driver, and the two of them would head out every day on some *important errand*. She kept a *switch* by her side and used it to get his attention when he made a mistake. Fortunately, I didn't see any welts on him when they returned from one of their trips, and it was Mama who went with him when he took his driving test (when not quite seventeen) and became a licensed Georgia driver.

In May of 1948, we bought a duplex apartment in Rahway and moved into our first house. It was a proud and happy couple who gave notice to the world that Mr. and Mrs. Silveo G. Colletti were in residence there.

Mama was present when each of our children was born and took over the household in Verna's absence. Supper would be ready when I returned from work, which I ate on the run having barely enough time to wash up and change my clothes, as I tried to be at the hospital the very first minute visiting hours began. I still fondly remember the first time she brewed *coffee* for me. She never drank coffee in her life so what she made was an undrinkable disaster, but I never let on. As you might have guessed, we developed a very warm, close relationship. I loved her and it was with sincerity when I called her "Mama."

22

FINAL THOUGHTS

In July of 1951 we made our first trip to Georgia to visit Verna's family; our first as husband and wife. Our eldest child, Courtney, was four years old and daughter Rita (who traveled in a basket) was five months old. Mama Atkinson and her son Edwin were the only occupants of the house that Verna had lived in, and which we buzzed that memorable day in late August 1943. Through the years, we have made the trip more than a dozen times, but the first one is the one which I will never forget.

Many times, I have tried to find the words to describe the overwhelming emotion I experienced when I saw, once again, the house with the tall sycamore tree in front that I knew so well from the air. That image, and the memory of being introduced to Red shortly thereafter, represents a turning point in my life. How little did we know.

Who could have predicted, that at that moment, we each had met the person who would become our lifetime partners; that we would have five children and be thankful for being given the rare opportunity of growing old together? Hollywood would have rejected a script with such a plot as an unbelievable fairy tale lacking credibility, and they probably would have been right. We, however, have lived and continue to live, our personal fairy tale.

While there we went for a walk, hand in hand, down the dirt road and continued until we reached the approximate spot where I had dropped down to fence post level, in August of 1943, and followed Lt. Simpson when we buzzed the Atkinson home. The memory was still so very fresh -- the excitement of doing something that was a *no-no* -- of the roar of the engine as I advanced the throttle, cleared the tree and made a tight, climbing turn -- the exaggerated sensation of speed due to being so close to the ground. Now I was standing where it had happened eight years ago, but a major change had taken place. The seventeen-year-old girl, who lived in that house in 1943, was here beside me, but now she was my wife and the mother of our two children.

Once again, what came to mind was a simple little song, sung by Patti Andrews, of the Andrews Sisters, that explained so clearly and completely what I was feeling:

"How Lucky You Are"[34]
As you walk, as you talk with the one you love
Do you know just how lucky you are?
When you stroll hand in hand, 'neath the moon above
Does your heart sing how lucky you are?
There're so many heartaches in this world of ours
But sometimes a dream will come true
When the one that you love is in love with you, that's the greatest of blessings by far
And you don't know how lucky you are.

After reading the preceding pages, you might have wondered how I was able to quote dates and places with some degree of precision. For the explanation, it is necessary to go back a few years.

In July of 1935, the city of Linden, New Jersey held its first model airplane competition at the high school athletic field. The city was one of the first anywhere in the United States that attempted to organize and bring together the so-called *air-minded* kids. Credit for this must be given to the first superintendent of recreation of the city, Frank Krysiak, for it was he who provided the driving force that made it possible.

There were nine contestants entered in the contest, and it was there that I met Carl Frank. He was fourteen years old, I was sixteen and we quickly became friends. (A friendship that has endured to this day.) We shared three major interests: aviation, model airplanes and photography, and it was one of his cameras, a 620 roll film Kodak, that I had with me throughout the war. I was the first to enter military service in 1941, and we soon began to correspond regularly.

A *few years later*, in the sixties, he paid me a visit and as he entered, I noticed that he was carrying a brown paper bag. I asked

"What's in the bag, Carl?"

He replied, "Take a look." I was amazed to see that he had saved almost all of the letters I had written to him! What a surprise! To read them again was to be transported back in time as I remembered where I had been and what I had done so many years ago. It was so very strange to read the postmarks and all my old return addresses complete with rank and serial number. Though many years had passed, I had no difficulty recalling the events I had experienced; but what was missing and had faded with time, were the little details and of course the dates. Thanks to him, that problem was solved.

Chapter 22

To my children
Collette, Gregory, Suzette, Rita and Courtney

My original intent, when I began this project, was to simply write of the days that I had been in uniform during World War II. At times, I had mentioned bits and pieces of my wartime experiences, but you never knew the complete story of where I had been and what I had done during the four-plus years that I had spent in the Army and Army Air Corps.

All went well until I had to tell of the event, in August of 1943, when *someone* came into my life, on Babcock Field in Georgia, and turned it upside down. It was then that I realized that I could not tell my story without including Verna Atkinson, since the two stories are linked together so completely.

Having read the previous pages, you have now come to know a little more about the two people who would become your parents, and how difficult it was for them to try to live a normal life during a very abnormal time. We met because of the war, but the war also kept us apart. Except for the few days we spent together, in 1943 and 1945, we were denied the opportunity to do what young people do: go to a movie, dance or just have fun without a cloud hanging over our heads. There always was the reminder that there was a war going on, so the mindset was to live for the moment and forget about making long-range plans. We missed out on the little things that young people do; holding hands while watching a movie -- being able to dance without someone cutting in. The feeling of excitement while dressing for a date in anticipation of going out with that special person -- of being able to get in your car and pick her up at her home, and have her sitting close while driving. Unfortunately, children find it difficult to accept the fact that there was a time when their parents were young and that they experienced all the emotions typical of their age. Certainly, we were not exceptions.

Your mother had a very unique way of informing me that there would be an addition to the family. She would wait for the right moment, hug my neck, look at me and say, "Hello Papa." The first time she said it, I started to say,

"I'm not your Pa--," but I never finished the word because I suddenly realized what she was telling me! No doubt about it, the redhead from Georgia is one of a kind, as you have already discovered. It is our fervent wish that someday you will be as fortunate as we and find the happiness which we have found.

Know this: I do not think any two people loved, and love each other more than we; and no children were more welcomed and equally loved than each of you. I am proud to say that we are a family, in every sense of the word, which is something that is slowly becoming a rather rare commodity. A family that regularly gathers for a sit down dinner in the old-fashioned way.

Perhaps the missing ingredient in today's world is the fact that relatively few people (compared to the thousands who served in WWII) know how painful it can be to love someone and be denied the opportunity to be together because of circumstances beyond their control.

To be thousands of miles apart, writing letters and wondering if *fate* would be kind enough to let you live to see the day when you would be together again. The fear, so difficult to suppress, that tomorrow might be the day when your luck would run out. To wait impatiently for mail call, in great anticipation, hoping that there would be something from that very special person. To read every letter, over and over, until they had almost been memorized, they being the only connecting link to the person you hoped would someday be part of your life. Afraid that the next letter might be a "Dear John letter," informing you that she had met someone else, which would put an end to all the dreams you had dared to dream. Wondering when the tormenting waiting would finally come to an end.

Ours was not an easy or conventional courtship. We were apart for two years, from November of 1943 to November of 1945 which was followed by another separation of seventeen months, so we could not be accused of acting on impulse. In addition, there were unforeseen obstacles to be overcome, but that just made it more wonderful when we finally put it all together that memorable day in April of 1947.

      You are all deeply loved,
      Your Dad

Chapter 22

And now to you, my One and Only.

On the day we met on Babcock Field, in August of 1943, you were introduced to me as "Red." Soon afterward, I learned that your name was Verna Atkinson and that you lived in the farmhouse which we had just buzzed.

When *the powers that be* decided to put us together in Valdosta, I began to think of you as "the Georgia Rebel" or "the Georgia Redhead."

Then the letter writing began, and without realizing what was happening, we slowly began to heat things up a bit. It was then that I started calling you "P38" after the Lockheed P38 fighter which was # 1. It was an easy choice because you had become my # 1.

Without a doubt, the name I liked more than any other, however, is "wife." I waited a long time before I could call you that, but it is an understatement to simply say that *it has been worth the wait*. (But I despise the word *wait* more than ever because it will always remind me of those unhappy days when we were apart.)

It has been an unbelievable, wonderful sixty-eight years of companionship, devotion, loyalty and most of all, love. What I have felt for you, you have returned over and over, and to use an overworked phrase, "This is as good as it gets." I thank you for being the mother of my children and making me happier than I could have ever imagined one could be. I dreamt a lot of dreams those years we were apart, but you have made every one of them come true.

Many years have passed since we took our wedding vows, but although the passing of time has slowed us down a bit, it has not been enough to take away the fun of chasing you around the house. The best part of the chase, however, is that you let me catch you, so to me you will always be "my P38." Nothing can ever change that.

In all probability, there were many skeptics who were of the opinion that after a year or so we would part and go our separate ways -- that we were doomed to fail. Fools! How could they possibly know how we felt about each other? That we had more in common than we ourselves realized? I hope they are not holding their breath while waiting for that to happen. We sure showed them, didn't we!

As much as ever, I love you Red,
Your Colletti

P.S. What are we having for supper tonight? I hope it is fried chicken, but this time I want the breast!

23

TODAY

Carl Frank and Silveo, Veteran's Day 2011

Chapter 23

Wade Schroeder and his son Wesley. 55th Reunion of the 22nd Bomb Group, Nashville, TN, October 2004

Rudy Riccio and Silveo. 65th Reunion of the 22nd Bomb Group, Denver, CO, October 2014

Wayne Baker for *The Westfield Leader* and *The Times*

BOMBS AWAY…Retired Air Force Major Silveo Coletti, right, of Westfield describes aspects of the operation of the Norden bombsight to Richard Stobaeus of Summit, center, and John Thoms, mayor of New Providence. Mr. Coletti served as bombardier on B-24's in the Pacific during World War II. Assemblyman Eric Munoz and his wife, Nancy, held the veterans' event on Sunday at their Summit home.

WWII Veterans Relive Norden Bombsight at Munoz Event

By WAYNE BAKER
Specially Written for The Westfield Leader and The Times

SUMMIT — Assemblyman Eric Munoz (LD-21, Summit) and his wife, Nancy, held a veterans-appreciation event at their home on Saturday. Guests of honor included former state assemblyman Joseph Azzolina, a Navy veteran who had spearheaded the effort to bring the Battleship *New Jersey* to the state, and Silveo Coletti, who served as a bombardier in the Pacific Theater during World War II.

Mr. Azzolina had served in the Navy beginning in WWII and continued to serve in the reserves into the 1980s. Mr. Azzolina expressed regret that he had been unable to arrange for the battleship to be permanently docked along the Hudson River. The ship is located on the Camden waterfront.

Mr. Coletti of Westfield, a retired Air Force Major, began his military career serving as a bombardier in B-24s during the World War II. Mr. Munoz owns a Norden bombsight and made it available during the event. The Norden sight helped bomber aircraft crews drop bombs accurately.

Mr. Coletti said of the bombsight, "The last time I looked through one of these, it was 1945." He gave a talk about his war experiences and later spoke to small groups of attendees that watched and listened as he demonstrated aspects of the sight's operation.

Mr. Coletti remembered how his training instructor described the sight, saying it allowed the airforce to "find the exact point in the sky where you need to release the bomb to hit the target." He described how accurate the device was, noting that in training he put six bombs into a 100-foot circle. However, he noted that such results were almost impossible in combat.

Other local politicians attended the event, including State Senator Tom Kean Jr. and Assemblyman Jon Bramnick (both LD-21, Westfield), New Providence Mayor John Thoms and Roselle Park Mayor Joe DeIorio.

Chapter 23

Verna and Silveo

For the Duration *plus* Six Months

24

MY DUTY TOURS, BASES AND DATES

October 20 - 23, 1941:	Drafted into Army from Linden, NJ, sent to Fort Dix, NJ.
October 23 – December 1941:	Camp Lee, Petersburg, VA.
December 1941:	To Langley Field, Hampton, VA. with medical detachment team assigned to Station Hospital.
August 1942:	To Walter Reed Army Medical Center, Washington DC for training as x-ray technician.
October 1942:	Graduated from Walter Reed and return to Langley Field. Assigned to x-ray lab as part of team.
December 1942:	Take aviation cadet qualification exam at Langley Field. Accepted into aviation cadet program after passing physical exam.
January 1943:	Leave Langley Field for Classification Center, Nashville Air Base, Nashville, TN. Qualify for pilot, navigator and bombardier training. Assigned to class 43-J for pilot training.
April 1943:	Maxwell Field, Montgomery, Alabama for preflight training. West Point system of upper and lower class designations and Honor Code is used.
May - June 1943:	Carlstrom Field, Arcadia, Florida to Embry Riddle School of Aviation for primary flight training in Stearman PT17.
July - August 1943:	Bainbridge Army Air Base, Bainbridge, GA for basic flight training in BT13.
September 1943:	Moody Field, Valdosta, GA for twin engine advanced pilot training. Eliminated two weeks before graduation day.
November 3, 1943	Tyndall Field, Panama City, FL for aerial gunnery training.
December 1943:	Left Tyndall Field for one week of air-to-air and air-to-ground training at Apalachicola, FL Auxiliary Field.
December 25, 1943:	Merry Christmas. Arrive Victorville Air Base, Victorville, CA at 4 AM for bombardier training. Assigned to class 44-6.

March 1944:	To Helendale, CA, on edge of Mojave Desert, for one week of training under field conditions.
April 29, 1944:	Graduated from Victorville with bombardier and dead reckoning navigator rating. Commissioned 2nd Lieutenant. Given leave plus travel time to NJ.
May 1944:	Report to air base in Fresno, CA. Board train for March Field, Riverside, CA for transition training in B24. Locate members of my crew aboard train.
June 1944:	Final phase of training at March Field in B24 Liberator bomber with my crew.
August 11, 1944:	Leave March Field for Hamilton Field, Fairfield, CA for movement overseas.
September 11, 1944:	Depart Hamilton Field for Hawaii in new B24. One night and two-day layover in Oahu.
September 14, 1944:	Depart Hawaii and fly to Canton, Tarawa and Guadalcanal Islands to final destination Garbutt Field, Townesville, Australia. Deliver aircraft and await assignment to combat unit.
September 1944:	Leave Townesville, Australia and sent to replacement depot at Nadzab on northern coast of New Guinea. Take three-day jungle survival training course with Australian guides. Assigned to 5th Air Force, 22nd Bomb Group, 408th Squadron.
October 1944:	Move up to base on Owi Island off the northwest coast of New Guinea. Fly first combat mission in B24, Oct. 20, 1944.
December 1944:	Unit moves northward to Anguar Island in the Palau Island Group.
January 1945:	Leave Anguar for Samar Island on the eastern coast of the Philippine Islands.
March 1945:	Leave Samar for Clark Field, Luzon on western coast of Philippine Islands. Fly combat missions to China, Formosa and other Philippine Islands.
June 1945:	Sent south to Morotai, in the Halmahera Islands, flying missions to the Celebes and Borneo. June 29th mission completes my duty tour and I am eligible to be sent home.
July 1945:	Return to Clark Field. Await orders to go home.
August 1945:	Off flying status. Orders delayed. Put aboard LST for ocean trip to Okinawa.

September 1945:	Orders finally received. Depart Okinawa on a war-weary B24 for trip back to Manila, Philippine Islands
October 1945:	Board Army transport ship, USS *Haskell* for ocean voyage home.
October 19, 1945:	Arrive San Francisco. Sent to Camp Stoneham, CA for processing and awaiting transportation home.
October 23, 1945:	Board train for trip to NJ.
October 27, 1945:	Arrive Fort Dix, NJ. Separated from Air Corps. Adding unused leave time to my time of service extends my official separation date to December 7, 1945.
October 29, 1945:	Separate from the Air Force, enlist in the Air Force Reserve and return home.
September 13, 1979:	Retired from US Air Force Reserve.

* * * * *

TOTAL (ACTIVE DUTY) MILITARY SERVICE: Four years, one month and seventeen days.

MY MILITARY ADDRESSES

October 1941:	Private Silveo Colletti, Company A, 4th Medical Training Battalion, T-651 Camp Lee, VA
December 1941:	Private Silveo Colletti, Medical Detachment, Station Hospital, Langley Field, VA
August 1942:	Corporal Silveo Colletti, Company B-1, S.M.D.T, Army Medical Center, Washington DC
November 1942:	Corporal Silveo Colletti, Medical Detachment, Station Hospital, Langley Field, VA
January 1943:	Aviation Cadet (A/C), Group 3, Squadron D, Army Air Forces Classification Center, Nashville, TN
March 1943:	A/C Silveo Colletti, Preflight School, Maxwell Field, Montgomery, AL.
April 1943:	A/C Silveo Colletti, Class 43-J, Carlstrom Field, Arcadia, FL
June 1943:	A/C Silveo Colletti, Class 43-J, Bainbridge Army Air Base, Bainbridge, GA
August 1943:	A/C Silveo Colletti, 32185829, Class 43-J, Squadron B., Moody Field, Valdosta, GA
October 1943:	A/C Silveo Colletti, 32185829, Bombardier Pool, Moody Field, Valdosta, GA
November 1943:	A/C Silveo Colletti, 32185829, Class 43-51, Cadet Det. Barracks 403 F.G.S. (Flight Gunnery School) Tyndall Field, Panama City, FL
December 1943:	A/C Silveo Colletti, 32185829, Class 44-6, Box E-54, V.A.A.F., Victorville, CA
May 1944:	2ndLt. Silveo G. Colletti, 0776632, 920 AAF Base Unit, Sqdn. T-1 March Field, CA
September 1944:	2ndLt. Silveo G. Colletti, 0776632, AAF, APO # 16409, A.B.3 C/O Postmaster, San Francisco, Cal. (Australia and Nadzab, New Guinea)
October 1944:	2ndLt. Silveo G. Colletti, 0776632, 408th Sqdn., 22nd Bomb Group APO 920 c/o Postmaster, San Francisco, CA (Owi Island, Dutch East Indies)
February 1945:	2ndLt. Silveo G. Colletti, 0776632, 408th Sqdn., 22nd Bomb Group APO 72, c/o Postmaster, San Francisco, CA (Samar, Philippine Is.)
June 1945:	1st Lt. Silveo G. Colletti, 0776632, 408th Sqdn., 22nd Bomb Group APO 74, c/o Postmaster San Francisco, CA (Clark Field, Luzon, Philippine Is.)
August 1945:	1st Lt. Silveo G. Colletti, 0776632, 408th Sqdn., 22nd Bomb Group APO 337, c/o Postmaster, San Francisco, CA (Okinawa)

Chapter 24

Biography

BORN:	September 13, 1919 411 2nd Avenue, New York City Moved to Linden, NJ, 1925.
PARENTS:	Father: James Salvatore Colletti, born Palermo, Sicily Mother: Rosalia Colletti, born Bivona, Sicily
FAMILY:	Brothers: Domenick, Salvatore and Joseph; Sister: Angelina
EDUCATION:	School # 2, Linden, NJ Linden Junior High School Linden High School, graduated 1937. Played on interclass softball team.
EMPLOYMENT:	After graduation, worked for a year in the office of the Linden Recreation Commission, doing clerical work. In 1935 accompanied Superintendent of Recreation, Frank Krysiak going to schools in Linden where we organized Model Aircraft Clubs and I taught the kids how to build model planes. Began working with father in jewelry business in New York on August 8, 1938
HOBBIES:	Building and flying free flight model airplanes. Original member of the Linden Model Aircraft Club which was established in 1935. Went with other club members to Washington DC in 1938, to assist in the founding of the Academy of Model Aeronautics. The LMAC was a charter member of the Academy. Photography; taking, developing and enlarging photographs. Playing the Tiple Ukulele, music.
SPORTS:	Softball, touch football, ice skating roller skating, pitching horseshoes.
MILITARY:	Drafted October 20, 1941 into the Medical Department. Went to Army Medical Center, Washington DC for training as an x-ray technician. Returned to Langley Field, VA as staff member in x-ray office. Entered the Army Air Force as Aviation Cadet in 1943. Went through Classification Center, preflight, primary and advanced pilot training. Eliminated. Went to aerial gunnery school and bombardier school. Commissioned 2nd Lt. upon graduation. After transition training in B24 aircraft, assigned to crew and flew overseas to

Australia. After a two-week stay moved north to Nadzab, New Guinea.

Assigned to 408th Squadron, 22 Bomb Group, 5th Air Force. Flew 39 missions to China, Formosa, the Philippines, Celebes and Borneo.

Separated from Army Air Force December 7, 1945. Enlisted in Air Force Reserve.

Retired from US Air Force Reserve September 13, 1979.

MARITAL STATUS: Married Verna Atkinson April 27, 1947. Five children.

HOME: Westfield, New Jersey

Notes

1. Irene LaFortune. 1946. "The Greatest Guy in the World was Aboard that Draft Train." *Welcome Home to Our Veterans*. Linden, NJ: Wolf Press, April 6.

2. Johnny Mercer, writer. *G.I. Jive*. (c) 1943 (Renewed) The Johnny Mercer Foundation. All Rights Administered by WB Music Corp. All Rights Reserved. Reprinted by Permission of Alfred Music Publishing.

3. Caesar Petrillo, Milton Isadore Samuels, and Nelson A. Shawn, writers. *Jim*. Copyright (c) 1941 Universal Music Corp. Copyright Renewed. All Rights Reserved. Used by Permission. Reprinted by Permission of Hal Leonard Corporation.

4. James Cavanaugh, John Redmond, and Frank Weldon, writers. *I Came, I Saw, I Conga'd*. Used by permission of Range Road Music, Inc. [and additional publishing information supplied by co-publisher(s)] Copyright (c) 1940 Quartet Music, Road Range Music, Inc. and Chappell & Co., Inc. Copyright Renewed. All Rights for Quartet Music Administered by BMG Rights Management (US) LLC. All Rights Reserved. Used by Permission. Reprinted by Permission of Hal Leonard Corporation.

5. John H. Mercer, and Victor Schertzinger, writers. *Tangerine* from *"The Fleet's In"* Paramount, 1942. Copyright (c) 1942 Sony/ATV Music Publishing LLC. Copyright Renewed. All Rights Administered by Sony/ATV Music Publishing LLC, 424 Church Street, Suite 1200, Nashville, TN 37219. International Copyright Secured. All Rights Reserved. Reprinted by Permission of Hal Leonard Corporation.

6. Harold Arlen, and Johnny Mercer, writers. *Blues in the Night: (My Mama Done Tol' Me)*. (c) 1941 (renewed) WB Music Corp. All Rights Reserved. Reprinted by Permission of Alfred Music Publishing.

7. Rube Bloom, and Mack David, writers. *Take Me*. Copyright (c) 1942 Universal - Polygram International Publishing, Inc., Bregman Vocco Conn, Inc. and Rube Bloom Music. Copyright Renewed. All Rights for Bregman Vocco Conn, Inc. Controlled and Administered by Universal - Polygram International Publishing, Inc. All Rights Reserved. Used by Permission. Reprinted by Permission of Hal Leonard Corporation and the Estate of Rube Bloom.

8. Johnny Mercer, writer. *Strip Polka*. (c) 1942 (Renewed) The Johnny Mercer Foundation. All Rights Administered by WB Music Corp. All Rights Reserved. Reprinted by Permission of Alfred Music Publishing.

9. Robert Crawford, writer. *The Army Air Corps, The U.S. Air Force Song*. Copyright (c) 1942, 1951 by Carl Fischer, Inc. Copyrights renewed. All rights assigned to Carl Fischer, LLC. All rights reserved. Used with permission.

10. Harry Hogan. 1943. "This Cadet Stuff." *Preflight*. Volume III. Montgomery, AL: The Paragon Press, April 1943.

11. Harold Arlen, and Johnny Mercer, writers. *That Old Black Magic* from *"Star Spangled Rhythm"* Columbia, 1942. Copyright (c) 1942 Sony/ATV Music Publishing LLC. Copyright Renewed. All Rights Administered by Sony/ATV Music Publishing LLC, 424 Church Street, Suite 1200, Nashville, TN 37219. International Copyright Secured. All Rights Reserved. Reprinted by Permission of Hal Leonard Corporation.

12. Arthur Altman, and Jack Lawrence, writers. *All or Nothing at All*. Columbia, 1943. Used by permission of Range Road Music, Inc.

13. Johnny S. Black, *Paper Doll*. Decca, 1930.

14. United States. Army Air Forces. War Department. 1945. *Bombardiers' Information File, BIF*.

15. United States. 1944. *Bombs Away*. Victorville, CA: Army Air Forces Bombardier School, Graduating Class 44-6.

16. United States. Army Air Forces. War Department. 1944. *Cadet Manual*.

17. Arthur Schwartz, and Frank Loesser, writers. *They're Either Too Young or Too Old*. (c) 1943 (Renewed) WB Music Corp. All Rights Administered by WB Music Corp. All Rights Reserved. Reprinted by Permission of Alfred Music Publishing.

18. Lawrence J. Hickey. 2001. *The 22nd Bombardment Group in World War II*. Photo Supplement 1941-1945. Edited by USAF (RET) Col. Don L. Evans. Vol. III. Huntsville, AL: 22nd BG Association, 226.

19. Hickey. 2001. *The 22nd Bombardment Group in World War II*, 226.

20. Hickey. 2001. *The 22nd Bombardment Group in World War II*, 226-227.

21. Hickey. 2001. *The 22nd Bombardment Group in World War II*, 227.

22. William C. Wilson. 1944. "Sink 13 Leyte Ships; 4,000 Japs Perish." *Daily News*. New York: Daily News, November 30.

23. Lawrence J. Hickey. 2001. *The 22nd Bombardment Group in World War II*, 228.

24. Hickey. 2001 *The 22nd Bombardment Group in World War II*, 228.

25. 22nd Bombardment Group. Red Raiders Logo.

26. Frank Loesser, writer. *Praise The Lord And Pass The Ammunition!* Copyright (c) 1942 Sony/ATV Music Publishing LLC. Copyright Renewed. All Rights Administered by Sony/ATV Music Publishing LLC, 424 Church Street, Suite 1200, Nashville, TN 37219. International Copyright Secured. All Rights Reserved. Reprinted by Permission of Hal Leonard Corporation.

27. Walt Gaylor. 2001. *The 22nd Bombardment Group in World War II*. 1941-1944 B-26 and B-25. Unedited. Vol. I. Huntsville, AL: 22nd BG Association, 608.

28. Hickey. 2001. *The 22nd Bombardment Group in World War II*, 229.

29. Hickey. 2001. *The 22nd Bombardment Group in World War II*, 230.

30. Crawford, *The Army Air Corps, The U.S. Air Force Song*.

31. "The Far East and the Pacific 1941." Ibiblio.org. Accessed September 6 Sept, 2015. http://www.ibiblio.org/himself/images/map_fareast1941.jpg.

32. Les Brown, and Ben Homer, writers. *Sentimental Journey*. (c) 1944 (Renewed) Morley Music Co. and Holliday Publishing. All Rights Reserved. *Reprinted by Permission of Hal Leonard Corporation*. (c) Copyright 1944, Renewed 1972. Holliday Publishing/ASCAP/Morley Music Co./ASCAP. All rights reserved. Used by permission.

33. Sammy Cahn and Jule Styne, writers. *It's Been a Long, Long Time*. (c) 1945 Morley Music Co. Copyright Renewed. Assigned to Morley Music Co. and Cahn Music Co. All Rights outside the United States Controlled by Morley Music Co. All Rights Reserved. Reprinted by Permission of Hal Leonard Corporation. Copyright (c) 1945 Cahn Music Co. (ASCAP) / Edwin H. Morris & Co. Inc. (ASCAP) Cahn Music Co. administered by Imagem Sounds (ASCAP). Used by Permission. International Copyright Secured. All Rights Reserved.

34. Eddie Cassen, and Des O'Connor, writers. *How Lucky You Are*. Copyright (c) 1947 Edward Kassner Music C.o Ltd. Copyright Renewed. All Rights in the U.S. Administered by Downtown DLJ Songs. All Rights Reserved. Used by Permission. Reprinted by Permission of Hal Leonard Corporation.

35. Wayne Baker. 2007. "WWII Veterans Relive Norden Bombsight at Munoz Event." *The Westfield Leader*, September 20: 3.

Bibliography

22nd Bombardment Group. Red Raiders Logo.

Altman, Arthur, and Jack Lawrence, writers. *All or Nothing at All*. Columbia, 1943. Used by permission of Range Road Music, Inc.

Arlen, Harold, and Johnny Mercer, writers. *That Old Black Magic* from "*Star Spangled Rhythm*" Columbia, 1942. Copyright (c) 1942 Sony/ATV Music Publishing LLC. Copyright Renewed. All Rights Administered by Sony/ATV Music Publishing LLC, 424 Church Street, Suite 1200, Nashville, TN 37219. International Copyright Secured. All Rights Reserved, Reprinted by Permission of Hal Leonard Corporation.

Arlen, Harold, and Johnny Mercer, writers. *Blues in the Night: (My Mama Done Tol' Me)*. (c) 1941 (renewed) WB Music Corp. All Rights Reserved. Reprinted by Permission of Alfred Music Publishing.

Baker, Wayne. 2007. "WWII Veterans Relive Norden Bombsight at Munoz Event." *The Westfield Leader*, September 20: 3.

Black, Johnny S. *Paper Doll*. Decca, 1930.

Bloom, Rube, and Mack David, writers. *Take Me*. Copyright (c) 1942 Universal - Polygram International Publishing, Inc., Bregman Vocco Conn, Inc. and Rube Bloom Music. Copyright Renewed. All Rights for Bregman Vocco Conn, Inc. Controlled and Administered by Universal - Polygram International Publishing, Inc. All Rights Reserved. Used by Permission. Reprinted by Permission of Hal Leonard Corporation and the Estate of Rube Bloom.

Brown, Les, and Ben Homer, writers. *Sentimental Journey*. (c) 1944 (Renewed) Morley Music Co. and Holliday Publishing. All Rights Reserved. Reprinted by Permission of Hal Leonard Corporation. (c) Copyright 1944, Renewed 1972. Holliday Publishing/ASCAP/Morley Music Co./ASCAP. All rights reserved. Used by permission.

Cahn, Sammy, and Jule Styne, writers. *It's Been a Long, Long Time*. (c) 1945 Morley Music Co. Copyright Renewed. Assigned to Morley Music Co. and Cahn Music Co. All Rights outside the United States Controlled by Morley Music Co. All Rights Reserved. Reprinted by Permission of Hal Leonard Corporation. Copyright (c) 1945 Cahn Music Co. (ASCAP) / Edwin H. Morris & Co. Inc. (ASCAP) Cahn Music Co. administered by Imagem Sounds (ASCAP). Used by Permission. International Copyright Secured. All Rights Reserved.

Cassen, Eddie, and Des O'Connor, writers. *How Lucky You Are*. Copyright (c) 1947 Edward Kassner Music Co Ltd. Copyright Renewed. All Rights in the U.S. Administered by Downtown DLJ Songs. All Rights Reserved. Used by Permission. Reprinted by Permission of Hal Leonard Corporation.

Cavanaugh, James, John Redmond, and Frank Weldon, writers. *I Came, I Saw, I Conga'd*. Used by permission of Range Road Music, Inc. [and additional publishing information supplied by co-publisher(s)] Copyright (c) 1940 Quartet Music, Road Range Music, Inc. and Chappell & Co., Inc. Copyright Renewed. All Rights for Quartet Music Administered by BMG Rights Management (US) LLC. All Rights Reserved. Used by Permission. Reprinted by Permission of Hal Leonard Corporation.

Crawford, Robert, writer. *The Army Air Corps, The U.S. Air Force Song.* Copyright (c) 1942, 1951 by Carl Fischer, Inc. Copyrights renewed. All rights assigned to Carl Fischer, LLC. All rights reserved. Used with permission.

"The Far East and the Pacific 1941." Ibiblio.org. Accessed September 6 Sept, 2015. http://www.ibiblio.org/himself/images/map_fareast1941.jpg

Gaylor, Walt. 2001. *The 22nd Bombardment Group in World War II.* 1941-1944 B-26 and B-25. Unedited. Vol. I. Huntsville, AL: 22nd BG Association, 608.

Hickey, Lawrence J. 2001. *The 22nd Bombardment Group in World War II.* Photo Supplement 1941-1945. Edited by USAF (RET) Col. Don L. Evans. Vol. III. Huntsville, AL: 22nd BG Association, 226-230.

Hogan, Harry. 1943. "This Cadet Stuff." *Preflight.* Volume III. Montgomery, AL: The Paragon Press, April 1943.

LaFortune, Irene. 1946. "The Greatest Guy in the World was Aboard that Draft Train." *Welcome Home to Our Veterans.* Linden, NJ: Wolf Press, April 6.

Loesser, Frank, writer. *Praise The Lord And Pass The Ammunition!* Copyright (c) 1942 Sony/ATV Music Publishing LLC. Copyright Renewed. All Rights Administered by Sony/ATV Music Publishing LLC, 424 Church Street, Suite 1200, Nashville, TN 37219. International Copyright Secured. All Rights Reserved. Reprinted by Permission of Hal Leonard Corporation.

Loesser, Frank, and Arthur Schwartz, writers. *They're Either Too Young or Too Old.* (c) 1943 (Renewed) WB Music Corp. All Rights Administered by WB Music Corp. All Rights Reserved. Reprinted by Permission of Alfred Music Publishing.

Mercer, John H., and Victor Schertzinger, writers. *Tangerine* from "*The Fleet's In*" Paramount, 1942. Copyright (c) 1942 Sony/ATV Music Publishing LLC. Copyright Renewed. All Rights Administered by Sony/ATV Music Publishing LLC, 424 Church Street, Suite 1200, Nashville, TN 37219. International Copyright Secured. All Rights Reserved. Reprinted by Permission of Hal Leonard Corporation.

Mercer, Johnny, writer. *G.I. Jive.* (c) 1943 (Renewed) The Johnny Mercer Foundation. All Rights Administered by WB Music Corp. All Rights Reserved. Reprinted by Permission of Alfred Music Publishing.

Mercer, Johnny, writer. *Strip Polka.* (c) 1942 (Renewed) The Johnny Mercer Foundation. All Rights Administered by WB Music Corp. All Rights Reserved. Reprinted by Permission of Alfred Music Publishing.

Petrillo, Caesar, Milton Isadore Samuels, and, Nelson A. Shawn, writers. *Jim*. Copyright (c) 1941 Universal Music Corp. Copyright Renewed. All Rights Reserved. Used by Permission. Reprinted by Permission of Hal Leonard Corporation.

United States. Army Air Forces. War Department. 1944. *Cadet Manual*.

United States. Army Air Forces. War Department. 1945. *Bombardiers' Information File, BIF*.

United States. 1944. *Bombs Away*. Victorville, CA: Army Air Forces Bombardier School, Graduating Class 44-6.

Wilson, William C. 1944. "Sink 13 Leyte Ships; 4,000 Japs Perish." *Daily News*. New York: Daily News, November 30.

Kilroy was here

CPSIA information can be obtained
at www.ICGtesting.com
Printed in the USA
LVOW04s0256090517
533708LV00005B/343/P